P.E.T. SHOWED PARENTS HOW TO
COMMUNICATE WITH CHILDREN.

STRAIGHT TALK SHOWS ADULTS
HOW TO COMMUNICATE WITH EVERYONE.

Based on the internationally famous Couple Communication Program that already has helped hundreds of thousands of men and women to talk and listen to each other, STRAIGHT TALK shows you how easy it is to convey what's on your mind and in your heart to another person.

You will learn how to assert yourself without being aggressive, how to criticize without hurting, how to talk with people and not at them, how to give voice to your most intimate feelings without awkwardness or embarrassment, and so much more. STRAIGHT TALK will not only change the way you talk. It will change the way you live—for the better.

SHEROD MILLER, Ph.D., is president and director of training for Interpersonal Communication Programs, Inc. He lectures widely on the subject of communication and frequently serves as a consultant to major corporations, government, and private industry.

DANIEL WACKMAN, Ph.D., is a full professor at the University of Minnesota's School of Journalism and Mass Communication. He is vice-president and director of family programs for Interpersonal Communication Programs, Inc.

ELAM NUNNALLY, Ph.D., is a marriage and family therapist, and an associate professor at the Universtiy of Wisconsin/Milwaukee's School of Social Welfare.

CAROL SALINE is a senior editor for *Philadelphia* Magazine, and a free-lance writer whose articles have appeared in major magazines, including *Redbook, McCalls,* and *Family Circle.* Her work has won several national journalism awards.

HELPFUL GUIDES

STRAIGHT TALK

---

*A New Way To Get
Closer To Others By Saying
What You Really Mean*

By
SHEROD MILLER, Ph.D.,
DANIEL WACKMAN, Ph.D.,
ELAM NUNNALLY, Ph.D., AND
CAROL SALINE

A SIGNET BOOK

NEW AMERICAN LIBRARY

Dedication

To our spouses: Phyllis, Kathy, Eeva, and Jack—
the most significant people in our lives.
To all those couples who have allowed us to share
excerpts of their dialogues in this book.

Contents

Introduction

I had never heard of Couple Communication when Eleanor Rawson contacted me to collaborate on a book about it. She had read several pieces I'd written in *Philadelphia Magazine* and thought my style matched the content of this program. Before I agreed to her offer, I took the course with my husband, and we were surprised to discover in four short weeks that we could learn a new and extremely valuable way to communicate when we already thought we were old pros.

I agreed to join the project as the writer and shortly afterward met Sherod Miller, Dan Wackman, and Elam Nunnally on the first of my several trips to Minnesota. From the first I was impressed to watch them lift the skills out of their course and use them as business partners and friends.

The core ideas in this book come from Couple Communication, a program developed at the start of the '70s to help people of the ME generation who did not believe that personal exploration was the only road to fulfillment. Instead of individuals, it focused on pairs and on particular ways that communication would improve relationships and deal with conflict.

In 1967 Sherod Miller had enrolled at the University of Minnesota Family Study Center to work on a Ph.D. in Family Sociology and was assigned to a project with a rangy, soft-spoken fellow named Elam Nunnally, a father of five who had taken a leave of absence from a family service agency in Milwaukee to study the sociology of families. Their task was to examine how families handle their rites of passage—those momentous and sometimes stormy bridges like marriage, birth, death, etc. They chose for their study couples at the stage between engagement and marriage and decided to concentrate on teaching them something useful. "What we realized," Nunnally recalls, "is that there were lots of topics—finances, sex, in-laws—that nobody had the skills to communicate about." Moreover, Miller had found in his counseling practice that people had difficulty talking out everyday concerns which, unattended, grew into the crises that drove them to his office. What they hoped to develop was a program that could teach couples how to talk more effectively on their own, to talk across the years and carry on a dialogue that created its own experience and added a robust richness to their relationship.

For their initial research they asked couples to discuss a topic of their choice: plan an activity, verbalize what irritates them about their partner, discuss what pleases them, and so on. They collected hundreds of hours of tapes and pored over them, examining every nuance. "We started to find," Miller says, "that people who made connections had certain skills. They talked differently from the ones who didn't connect. I don't mean they were more dramatic or more articulate or smarter. They were somehow able to understand others and be understood themselves. It was fascinating."

Miller and Nunnally knew they were on to something special. By now it was 1969 and their project had been extended to include married couples. From the data they had collected they had formulated a program that could actually show people how to alter their communication, and the feedback was that the skills they taught were lasting ones. Unlike the "high" of a weekend encounter, so hard to sustain in subsequent months, they were teaching practical techniques to tackle everyday situations. And like a new pipe that seasons with each smoke, their skills improved the more they were used.

What they lacked at that point was an organizer to systematize their material, fill in the holes, and create an overall mold to house all the pieces. Enter Dan Wackman, who rolled into the Family Study Center in Minnesota at the ripe old age of twenty-nine with two masters degrees—one in political science and one in journalism—plus a doctorate in mass communication. His forte was research and he was interested in learning more about family communication. "There were some pretty important people then," he remembers, "who were saying it was impossible to teach people to communicate. That set up a challenge for me." His expertise balanced the field work of Miller and Nunnally and they joined forces.

Within a short time the trio developed a complete communication program with funds provided by the Family and Children's Service of Minneapolis and the National Institute of Mental Health. Their finished work was summarized into a 150-page report, and seventy-five printed copies of that report, bound with a bright orange cover, were distributed to people who had contributed to the project. Miller, Nunnally, and Wackman went their separate ways, never suspecting their summary would soon be circulating like hot gossip at professional meetings and that calls would be forthcoming from Salt Lake City, Atlanta, Los Angeles. "Come out and do a workshop. Teach us how to teach communication."

That was the germination of the Minnesota Couple Communication Program. Miller, Nunnally, and Wackman reunited, formed a corporation, Interpersonal Communications Programs, Inc., to distribute their offspring, and authored a textbook, *Alive and Aware,* that's sold over 100,000 copies and is a resource in over 300 colleges and universities offering courses in communication, family dynamics, and human services.

Since its inception, over 75,000 couples have taken Couple Communication and the program has won achievement awards from the National Council on Family Relations and the Association of Couples for Marriage Enrichment. Some twenty-five studies conducted at major universities to test the impact of Couple Communication have found consistent positive results. Almost everybody comes away from the course having learned the skills to be a better communicator. Today, besides the Couple Communication Program, ICP has added new programs for families and businesses.

It isn't easy for four people to collaborate on a book, especially when two are in Minnesota, one is in Wisconsin, one in New Jersey, and the publisher adds a fifth voice in New York. I'm convinced the reason we were able to work together so amiably is because the very contents of this book gave us a means to settle our differences and enjoy our similarities.

I want to thank Alan Halpern, my editor at *Philadelphia Magazine,* for allowing me the time to write *Straight Talk,* and for his encouragement and support to me as a writer. My gratitude also to Dr. William Stayton and Ann Wiens-Stephenson for their contributions to the chapter on sexual communication, and to Dallas and Nancy Demmitt for their contributions to the chapter on communication at work. To my husband, Jack, my children, Sharon and Matthew, my sister and my parents, a very special thank you for helping me to appreciate the benefits of Straight Talk and to experience the joys of connecting. I hope—no, I'm certain—that our book will show you how to connect and enrich your life, too.

—CAROL SALINE

STRAIGHT TALK

PART I

The Style and the Substance

1
Talk about Talk

Stop the first hundred people strolling down any street in any city and ask them what they want out of life. You'll get a hundred different answers ranging from health to wealth to a good night's sleep. But if you dig to the core of their responses, in some form or another they are saying, "I want to be happy." Beyond our dreams and fantasies what gives us happiness in our everyday lives is the capacity to form and sustain good, positive relationships. And it is communication that creates and nurtures such relationships.

In its fullest definition, to communicate means to make known; to give to another; to interchange thoughts, feelings, and information; to participate; to share; to form a connecting link. Thus, communication creates, maintains, alters, or destroys human relationships. Beginning with the verbal initiation of "hello," language nourishes or starves whatever grows between two people. That's why we can make the very bold statement that if you can learn how to talk, you can be happy.

Forget oil and gold. Talk is our most precious commodity. Yet it's been virtually ignored as a thermometer for monitoring the temperature of a relationship. Limited research shows that it's an excellent guide to the quality people ascribe to their life together. When surveys ask couples, "Are you satisfied with your relationship?" those who respond "yes" also answer "yes" to the question, "Do you consider that you communicate well with your partner?"

The quality of communication has nothing to do with the quantity of conversation. The way we all run around to meetings, jobs, racquetball, bridge games, volunteer work, self-awareness seminars and lessons, we couldn't rely on the quantity of talk to cement our relationships even if we wanted to. When we are able to connect in brief moments, we know how priceless quality exchanges are and how meaningless quantity can be.

Several years ago, Dr. Ray Birdwhistel, the anthropologist who coined the term "body language," conducted a study to see how much time married couples spend talking to each other in the course of a week. He studied one hundred couples who had been married at least five years and considered their marriage reasonably successful. For a year he equipped them with voice-activated body microphones which they carried whenever they were together. Then he sat down to measure his data.

He immediately discounted certain kinds of talk: one-way comments, grunts, "yes, dear" responses, "dinner's-on-the-table" type announcements, etc. The content didn't matter either as long as there was some sort of two-way dialogue. When those exchanges were added up, the median came to 27½ minutes per week. Less than a half hour! And it was that high, Birdwhistel says, because many of the couples in his sample were fairly social and spent time talking in the car as they shuttled about.

Ultimately, Birdwhistel concluded that the amount of talk between pairs is no barometer of their happiness. Moreover, there's no way to measure couples' nonverbal communication, since every motion we make from a grin to a grimace, a wave to a slap, a saunter to a slouch transmits some message. However, such messages aren't always clear. You may interpret someone's silence as boredom or withdrawal when he or she is simply feeling pensive. You may read the grip of a strong handshake as aggressive when it's meant to be friendly. Nonverbal language has another limitation: it cannot describe anything but the here-and-now. Even the gifted mime Marcel Marceau would have difficulty conveying wordlessly something that happened yesterday or his expectations for tomorrow.

Body language provides clues without a context. For detail, color, background, and clarification, nothing replaces the spoken word. The first time a baby strings together a few sounds to form a recognizable word, the family is elated. During a group conversation about language a woman whose children were in college recalled, "My son's first word was cookie and I was so thrilled you'd have thought the Gettysburg Address poured out of his year-and-a-half-old mouth. I telephoned my husband, my mother, *and* sister."

As we wobble from the cradle toward adulthood, the initial importance ascribed to words diminishes, and it's replaced somewhere along the line with the notion that talk is cheap. Words lose their value and, under the current protective umbrella of self-expression, it's become fashionable to blurt out almost anything without censorship. And we forget that words come back to haunt us as well as to hallow us.

Haven't you been in a situation where you failed to speak when you should have. Where you opened your mouth and unintentionally stuck your foot in it. Where you made a promise you knew you couldn't keep. Where you learned Aunt Grace had cancer and you meant to tell her what a valued friend she'd been to you, but she died before you got around to it. Where you told your husband or wife in the heat of anger that you'd have left years ago if it hadn't been for the children. Where you lashed out with your fist or your tongue and wanted to say afterward, "I'm sorry," but you couldn't summon the courage. Where you watched somebody cry and wanted to touch them and say something comforting, but you kept silent. Where you babbled some malicious gossip and wished your mouth were a tape recorder so you could erase the words. Where a kind word, a can-I-help-you, would have made all the difference, but you didn't take the time to say it. Or you did! Where you and your roommate started the day with a quarrel and as a result you jumped on everybody at the office. Where you tried so hard to say it but the words got in the way.

You see, talk isn't cheap at all.

WHY COMMUNICATION IS SO DIFFICULT

If you've heard it once, you've heard it a thousand times: "We just can't communicate."

Kids mumble, "I can't talk to my parents. They don't understand me."

Parents wail, "I can't talk to my kids. The only thing we have in common is that we speak the same language."

A woman confides to a friend, "I don't know what's the

matter with my marriage. We aren't on the same wavelength. We can't talk to each other."

A husband comes home from work, pecks his wife on the cheek, and asks, "What's new?" She replied, "Not much. I had a typical day. Shopping, the kids, a PTA board meeting. Nothing special." They both complain they have nothing meaningful to talk about.

A couple mutually agrees to separate after twenty years of marriage and three children. He tells a friend, "I don't think she ever really knew me. I was never able to tell her who I am."

An employer learns a key manager is leaving and asks, "Why didn't you come talk to me if you were unhappy?" The employee replies, "I've tried in the past, but we have a communication problem."

Actually, all these people are communicating at some level. You cannot *not* communicate. Even silence says something. What they are not doing is connecting. Isn't it ironic that in an era where we've discovered so much about human behavior and we've got a word for practically everything, we still continue to communicate in the same old ways. Like our grandparents and our parents, we speak from positions of authority rather than equality, from distance rather than intimacy, from restraint rather than receptivity.

Moreover, we unquestionably accept the truisms handed down from generation to generation that maintain the very barriers to communication that we need to topple. Do you remember, when you were a small child, that the magic of love was having one person in your life who knew exactly what you wanted and needed? Whether it was your mother, your father, or your grandmother, that special person somehow always knew—when you needed a hug, when you were sad or angry, what you wanted, what you were thinking, how you felt. Back then, somewhere in your mind a little seed was planted: if somebody really loves me, they'll *know* what's going on inside me; I won't ever have to tell them.

Over the years that seed blossoms into a full-grown myth: when people care about you they understand you totally. You don't have to tell them you like flowers on Valentine's Day and movies with happy endings; they'll know. You don't have to reveal your private thoughts because people who are close know each other intuitively.

It would be wonderful if relationships were that simple and

people that transparent, but most of us are too complex and our lives too varied for such assumptions to be anything more than wishful thinking. Unfortunately, these very myths and truisms create the impasses to adult communication:

- Don't say what you really think.
- Children should be seen and not heard.
- If you ignore problems, they go away.
- Familiarity breeds contempt.
- What you don't know won't hurt you.
- Silence is golden.
- We think alike and that's why we get along.

Blocked by shopworn clichés and deprived of models to follow, we've been led to believe that good communication is difficult at best and frequently impossible. But even were we able to do away with these myths we would continue to have trouble opening ourselves to others because at a gut level we are afraid of speaking up and speaking out.

FACING THE FOUR FEARS

Much of what we say or don't say and the way we say it is governed by some kind of fear. Sometimes fears are grounded in reality; sometimes they're justified; sometimes they are totally irrational, based on myths we've come to accept as truth. What matters is that our fears are real to us and they influence the way we communicate. In our experience with thousands of couples we've isolated four basic fears that inhibit communication. Although we cannot eradicate fear, we can only agree with Franklin D. Roosevelt that you have nothing to fear but fear itself. You can let fears and doubts limit your life, or you can face them with the skills we will be teaching and move beyond them.

The Fear of Speaking Out
Many of us bite our tongues and swallow the words we desperately want to tell somebody because we're afraid. Afraid of sounding dumb or silly. Afraid of being disliked for something we've said. Afraid that if we're honest and forthright we'll hurt someone's feelings, insult them, or wound their pride. And we believe the myth that says when we hurt others, they'll reject us and we'll only end up hurting ourselves

more. So we keep silent. Lila is typical of those who took our course and found a way to conquer this fear.

"I never was able to be straightforward with people. I always worried about offending someone and I assumed my close friends would just know what I wanted. After Couple Communication, I had to arrange an all-day workshop. There was a lot of detail work to be done and it was falling on me. I called a friend who'd agreed to assist me to tell her that I was holding a meeting later in the week at my home. She started to offer the excuse that her mother was coming to visit. I decided to try what I'd learned and come out and say what I wanted.

"Let me tell you, my heart was in my mouth. I said, 'I need you to share some of this responsibility. I'd appreciate it if you'd come because there's more here than I can handle myself.' You know what? She came. And later she told me she'd realized that she'd let me down. It was really neat to see her at that meeting and to feel we'd been able to communicate."

The Fear of Fighting

Not everybody is afraid to fight. Those who learn to spar positively find that fights don't necessarily pollute the atmosphere. They can blow the clouds apart and clear the air. But suppose, like Marion, you were raised in a home where your parents never had a cross word and you came to believe that fighting was a sign that your marriage was doomed. Marion told us:

"Shortly before I was married, my mother told me, 'Your father and I have never had a disagreement.' I assumed she was uttering the gospel truth, and that if Eric and I disagreed, our whole marriage would fall apart. I thought, 'If we don't agree, well, where's the love?' We had a hard time in the beginning because I hid myself from him so we wouldn't fight. I had to learn that it's okay to argue, and I couldn't do that until the course taught me a style for disagreeing that freed me to say the things that were really on my mind. I can say what I feel, what I want, and what I think, as long as I don't accuse or blame Eric or make him the cause."

Fred and Linda had the opposite problem. In the early years of their marriage they clashed like enemy battleships, but they rarely tasted the sweetness of victory. Their arguments inevitably ended in a stalemate, adding calluses to old wounds. Because their fights created so much pain, they decided to avoid discussing issues and settled into an uneasy truce of coexistence. When they came to our group they were choking on bottled-up anger. We introduced them to the Straight Talk style and showed them that issues don't have to smolder unresolved, only to flare up when someone throws a match on the ashes. They learned to use disagreement as a catalyst for change. One night after the group had ended, Fred called to tell us:

> "Linda and I still fight now and then, but what a difference. We had a whopper last week just before Timmy's hockey game. When we got to the rink we were so mad at each other that we went to opposite ends of the arena to sizzle down. By the second period we'd cooled enough to sit together, and we were both mad—but oddly optimistic. We knew we'd learned to talk things out when we were ready and that blew our old hopelessness away."

The Fear of Intimacy

Someone once described the beginning of true friendship as the moment two people reveal equally dangerous secrets about themselves. The willingness to lift the curtain and let somebody peek at the inner you is certainly an invitation to intimacy, and it's one that many people are very timid about offering. We tend to believe that our deep, dark secrets are unique, that no one else harbors desires or thoughts quite like our own—however bizarre or beautiful they may be. If we reveal our real selves, point out the location of our soft spots, we're afraid we'll look foolish, mean, or even perverted, and we'll lose the respect and love of our partner or friend.

However, we've found that when people risk revealing themselves through a tool we call the Awareness Wheel, they're surprised and relieved to discover that they're not very different from anybody else. More often than not, they experience acceptance where they had anticipated rejection. Roger told us how fearful he used to be about opening up to his wife:

> "I believed men had to be strong and make decisions on their own. When I was offered the promotion to the job I have now, my main concern was that I wasn't qualified to handle it, that I couldn't make the grade. I certainly didn't want to tell my boss and I couldn't tell Marie because I

didn't want her to know I was unsure of myself. I was afraid
to let her know I thought I might be inadequate. Our society
is so success-oriented. There's so much pressure about getting ahead. I worried that if I expressed my fears to her she
would say, 'What's wrong with you? It's not natural to be
like that.' And maybe she'd say to herself, 'I married the
wrong kind of guy.' I was afraid she wouldn't be proud of
me. I'd lose her respect.

"So I stewed about it to myself for a couple of weeks. I was
pretty irritable and tense, but she didn't know why. In fact
she didn't know a thing about the promotion until I came
home and told her I had a new position. She was floored. I
really wished I could have talked to her about all this. It was
an awful burden for me to carry alone, but I just didn't have
the technique then for approaching her."

Not everybody shares Roger's type of fear. Others fear that
if they get too close in a relationship they'll lose themselves
and their freedom. To preserve their identity they keep their
shades drawn and maintain a safe distance. We aren't suggesting there are no risks to intimacy. There are. But there
are also precious rewards from sharing, and in this book you
will learn how to share yourself when and if you want to.

It's our firm belief that sharing yourself with another person is crucial to your growth as an individual as well as to
the growth of your relationships. We all need someone to talk
to, to trade our hopes and dreams with as well as our fears
and sorrows; someone who will listen to us and take us seriously.

The Fear of Commitment

It's commonly believed that a verbal agreement to do something irrevocably locks us into meeting that commitment. Unfortunately, it isn't always possible to fulfill a promise and,
rather than risk the blame or criticism for failing to follow
through, it becomes easier to say nothing.

In an emotional moment at his father's funeral, Harold
told his sisters he would give the lion's share of support to his
widowed mother. A year later when his business suffered re-
verses, he went to his sisters and asked them to increase their
aid. They reacted with indignation. "You promised. A promise is forever. If you didn't mean it, you never should have
committed yourself."

Let's face it, things change. And reactions like that of

Harold's sisters are precisely why people fear saying "I will." Commitments are especially risky with people who have witnessed your past performance and are likely to be around in the future to applaud or hiss your encore. Harold's impulsive kindness was their undoing, but it isn't an argument for ducking commitments. Consider commitments as choices. When you say what you will do, you can also say what you will not do. And when you learn to use the Awareness Wheel in Chapter 4 you will discover how to commit yourself to reasonable expectations, how to say no when you mean no, and how to appropriately qualify the word "yes."

YOU CAN DO IT

Although these fears and doubts can thwart your potential to connect, you *can* confront them and move beyond them. The main reason you aren't more successful right now is that you haven't been taught the proper skills, and Straight Talk is designed to fill that void. Our experience indicates that fears rarely, if ever, materialize when people speak in a style that genuinely expresses their thoughts, feelings, and wants without blaming or demanding. From this moment on, we want you to believe that you are capable of relinquishing worthless myths, conquering inhibiting fears, and becoming a clear communicator who uses words to build bridges to connect with others.

The success of our program has convinced us that anybody who wants to can learn new and better ways to communicate. Everyone can be taught to enrich a relationship and establish a base of shared esteem. We've come to believe that intimacy isn't an impossible dream but a reality achieved through a communication process that encourages mutual sharing. We've found, too, that when people learn the skills to talk out their day-to-day concerns, they begin to bypass the roadblocks that lead to major crashes.

We keep repeating the term *skills* because this is the missing ingredient in the wave of knowledge about behavior that's flooded both professional journals and mass media over the last decade. Pick up a magazine or turn on a TV talk show and there's Dr. So-and-So telling us why our teenagers rebel, why men go through periods of crisis, why older women are dating younger men, why we must deal with stress before it deals us in. Certainly it's important to understand why we are the way we are. But the value of mere insight has been over-played. It's been touted as the magic potion that can create instant change, but it's disappointed all those who weren't in-formed that insight is only the first step. If you are over-weight, it surely helps to understand that you gorge yourself when you are depressed because your mother gave you lol-lipops and cookies to cheer you up as a child. However, until you master the skills to change your eating habits, you can't permanently shed pounds. It's the same for human relation-ships. If you lack the skills to clearly convey what you think and feel and want, your insights may be revealing—even in-teresting—but not particularly productive.

In some respects, we professionals are partly responsible for underestimating the capacity of people to master commu-nication skills and use them to take charge of their lives. The rapid growth of the human services field has created the im-pression that professionals have all the answers and that only under their guidance can you alter your behavior. In many cases professional assistance *is* necessary. Yet our course (and others) proves that most people are able to help them-selves—and a book like this may be the only tool they need to begin.

How can we make such grand promises? Because we've seen amazing results with the nearly 75,000 couples who've taken our Couple Communication course. Since 1971 all across the United States, in Canada, Europe, and Australia, we have been demonstrating that it is possible to accept and appreciate differences between partners, to convey joyous as well as painful information clearly, to learn how to listen and be listened to. We've done it by teaching skills well within the reach of everyone's ability.

It's an exciting process to witness. Five to seven couples of all ages gather together for a three-hour session one night a week for four weeks. Most are married, some engaged, some living together. They live on farms and in high-rise apart-ments. They work as teachers, firemen, lawyers, nurses, cor-porate executives, homemakers. Their only common denominator is an interest in improving relationships through communication, and that desire cuts across the barriers of age, race, faith, and social status.

Our basic program involves observation, participation, dis-cussion, and reading to help people identify how they communicate and teach them special skills. During each session the instructors—a couple who have gone through our instructor training program—explain and demonstrate a particular skill. Then the participating couples discuss some current issue in their lives for two minutes, using the skill just introduced as well as the preceding ones. The exchanges are purposely kept short because, unlike group therapy, we aren't interested in solving problems on the spot. Whether couples discuss money, in-law problems, time together, or a trip to the moon is entirely up to them and irrelevant to us. The issues are merely vehicles to practice the skills; then couples can use them to resolve the issue in the privacy of their homes.

If couples want feedback on their use of the skills, the group provides it. Did they steer away from blaming and accusing each other? Did they respect each other? Did each one express feelings, thoughts, and desires? Did they hold back because they assumed their partner intuitively knew their position or feelings?

When the twelve hours are completed, most graduates are like late readers who've found the missing link and had a whole new world open for them. A chemistry teacher in St. Paul said:

"I learned more about my husband and the way we relate in the four weeks of this course than in twelve years of marriage."

An auto salesman in Detroit said:

"There have been positive changes in my marriage and carryover into my relationship with others."

An occupational nurse who has been married thirty years discovered:

"Nothing is so big I can't talk about it now, and that means it's possible to work anything out."

Perhaps the most poignant comment we ever received came from a woman who wrote us a year and a half after she and her husband had taken the course.

"Shortly after we finished Couple Communication, my husband learned he had terminal cancer. Because of the skills and principles you taught us, we were able to say all the things to each other in our last months together that we'd been too afraid or too anxious to say before. Maybe we just would not have known where to begin. When he died we had no unfinished business between us and that has made his death easier for me to bear. Thank you."

A PREVIEW OF COMING ATTRACTIONS

What our course has taught thousands, this book can teach you. There are no technical phrases or scientific jargon to confuse you. We'll be explaining broad concepts, backing them up with specific skills, and illustrating their application in a variety of situations. We won't just tell all; we'll show and tell and then we'll present some short exercises to help you test your understanding.

We begin by introducing the three common conversational styles that mark most of our daily exchanges. Then, in Chapter 5, we will show you a fourth and probably unfamiliar style that examines the little pebbles which, when ignored, lead to emotional landslides. You will learn to recognize your predominant style, if you have one; why that style may be creating problems; and why changing *how* you talk is more effective than changing *what* you talk about. You might see yourself as Mark did when he took our course:

"Boy, I come on strong to people. Nearly everything I say sounds like I'm the undisputed authority, even when I don't know much about it. You helped me see how many of my sentences start with 'You should do this' or 'You ought to do that.' No wonder people turn me off. Just learning to say 'I'd like you to' instead has already made a difference in my family life. That may not sound like a big deal, but changing the way I phrase something somehow makes me see a situation differently. I'm finding I demand less now and I'm getting more."

In Chapters 3 and 4 we give you the most valuable tool you'll ever own: the Awareness Wheel. The cornerstone of Couple Communication, the Awareness Wheel puts you in touch with the inner you and helps you translate what you *see* and *hear*, what you *think* and *want*, how you *feel*, and what *actions* you might take. You will learn how to hook into the information inside yourself and use it to communicate honestly and clearly with others.

Chapters 7, 8, 9, and 12 concentrate on skills—speaking

skills, listening skills, and problem-solving skills. These chapters are crammed with dos and don'ts, tips, insights, and how-to examples. Chapter 10 explains how communication reflects your self-esteem and the esteem you have for others, and demonstrates four ways that our spoken words can mirror these attitudes. The final four chapters pull everything together and show you how you can apply these new skills to the vital aspects of your life: your sex life, your children, your work, and, ultimately, your spiritual life.

When you finish *Straight Talk,* you will:

- Understand how you talk and how you can increase your conversational range by adding alternative styles to your repertoire that you may never have considered before.
- Learn how to talk safely about explosive or delicate issues in your life.
- Increase your choices for relating to people.
- Make deliberate connections rather than accidental ones.
- Use communication to raise your self-esteem and show esteem for others.

FOLLOW THE LEADER

You hold in your hands the power to initiate and maintain connections. Although you cannot force someone to tell you what you want to hear, nor can you control how they'll answer you, you do not have to follow their lead and succumb to their style. You might even draw them into yours. In other words, communication is influenced and directed by the receiver of a message as well as by the sender. Instead of being sucked into a whirlpool, you can pull the plug. For example, you will learn that when you're attacked there are better ways to respond than by counterattack.

Suppose you were expected home at 5 P.M. and you arrived at 5:30, assaulted by the volley, "Don't you wear a watch? You knew we had to be at the doctor by 5:15. How can you be so irresponsible?" Normally, you might take the bait and jab back defensively, "Well, you're not perfect either. It wasn't my fault anyway. The traffic was heavy." But you could change the tone of the whole conversation by responding, "I know I'm late. I didn't expect to encounter such heavy traffic. I'm sorry I worried you. Let me call the doctor and see if he's still there." A change in tone or style can be that simple and can refocus an entire conversation in a more pleasant vein.

Too often people react when they ought to act, and they are lured into playing follow-the-leader instead of being the leader. We often hear stories like this one from a woman in her mid-forties:

"My husband seems more interested in watching TV than in talking to me. I can't tell you how many nights I'll sit beside him on the sofa, and I can't get his attention off the blasted tube. The more I nag him about it, the more he withdraws. Then he complains I'm a nag. Well, I can't do anything but nag because otherwise he ignores me."

"I do this because he does that." People engage in follow-the-leader because they think it's the only game in town. Blinded by myopic communication, their eyes focus solely on the object of their attention, which prevents them from seeing other possibilities or choices. Starting now, we want you to broaden your glance and include yourself in your line of vision. You will discover you don't have to pursue a bad lead. You can set your own course, keeping in mind that although you cannot control others, you can choose not to surrender control of yourself.

The harness of control is invariably ill-fitting. We don't want to be controllers because controlling types are thought to be dominating, hovering, grasping, clutching, smothering—a host of undesirable adjectives. Nor do we want to be controlled by others because that suggests we're spineless pushovers with no opinions of our own and no gumption to support them. But if we try to avoid being controlled, we face the accusation that we're cold or remote, withdrawn or withholding. And who has not experienced the chilly apprehension of losing control, where we tremble for fear of hurting others or embarrassing ourselves.

Losing control, being controlled, controlling others—these are simply the realities of human behavior. It's the way people have always been and will probably continue to be. Although you can't totally escape some form of control, you *can* be aware of it and recognize which control pattern you typically use in your interactions with others. Armed with that awareness, you can use the skills in *Straight Talk* to deal effectively with control.

Control is dangerous because it separates people. Whether

you are controlling or being controlled, you are locked in opposition; it's you *versus* someone else. We do not believe in adversary communication and this book is a plea for collaboration; it's about you *and* someone else. Throughout, we stress ways to connect, first with yourself and, then, equally important ways to use that knowledge to conect with others. Our goal is to reduce the conflicts that separate people by teaching how to participate confidently in relationships as an equal partner.

Perhaps that sounds like a tall order, but you'll find it happening naturally as you lift the skills from these pages and apply them with your mate, your family, your friends, and your co-workers. We think you'll find your life running more smoothly because we've designed *Straight Talk* to help you ward off trouble. We're concerned about prevention. We intend to prevent breakdown in relationships by equipping you with communication skills and knowledge to assist you at every step along the sometimes rocky way.

Problems in relationships often occur because people fail to recognize what angers, disappoints, frightens, or pleases them. Even when they do, they often can't or won't talk about these feelings, and what is left unexpressed festers and hardens. The earlier you can identify and talk out your everyday concerns, the greater chance you will have to prevent them from building up inside and exploding.

Connecting doesn't have to be difficult. Often, it happens unconsciously when a spark ignites between two people. You are accustomed to experiencing the glow and intensity of connecting in a surge of love, but you can connect in almost any way: when you're crying, playing, grieving, agreeing, disagreeing, sharing good feelings. You connect when you're joking and laughing. You connect over a whopping fight, as long as both of you are on equal footing. You connect when you dream with someone, scheme with someone, hold hands by a sickbed or watch a sunset. You connect by communicating and by facing the reality that maintaining relationships is highly variable: sex, money, careers, children, vacations, with bad and accepting the fact that will be both—not necessarily evenly distributed.

The need to communicate is one of the most powerful human drives. By improving your awareness of how you talk and learning the skills to communicate fully and clearly, you can literally make connections happen. If we were to teach you nothing more than ways to handle your present issues and to head off some of tomorrow's problems at home, at work, and at play, *Straight Talk* could be the most useful book you'll read this year. But that's not enough for us.

We think life was meant to be savored in the joy of intimacy. As you read *Straight Talk* you will gain the confidence to peel away your protective shield and reveal your vulnerable parts to those you love. That is the true sharing of communication. The more you are able to share at an intimate level, the more connected you will feel. And the more often you can connect, the richer your life will become.

2

A Sense of Style

Communication is a combination of what people talk about and how they talk to each other. The *what* is content, and it is highly variable: sex, money, careers, children, vacations, politics, sports, the weather. The *how* is style: tone of voice, attitude, method of expression. Think of content as raw material and style as the many different things you can do with it. If the content is potatoes, style depends on whether you bake them, mash them, add cheese or chives for extra flavor, cut them up and fry them, or toss them in a salad.

Matching style to content is an integral part of effective communication. Although most of us give a great deal of thought to the content of our conversations, we tend to take style for granted, and we rarely recognize the enormous impact it has on the quality and clarity of our communication. Your style lets others know if you're joking, serious, angry, happy, puzzled, depressed. It fleshes out content, adding nuances and clues that tell others a great deal more about your feelings and thoughts than your words do.

When style doesn't match content, you're apt to confuse your listeners or be misunderstood. You probably know people who are one- or two-dimensional in style, and conversations with them may be uncomfortable because their style is so obviously inappropriate to the situation. People like glad-hand Bill who meets a pal on the street, slaps him on the back, and says cheerily, "How ya doing, old buddy? I hear your mom's in the hospital?" Or people like bearded Brad, who graduated with honors from all the human potential courses. He bumps into friends in a restaurant or on the street, takes their hands in his, peers into their eyes, and asks, with a gravity generally reserved for reading wills or signing treaties, "How have you been? Please share with me what's going on in your life."

At best, style and content have a hand-in-glove relationship. But too often, people get locked into one or two predominant styles and their communication suffers as a result. Couples often come to our group complaining:

"We seem to talk past each other."
"I can't get a word in edgewise."
"Talk? Are you kidding? All we ever do is argue."
"We seem to be on different wavelengths."

The earliest study of communication styles was done by Professor William Fawcett Hill. From his work and from our twelve years of observing how people exchange information, we've identified four basic styles of interaction. The first three will probably be quite familiar to you. There's Small Talk: the chatty style that meets, greets, and runs most of our daily lives; Control Talk: the bossy, take-charge style; and Search Talk: the reflective style that wonders why out loud. The fourth style, Straight Talk, which we'll discuss at length in Chapter 5, may be quite unfamiliar to you, but it's a style we will be emphasizing because it's the best one for dealing with difficult issues and personal concerns.

It's fairly easy to identify a style by examining two essential ingredients: the intentions and the behavior. What's the aim of the remark and what conduct supports it? When you want something done quickly, you're likely to bark a crisp order. That's one aspect of Control Talk. When you're furious at being picked up a half hour late, you're likely to come off blaming. That's another side of Control Talk. When you're feeling on top of the world and don't want anything to knock you off, you use Small Talk to broadcast your mood. You might turn to Search Talk if you're trying to decide whether to keep your present job or go back to school. And when you've finished this book you'll know how to use Straight Talk, the style that defuses conflict and makes it possible for you to connect with everyone in your life in new and intimate ways.

As you read about these four styles, the light bulb in your brain will begin to flash off and on like a strobe: Hey, that sounds like me, like Ethel, like Uncle Harry, like my boss. Although the styles are not normally as clear-cut as we present them, we make a point of isolating the characteristics so you can appreciate the differences.

You'll begin to wonder, how do I typically operate? Am I a Small Talker? Can I control my Control Talk? Am I willing to use Search Talk when I'm stymied? Can I learn Straight Talk to help me connect? You may realize you're terrific at chitchat and argue with brilliance, but find yourself groping for words when you want to express fear or sympathy. Or you may be so skilled at one or two styles that you wrap yourself in them like a favorite bathrobe because they're comfortable and familiar.

Through our work with groups, we've found that couples who learn the art of aligning style and content become better communicators. And the first step in this progress is becoming aware that you have alternative styles. Suppose you've just been introduced to someone. You might effusively gush, "Hi there, delighted to meet you," or shyly mumble, "Hello." You could extend your hand or avert your eyes. You might say, "Gee, you have a friendly smile" or "Don't you hate cocktail parties." Each of these responses is quite different, and depending on which one you choose, the outcome of the meeting is likely to be quite different as well.

Flexibility of style creates choices. Remember how you were taught to read by looking at each word on a page. Then along came speed reading and you were told the only way to read was in clusters. Well, in fact, both modes have their place. It's fine to zip through a newspaper, but a beautifully written novel should be savored slowly. Communication should also be flexible. A good communicator recognizes choices and knows when and how to use each style appropriately.

Human beings are creatures of habit, and one of our aims in this book is to help you break out of your style habits by showing you the range of your choices. We think you'll find that learning to match and switch styles will have a more dramatic effect on your relationships than changing subjects ever did. As you refine your knack for assessing situations and matching them with appropriate styles and skills, you'll find your connections to others increasing.

STYLE I: SMALL TALK

Small Talk is the chatty, sociable conversation that fills most of life. The mode is easy-breezy, suitable to the casual content. Nobody has to learn Small Talk. It's a style almost as automatic as breathing because it's spoon-fed to us at home right along with Pablum, handed out in school with books and pencils, delivered with birthday gifts by aunts and uncles, and babbled in the family room as tots mimic their elders while they play house. Even people who complain they're no good at Small Talk admit, when pressed, that it's not for lack of knowing what it is.

Small Talk is perfect for making contact when you walk in the door or pick up a telephone. It's good for calling attention to routine matters such as service appointments or broken appliances. You Small Talk your opinion of a movie, the details of an article you read in the paper, or a football pool you bet and lost. Despite its casual nature, Small Talk has an important impact on couples. Indirectly, you and your partner demonstrate fondness and affection as you catch each other up on the events of the day, prattle about people you know, or pass on a good story you heard at work. You show mutual enjoyment of each other without saying directly, "I like you. I have fun with you."

When two people agree on something but have to discuss plans for executing it—picking up a baby-sitter, planting a vegetable garden, or arranging a car pool—Style I, Small Talk, is a most efficient way to handle it. Small Talk oils the wheels of daily life and keeps us rolling. Its characteristics are:

- The content is common, ordinary, everyday fare.
- Expectations are clear and agreed upon by both parties.
- Little or no tension exists. Emotions are on an even keel.
- Feelings are not expressed. Since little intensity is stirred up by the content of Small Talk, there isn't much to get emotional about. The focus tends to rest on something you or someone else said or thought.
- The tone of voice and pace of speech are normal, relaxed, friendly, and even-handed.

When to Use Small Talk
The intention of Small Talk is to maintain the status quo

and keep things pleasant and genial. You would use Small Talk in any of the following ways:

- *Reporting events and factual information:* "The car stalls every time it rains. Probably needs a tune-up."
- *Keeping informed:* "How did the interview go yesterday?"
- *Joking and storytelling:* "I heard a good one today. It seems that . . ."
- *Routine questions:* "Is your office closed for the holiday?"
- *Simple descriptions:* "I see you painted your house."
- *Making unelaborate statements about yourself:* "I was born in Kansas."
- *Your habits:* "I usually drink wine with dinner."
- *Your preferences:* "I'd rather have the vanilla, please."
- *Your likes and dislikes:* "I hate classical music. Give me country-western any day."
- *Your opinions:* "I'm a believer in a day's work for a day's pay."
- *Your physical state:* "I'm ready to fall into bed."
- *Your actions:* "I wrote to Sharon today."
- *Your friends:* "Connie never forgets to send me a birthday card; she's so thoughtful."

Small Talk may be dull, zesty, or even boastful: "Did I act my way out of a tight corner yesterday. I was superb." The lighthearted joking of Small Talk is also a great way to put an absurd situation into perspective, to cut through tension, or to make a point without blaming or attacking. The jibes of Style I are intended to hit their targets like a pillow, not a bullet. They jostle; they don't wound.

You are going to a party and your husband hasn't shaved since morning. You'd like him to give his face a once-over, but you know he's likely to get annoyed if you come on like Big Mama and tell him he needs a shave. So you kid him: "Hey, hon, did you remember to set the alarm for your five o'clock shadow?"

Your wife has been acting like a witch all evening. You need a way to let her know it without creating a hassle. You walk to the utility closet, hand her a broom, and, with a twinkle in your eye, suggest she go out for a short ride.

This Is Not the Time for Small Talk
Although Small Talk serves an important function in our interpersonal relationships, it is totally inadequate for handling strong differences or important issues. However, it re-

mains the most widely used conversational style, even in situations where it is inappropriate, simply because it doesn't make waves or precipitate emotional upheaval. If swimming in unfamiliar waters makes you nervous, you're liable to retreat to the safety of Small Talk when you'd be better off exploring the territory with Search Talk. And if you're uncomfortable with emotional outbursts, you're likely to try to defuse an unpleasant situation with some Style I lighthearted joking.

But it's awfully frustrating to try to talk seriously with someone who won't move beyond the pleasantries of Small Talk. You want to shake that person by the shoulder and holler, "Can't you ever get involved?" Recall the last time you tried to discuss something really important with somebody who chitchatted and joked in response. Aggravating, wasn't it?

Because it's easier to gloss over a difference than to take the time or risk the pain of talking it out, couples frequently resort to Small Talk to sidestep issues. But issues are like weeds. They don't go away unless you pull them out and, left alone, they can choke your entire garden. People who communicate almost exclusively in Style I cheat themselves. Their partners begin to think it's not worth bringing up issues because nothing ever seems to get settled. Worse, a relationship that doesn't move beyond the superficial level eventually loses its fizz and becomes stale.

STYLE II: CONTROL TALK

None of us needs lessons in recognizing Control Talk. We've all been told what to do by a parent, a boss, a spouse, or a friend, and we know how irritating certain kinds of directives or advice can be. We've done our share of manning the controls, too; telling others what they should think or do. Control Talk, in any of its many forms, carries one implicit message: "I'm in control here and I know what's right for me *and* for you. I'll direct; you follow. We'll do it my way." Unlike Small Talk, which attempts to maintain the status quo and keep things moving smoothly, Control Talk takes charge and alters the course.

In many circumstances Control Talk is necessary and useful. Teams need captains to direct their play. Classrooms need teachers to instruct and to prevent mayhem. Control is troublesome in relationships only when those involved struggle over who's holding the reins. When one person tries to force a change of action or opinion by barking orders and hurling labels and accusations, the other person naturally tries to resist. The content of the message is completely obscured as both parties channel all their energy into a destructive battle of wills.

Once your verbal guns are poised for attack, you're almost certain to be hit by return fire. For example:

If one says: "If you hadn't taken so long to put on your makeup, we wouldn't be late again, as usual."

The other shoots back: "Half the time we're late, it's your fault. You drive like a turtle."

If one says: "You never pay attention when I talk to you. All you care about is the stupid TV."

The other shoots back: "If you had something worthwhile to say, maybe I'd listen."

If one says: "You should call your sister more often."

The other shoots back: "If you're so fond of my sister, you call her."

Sadly, that kind of Control Talk repartee is quite common. The content may change, but the underlying control message inevitably triggers a contest in one-upsmanship.

However, not all Control Talk is inherently negative. One aspect, Light Control Talk, facilitates a particular end and is expedient and helpful. It's the blaming and coercive component of Heavy Control Talk that causes problems between people. Let's look at the differences.

LIGHT CONTROL TALK: EASY DOES IT

When the pressure valve rests on low and the tension level between people is at a minimum, the pragmatic, nonhostile directives of Light Control Talk generate action. The precondition for successful Light Control Talk is a willingness to cooperate. Although usually spoken in a normal voice, the instructions or directions of Light Control Talk have a firm,

authoritative tone. You would use Light Control Talk when
your intentions are:

- To persuade
- To direct
- To seek *but not force* agreement
- To use legitimate authority

Good salesmen and successful politicians are masters of
Light Control Talk—the art of gentle persuasion. When you
vote for Senator X instead of Y, or pedal home from the bike
shop with a ten-speed when you had planned on buying a
three-speed, it's because persuasion conquered your opposition. The preacher on the pulpit sermonizes with Light Control Talk; so does the public relations man who convinces
you to contribute to the Heart Fund. And when you want to
try hang-gliding and your friend backs off, you may urge,
"Come on. Let's try it just once." That's a form of Light
Control Talk, too.

Light Control Talk is the natural and preferred style in a
variety of situations:

- *It instructs:* Teacher to students—"Today we will discuss
  the principles of Euclidean geometry." Office manager to
  new clerk—"File paid bills in this cabinet, but put the ac-
  counts receivable in that box over there."
- *It cautions:* "No candy, Benji, it's almost time for dinner."
  "Don't swim right after you eat. You'll get cramps."
- *It establishes expectations:* "Church starts at 9:30. We'll
  all go in my car." "Make sure I have this report no later
  than 3 P.M."
- *It directs:* "Take the lawnmower for new blades." "Brush
  your teeth and go straight to bed."
- *It signals rising tensions:* "The next time you're going to
  be delayed, give me a call."
- *It praises:* "Blue is your color. It matches your eyes. You
  should wear it more often."
- *It advises:* "If I were in your shoes, I'd probably buy the
  house instead of renting the apartment."

As long as there is no compulsion attached, Light Control
Talk is efficient and functional. However, when advice or
directions reek of indisputable authority, you've crossed the
line into Heavy Control Talk: "Look, I've been in real estate
for years and I know what I'm talking about. You'd be foolish not to do what I tell you. Buy the house. Don't rent the

apartment." The difference is subtle but powerful, and unfortunately, Light Control Talk can all too easily escalate into the arm-twisting pressure of Heavy Control.

HEAVY CONTROL TALK:
THE HARD LINE

People gravitate to Heavy Control Talk when they are caught in a tense situation or when their emotions heat from simmer to boil. Driven by a desire to get their own way, establish their primacy, protect themselves, or stay in charge of a situation that's getting out of hand, they resort to control as the means to their particular end. Control Talk is demanding and aggressive, accusing and abusing. Its tone is harsh, stern, and threatening. It seeks nothing less than agreement and compliance, and it's self-centered, in that it considers only the speaker's point of view.

Although we don't normally think of words as instruments of attack, a direct hit by Heavy Control Talk always wounds. We are all guilty of Heavy Control Talk at one time or another, especially its most common form: blaming. When someone flings an accusation, the victim becomes defensive and counterattacks in an attempt to justify his or her position. The following exchange between Beth and Phil, taped when their marriage was shaky and full of tension, is typical of Heavy Control Talk.

PHIL: Why don't you just lay off! You're always on my back about something.
BETH: You're the one on my back for everything I do. Yesterday, when I was carrying bottles in from the car, you said, "You're gonna drop them." When I went out to start the car in the snow you said, "You'll never get it started. You'll just run the battery down again." And you always use a blaming tone of voice.
PHIL: Well, you do run the battery down.
BETH: Rarely. But you're always accusing me of not doing things right. When I go on a diet you say, "I know you won't lose any weight."
PHIL: Well, you never have. Every diet you go on turns out to be a farce.
BETH: Yeh, because you never give me any encouragement. You assume I won't stick to it.

PHIL: Well, do you? How many times have I caught you with a spoonful of ice cream in your mouth?

Round and round they go in a Heavy Control Talk war of the words: "I'm right; you're wrong." "No, I'm right and you're wrong." The pressure to comply is met with equal pressure to resist. People don't like to be told what to do or what's right for them, and that's exactly what happens in Heavy Control Talk. The attacked person gets the message: "You're not very important. What *I* think and feel has value. What *you* think and feel hardly counts."

When people have a mutual problem to solve, they mistakenly turn to Heavy Control Talk to press for a solution that suits each of them, instead of searching for a way out that might satisfy both. Heavy Control Talk is equally popular when you're seeking some kind of change and only a threat or order seems likely to produce the results you want. Jack and Sue are at a party and Jack has tippled one too many. In a steely voice, Sue attacks him:

"Don't dare take another drink. You're making an idiot of yourself. If I see you with a glass in your hand, I'm taking the car and leaving."

As soon as she walks away, Jack heads for the bar. It's the only way he knows to fight back.

Whether Heavy Control Talk is used to blame, attack, demean, coerce, threaten, or demand, it has the following underlying characteristics. By becoming aware of them, you have a better chance of eluding their stranglehold:

- People act out their feelings and desires instead of recognizing and coping with them.
- People focus on getting their own way instead of looking for acceptable solutions. And since it's assumed that only one person can be in charge, choices are eliminated.
- Tone of voice and choice of words signal tension and abuse feelings.
- Both parties try to blame each other for the problem, rather than considering how each has contributed to it.
- Introspection is completely bypassed as both people look outside for answers.
- Compliance is the motivating factor and the only outcome that seems to matter.

THE TWO FACES OF HEAVY CONTROL

Like the comedy/tragedy mask that symbolizes theater, Heavy Control has two distinct aspects. When it's direct and obvious, we call it Active. When it's indirect and subtle, we call it Passive.

Active Heavy Control: The Iron Fist

Active Heavy Control Talk is a sledgehammer; when it hits you, you know it. It's fairly easy to spot by its cutting edge, its demanding tone, the assertiveness of its "you do this" orders. It's acted out daily in a hundred different ways:

- *Labeling:* "That's a totally irresponsible statement."
- *Name-Calling:* "You're a coward."
- *Mind-Reading:* "You don't believe in that nonsense, do you?"
- *Blaming:* "This wouldn't have happened if you'd thought of someone besides yourself."
- *Accusing:* "Your eyes never left him once during dinner."
- *Threatening:* "This is your last chance."
- *Demanding:* "Just shut up."
- *Evaluating:* "You're wrong again."
- *Putting-Down:* "Only a woman would come to that conclusion."
- *Ventilating:* "Don't tell me how to drive."
- *Ordering:* "Don't leave until you've finished."
- *Taunting:* "Oh, your mother could never do anything to hurt her golden boy; her son, the doctor."
- *Ridiculing:* "That's your idea of dressing for success?"
- *Criticizing:* "Look, that approach will get you nowhere. Why don't you learn to stand up to her."
- *Nagging:* "Do I always have to remind you to take a shower?"
- *Lying:* "Well, we were going to invite you along. In fact we tried, but the line was busy. You must have been using it or maybe somebody was calling you. But we did try, honest."
- *Sarcasm:* "Well, well. Look who has graced us with his presence."

Passive Heavy Control: The Velvet Glove

The slippery subtlety of Passive Heavy Control Talk can be even more powerful than the direct hits of Active Heavy

Control Talk. Its tacticians employ weakness and dependency to get their way, making themselves appear victimized or inadequate. Unlike Active Control Talk, whose directness incites you to fight fire with fire, Passive Control Talk is so underhanded that you don't even know why you're angry. You aren't sure what's hooked you—guilt or pity—and you don't quite know how to respond. Look for the tentacles of Passive Control Talk in the following behaviors:

- *Complaining:* "I do all the dirty work around here and never get any help."
- *Whining:* "I can't seem to get the hang of anything."
- *Denying:* "That's not what I said."
- *Disqualifying:* "I didn't mean to upset you. I would never deliberately insult your artwork."
- *Withholding:* "I told you once. I'm not going to repeat myself."
- *Poor Me:* "Just once I wish things would go my way."
- *Pseudo-Questions:* "Will you tell me what's so terrible about wanting to have a little fun now and then."
- *Foot-Dragging:* "I know I said I'd do it and when I have time, I'll get around to it."
- *Assuming Blame:* "You're right. If I had any sense, I'd have quit."
- *Playing the Martyr:* "It doesn't matter. I'll get over it. I can take the heat. I always do."
- *Self Put-Downs:* "I'm incompetent. Anybody else would read these instructions and put the dollhouse together in an hour. I wouldn't get it if it took all day."
- *Excuses:* "If I felt better, I'd be out there shoveling too."
- *Changing Topics:* "Anything special on TV tonight?"
- *Self-Righteousness:* "And what makes you the authority, may I ask?"
- *Sweetness and Light:* "I baked all day to make you those chocolate cookies you adore because I love doing things to make you happy. That smile on your face is all the reward I need."
- *Keeping Score:* "I bought lunch last time."

Passive Control Talk is actually the iron fist disguised by a velvet glove. The verbal blasts are less powerful than those commonly used in Active Control, but this style is marked by physical signals that convey the same message: dramatic eyerolling, slouching shoulders, stony silence, hangdog looks. There's great strength in feigning weakness as an indirect expression of resentment or resistance.

WHAT'S BEHIND THE STRIKE FORCE
OF THE IRON FIST

Despite its many destructive aspects, Control Talk has become a fixture in our society. We lapse into it almost unconsciously, as one of our CC instructors learned on a motor trip from Philadelphia to New York. She had just finished her training and thought the two-hour drive would be a good time to review her material, so she asked her eight-year-old son, who was a precocious reader, to quiz her on the characteristics of Style II. She went down the list: blaming, accusing, fault-finding, and so on while he checked her off. About an hour later the boy was eating a candy bar in the back seat and making a mess. She turned to him and said, "Pick up those papers and stop licking your fingers. Why can't you learn to be neat?" He looked at her with his innocent eight-year-old eyes and said, "Hey, Mommy, you're in Heavy Control Talk and that's not nice."

We slip into Heavy Control Talk because, since early childhood, we've been plugged into a system that points fingers and looks for culprits. Who broke the ashtray? Who left the stove on? Who brought the cold germs to the classroom? Who forgot to bring in the paper? Who was the last one to use the car keys? Who dunnit? And since we humans are fast learners, we learn to hit back, or even better, to strike first.

Digging Beneath Anger
But Control Talk is more than a conditioned reflex; it's an outburst that the world perceives as anger, yet anger is just the tip of the iceberg. Underneath are a whole range of feelings that are sometimes quite apparent to us. But at other times, our feelings are buried so deeply in our subconscious that we act on what seems like impulse because we have no idea of the real motivation. In either case, we turn to Control Talk to master these feelings, using either the verbal blasts of Active Control or the manipulative whining of Passive Control.

Broken Expectations
Control Talk is often generated by the annoyance or irritability we feel when things don't go the way they are supposed

to. At home, at work, or at play, we all have certain established routines, patterns, and expectations which generally remain unspoken, although we tend to assume that those around us understand and recognize our personal rhythms. When someone suddenly violates these expectations, even inadvertently, we overreact.

The family is leaving for Grandma's. Each member has get-ready chores. Your son's job is to put the dog in the pen, but he's careless; the dog breaks loose and takes off. You and your spouse shout to bring him back. No luck. Your son chases after him but he's not fast enough. You look at your watch and realize you'll be late, delaying dinner. Almost automatically, you look for someone to blame and rip into your son with Heavy Control Talk.

"What's the matter with you? Why didn't you hold the leash tighter? Now we'll all be late because of you. You know how Grandpa gets when he has to wait to eat. Can't you do anything right?"

In the disruption of ordinary activities, we're thrown off balance by broken expectations. We become angry and begin to accuse: you're late; you're too early; you're careless; you're sloppy. We take charge and restore order with Heavy Control Talk.

Sheer Frustration

We also develop certain expectations about anticipated changes. When our hopes are dashed and we don't get what we want, we're frustrated and we show it through the anger of Control Talk. We might feel wronged because a friend or lover reneged on a promise, or disappointed because we'd hoped for pearls and ended up with an oyster.

Often, this kind of frustration can be avoided if you verbalize your expectations. For example, the anniversary of your first date holds great sentimental importance for you. It means nothing special to your fiancé. He forgets it: you're blue. Then, you begin to feel slighted, decide he's thoughtless, and attack him for not caring. He's shocked because you never told him what you wanted.

Often, frustration develops because you'd like to make some changes that you feel powerless to enforce. You wish your mother would be the kind of person who'd call you once in a while. You'd like your kids to clear the table without a reminder from you every single time. Or you'd like your partner to initiate sex more often. And when you don't get the changes you want, you search for a scapegoat on whom you can vent your frustrations and disappointment—and let loose with Control Talk blaming.

Fear of Falling

Fear also triggers the anger of Control Talk. When you believe that you're threatened or vulnerable, open to criticism or blame, you try to protect yourself by hiding behind Control Talk.

You did something that turned out badly and you're worried about being put down for it. The seminar you arranged bombed and now you'll surely be accused of poor planning and organization.

You don't have enough skill or knowledge to handle certain situations and you're afraid that someone will discover your limitations. You never should have accepted that promotion. You weren't ready to handle forty subordinates.

You're frightened of losing the love and respect of your partner. You don't earn the kind of living she expected you would, and you can't keep her in the style her parents did.

You're feeling incompetent about your ability to do something and someone makes an offhand comment that reinforces your doubt. You should never have agreed to go disco dancing with this crowd. You've only taken two lessons and you still feel awkward. Still, they don't have to make it so obvious that you can't keep up with them.

There are innumerable ways to feel threatened and we've all suffered through some of them. In an effort to stay on top of the situation, it's common to turn the tables and, like a good military strategist, attack first. Rather than face your fear of vulnerability, you protect your ego or position by defending yourself. Sometimes, you might simply withdraw, retreat into silence, or actually leave. At other times, you might become boisterous, hiding your vulnerability behind a mask of humor or laughter. Or, you might change the subject. But most likely, you'll fight your way out of the paper bag with Heavy Control Talk:

"The seminar would have been great if the guy I hired didn't cancel on me."

"If the people in my department weren't so lazy, I'd be able to get my work out on time."

"What good was all your parents' money? All it did was spoil you."

"I've got a headache and don't really feel like dancing. I'll call a cab and go home by myself."

Similarly, you may try to whitewash your fear by assuming an attitude of superiority to cover the inferiority you are actually experiencing:

"I don't know why I bothered to arrange that seminar. I've got far more important matters to think about."

"This position is merely a stepping-stone. In no time, I expect to move higher because it doesn't utilize my talents."

"Materialism poisons relationships. You should appreciate me for what I am, not for what I earn."

"Don't you think dancing is a mindless activity? I'd rather be home doing something meaningful, like curling up with a good book."

And you may try to escape your own feelings of vulnerability by finding fault with someone else:

You went out today to buy a new car with every intention of driving home with a four-door station wagon. Instead, you succumbed to the magic of a convertible sport coupe, spending far more than you could afford and denying the family a comfortable new car. To cover your guilt, you unconsciously look for a way to criticize your wife to keep the attention off yourself and balance the score. After dinner, she gossips on the phone for nearly an hour with a friend, and when she hangs up, you ridicule her for being a busybody and wasting her time. What you're really doing is covering your fear that she'll attack you for splurging on the car.

All of these Control Talk tactics keep us from recognizing or dealing with our fear of vulnerability. By knocking others off center, we attempt to take ourselves off the hook. But anger simply pushes people away. Although it's easier to blame someone else when we're ashamed, scared, or worried, Control Talk eventually alienates others and we may find ourselves mounting a defense when there are no attackers left.

Up Against the Wall

Sometimes, the abusive quality of Heavy Control Talk grows out of desperation. Overcome by feelings of hopelessness in a situation that seems to present no solutions, the angry denunciations of Control Talk may seem like the only choice available. When people feel desperate they will do anything to get attention. They may overeat, drink too much, develop drug dependencies, even attempt suicide. And those "notice me" cries are often voiced in either Active or Passive Control Talk.

Sad But True

When you cut through all the anger and fear, you will find at the nadir an unexpected feeling: sadness. A sense of profound loss—whether it's the loss of a person or a goal—fed by the feeling that you are powerless to change your circumstances, produces sorrow. You married a woman who seemed content to have babies and bake bread. Now, at forty, she's gotten a degree in journalism and taken a job with the local paper. You've lost the homebody you once loved, and the career woman you have now isn't what you wanted. . . . All your life you dreamed of having your very own dress shop. But at age fifty-five you realize you'll never rise above being sales manager for someone else. . . . Your fiancé has cold feet a month before the marriage. You've been dating since eighth grade. He says he wants a chance to travel before he settles down. You're devastated. He's the only boy you think you could ever love. One way to cope with the sadness of lost dreams or shattered hopes is to rail at the world through Heavy Control Talk.

We're Only Human

Finally, we often lapse into Control Talk because, being human, our goals in life are not always lofty or egalitarian. The bottom line is that there are times when we want:

- To win
- To make someone feel guilty
- To force change or resist it

Suppose you want to go to a movie on a Friday night. You suggest a spy picture to your mate or your friend. The answer is, "No, I'm too tired." You try a little persuasion in Light Control Talk. "Aw, c'mon. We'll make the early show.

It's supposed to be a dynamite film." The response is a dull
"Do we have to?" Now you're getting irritated and you begin
to push harder in Heavy Control. "I don't see why you make
such a big deal about going to a movie. You don't have to
work tomorrow. You never want to go anywhere these days.
Why are you so difficult? Once we get there, you'll enjoy it."

It's just that easy for Light Control Talk to slip into Heavy
Control, and soon you are in the midst of an argument over
something as trivial as a movie. The lack of alternative styles
to settle small disputes as well as major problems causes too
many of us to raise the iron fist of Heavy Control. And, inevitably, we get clobbered. The style doesn't match the situation. It divides partners and solves nothing. Those who can't
extricate themselves from the control trap of attack/ defend/
counterattack eventually lose faith in their ability to resolve
problems. Any differences, large or small, seem to spark a
fight.

Sadly, we often unleash Control Talk against those we love
the most—our families. We feel free to blurt out remarks
that we wouldn't dare utter publicly, and most of us have
never gotten angrier, yelled louder, or said more terrible
things than we have within the intimacy and privacy of our
homes. Our friends can stop calling and turn their backs on
us. Our bosses can fire us. Acquaintances can shun us. But
our families are forever. And our confidence in the endur-
ance of that bond allows us to engage in some fairly awful
behavior. Usually, that behavior isn't meant to destroy but to
deceive. We believe that we will lose stature in the eyes of
others if we reveal our true nature and expose our
weaknesses. And the closer and more valued a relationship is,
the greater the risk of losing it should the less-than-perfect
parts of our inner selves leak out. So we hide behind the invisible shield of Heavy Control Talk without realizing that after a while people see through us anyway.

If, over the years, you or someone you care about has consistently retreated to Heavy Control Talk to dump feelings of
anger, frustration, or despair, you know that this style always
exacerbates situations. It serves no purpose whatsoever and
only makes people feel worthless. The person using Heavy
Control feels awful for having spoken so sharply and the person under attack suffers from the verbal blows. Moreover,
once Heavy Control Talk becomes a habit, it's a tough one to
break.

When people begin our communication workshop, they immediately identify with both Small Talk and Control Talk. Many complain that they simply don't know any other ways to talk to each other. There are, fortunately, two other styles for *acting on* your feelings instead of acting them out. The first, Search Talk, which we'll describe next, may be familiar, and you can begin to use it productively, now, as an alternative to the hurtful grip of Control. The other, Straight Talk, will be discussed in depth in Chapter 5.

STYLE III: SEARCH TALK

Search Talk is the vehicle to board when you want to test the waters. It's very different from Small Talk, a style that doesn't make waves, and Control Talk, a style that tries to change the tides. In the nonthreatening atmosphere of Search Talk you can explore, analyze, and speculate about the "what-ifs" and "I-wonder-whys" of the past and the future with no pressure to make decisions or take any action. When you are stumped, anxious, or uncertain, Style III helps you stop your world, get off, and take a detached look at possible causes and effects.

Search Talk pokes around for information, but not with the accusing tone of an inquisitor. It's cautious and tentative—never blaming—and sometimes it leads nowhere. But don't discount the value of aimless meandering to hunt for insights which might ordinarily elude you. In the unstructured probing of Style III you uncover choices and ideas which you might otherwise be afraid to consider. Because Style III neither demands nor promises, it's practical for gaining an overview of a situation, reflecting on possible causes of dynamics, and contemplating various solutions.

Usually, you'll turn to Search Talk when there's an issue at hand—an issue being anything of concern. Whether the dog should be sold or sent to obedience school. How to tell your son (who loves the dog) that you've decided she's a destructive pet and must be given away. In fact, Style III is a particularly useful tool for beginning to deal with issues because it opens up possibilities and expands options without any commitment to a course of action.

Let's look at the way Sarah and Carl step into the think tank of Search Talk:

Sarah was in the kitchen finishing the dishes after a holiday dinner. It had been a hectic day for her, but she enjoyed cooking a special dinner and having the family over. As she wrapped the leftover turkey in foil she heard her husband bellowing at the kids for playing the TV too loud. "I wondered how long it would take this time," she said to herself. She dried her hands and walked into the den where he was reading the paper.

"Carl," she said hesitantly, "I've noticed something. Nearly every holiday we start out having a lovely day. But after dinner, after your parents leave, you seem to fall into a foul mood. I wonder why?"

Carl looked at her and thought a moment. "I don't know. It never seems to happen when it's just your family. Only when my folks come over."

"Do you have any idea what the difference is?"

"Maybe my folks make me nervous. Embarrassed. They're always putting everything down. Criticizing, you know. They don't seem to have anything decent to say about anybody. I guess being around them sets me off."

"It could be you've changed and you're more conscious of their attitudes than you used to be. Noticing how negative they are disturbs you now when it didn't before."

"That's possible. I think maybe if we had them over with more people, to help dilute the atmosphere, it might be better for me. I have to think more about this."

Character Traits

Search Talk is sometimes confused with Small Talk because their tones are similar. However, their characteristics are quite different.

- Style III always revolves around an issue, however fuzzy and undefined that issue may be. Small Talk only considers issues insofar as it's necessary to make routine decisions. And though Small Talk may include background information, it's usually part of the reporting of an event and doesn't lead to the deeper understanding that occurs in Style III.
- Like Style I and Style II, Style III concentrates on other people and outside events and omits direct expression of personal feelings, although it can explore them in an impersonal way.
- Search Talk examines like an intellectual fact-finder. Why

is this happening? What caused it? "Do I overeat because my mother always said a good eater finishes everything on his plate?" "Do I shout at my wife because I can't yell back at my boss?"

- Though a variety of solutions may surface as part of the examination process, Search Talk precludes a definite commitment to any one of them. It's not the style for making decisions.

- Search Talk conversations have a slow pace and a hesitancy full of ummms and pauses. The tone is quiet and thoughtful, and what little emotion exists is expressed cautiously.

- To avoid any note of finality, Search Talk conversations are liberally salted with qualifying words which give them a tentative flavor. As soon as you hear: sometimes, maybe, perhaps, probably, could be, might, hopefully, what if, suppose, possibly, you've got the verbal cue that you're in the think tank.

THE PAUSE THAT RESEARCHES

The speculative nature of Search Talk is ideal for those situations in which you want to:

A. *Examine background information:*
Ron, a forty-five-year-old broker, came home one night, barely said a word through dinner, and buried himself in a book most of the evening. As he was climbing into bed, his wife, Jean, said, "You seem to have the blahs. Did anything happen to you today?"

"Nothing special," Ron replied. "I had a pretty normal day. My boss even complimented me on the deal I put together to finance the shopping center. No, it isn't work. It must be something else."

"Maybe you got some bad news?"

"I can't remember any, unless it was that story I heard at lunch."

"What was that?" Jean asked.

"Well, I heard about this guy, same age as me, who dropped dead at the football game yesterday. He had a heart attack. Sitting right there in his seat. Slumped over and that was it. He was exactly my age."

"I wonder if that's what's been on your mind all night. Have you been having those chest pains again?" Jean asked.

"No," Ron answered. "It's just the idea that a guy my age could die so fast with no warning. I haven't been able to get that image out of my mind. Could be that's just what has me down."

B. Ask for advice:
Carla's father is an alcoholic who's been abandoned by everyone in the family except her. Yet when she calls to see how he's doing, he sometimes becomes abusive, and she regrets having made the effort to care. Over lunch she asks her friend Nora what to do.

"Should I stop calling him altogether? Do you think that's the answer?"

"Well, that's certainly one possibility," Nora says. "Is he always nasty when you call?"

"Oh no," Carla responds. "When he's sober we have wonderful conversations."

"Then you don't want to stop calling completely, do you?"

"I guess I don't," Carla admits.

C. Speculate on possible solutions:
"Maybe you could have your father call you only when he's sober," Nora suggests.

"That's a possibility," Carla says. "But he's never been one to follow guidelines. He might end up calling me every day."

"Maybe you could set the rules then. Possibly tell him you'll call every week but you won't stay on the phone if he's drunk and ugly."

"Hmm. I hadn't thought of it. You mean I might take charge?" Carla asks.

"Yes, something like that. It might work, you know," Nora says.

D. Clarify an incident:
Bill and Ann, graduate students who'd been living together for nearly a year, aired this Search Talk exchange as an example before a group.

BILL: I've been thinking about that party last night and I'd like to ask you something.

ANN: Sure, fire away.

BILL: You seemed to spend a lot of time talking to that lawyer cousin of Carter's. I wonder if you were attracted to him?

ANN: Well, I guess I was kind of. He was telling me about a labor contract he was negotiating and it was fascinating. He was quite an eloquent storyteller and I was really into the strategies he was describing. Did you think he turned me on?

BILL: It looked that way to me.

ANN: I don't think you have anything to worry about. I just found him interesting.

Notice that Bill didn't begin by blaming Ann with a Control Talk blast: "You were flirting with that lawyer last night at the party. I know he turned you on." Instead, with Search Talk, he cleared up an issue by checking out whether there was anything to worry about in the first place.

Still another use of Style III is *brainstorming*, bouncing ideas back and forth without settling on any one in particular. The expansive, uncensored wanderings of brainstorming broaden the perspective on an issue. Some of the ideas are worthless; one may be a gem. In this style, no judgments are made. You simply scatter seeds and later pick the healthiest plants from the ones that rooted.

THE ADVANTAGES OF SEARCH TALK

Although too much procrastinating in the whys and wherefores of Search Talk can become frustrating, Style III has many appealing advantages as a shelter where you can lay out an issue away from the heat. Let's say you and your partner are schoolteachers and spring vacation is quickly approaching. In the past you've always gone on some type of trip. Assuming this year is no different, you bring up the things you'd like to do. You mention camping. The response is negative. You suggest a visit to your sister in California.

"No."

"Well, how about your brother in Vermont? We might still have enough snow to ski."

"I don't think so," is the answer. You're becoming annoyed and uneasy. Hop into the think tank of Search Talk and check out what's happening. You could discover that your mate has lost the vacation money in a bad investment and has been afraid to tell you. Perhaps he or she would prefer to spend the vacation at home for a change, puttering and fixing up, but doesn't want to disappoint you. Whatever the reasons, Search Talk is the mode to look for them because it gives you considerable freedom to probe with no pressure to act.

In sum, think of Search Talk when your intention is to:

- Check out uncertainties.
- Share impressions and hunt for explanations.
- Examine possible causes.
- Pose tentative solutions.

WHY YOU NEED MORE THAN ONE STYLE

When you have several styles at your disposal, your personal and business relationships are likely to become stronger and more enduring. Generally, the mark of a weak or troubled relationship is its limited choice of styles. When you lack a spectrum of styles, you have no way to express your feelings or thoughts honestly. Your intentions are often unclear, and issues can remain unresolved because you don't have an effective mode for tackling them.

Understanding the differences between the styles is the first step to better communication—and it's an important and necessary one. The next step involves a bit of exploration into the inner you. In order to express yourself completely and clearly, and invite a similar response, you have to know what you want, what you think, what you feel, what sort of action you'd like to take. Complete awareness is vital before you can begin translating your inner experience to the outside world. And that's what you'll be learning in the next chapter.

QUIZ: IDENTIFYING COMMUNICATION STYLES

For each of the statements below, indicate which style you think is being used: Style I, Small Talk; Style II, Control Talk: (a) Light Control, (b) Heavy Control; or Style III, Search Talk.

1. Daylight saving ends tomorrow. Did you set the clock back? _____

2. I'm wondering why we seem to have arguments mostly on Sundays. You have any ideas about that? _____

3. I was probably pretty sore at you at the time. _____

4. You had to make that crack about my friends, didn't you? _____

5. What a snob! He wouldn't give you the time of day if his life depended on it. _____

6. I've been trying to figure out why I react to Sally the way I do. Maybe it's the way she so often tops whatever anyone is saying. _____

7. Were we planning to go out with them this Friday or next? _____

8. Can't you ever remember anything? _____

9. You really did a great job handling Mary's tantrum at the supermarket. _____

10. We have these arguments all the time because you never really listen to me! _____

11. What I like most about Sundays is lolling in bed and reading the entire paper. _____

12. We should get up in time to go to church. _____

Answers: 1. I; 2. III; 3. III; 4. IIb; 5. IIb; 6. III; 7. I; 8. IIb; 9. IIa; 10. IIb; 11. I; 12. IIa

EXERCISE: EXPERIMENTING WITH STYLES

Choose a topic to discuss with a partner. Talk about it in Small Talk (Style I) for one minute. Shift into Control Talk

(Style II) and continue the discussion for another minute. Finally, switch to Search Talk (Style III) and continue to talk for not more than two minutes. Was one style more comfortable than the others?

This is a good exercise to tape-record. If you do tape it, discuss the dialogue before replaying the tape. Then listen to the tape, and pay particular attention to distinguishing one style from another. Make note of the key words and phrases that identify each of the three styles.

3

Tuning in
to the Inner You:
The Awareness Wheel

How do you feel when you come home from work expecting a warm hello and a relaxed family dinner, and instead, before your coat is even unbuttoned, your son starts to complain about his rotten tennis lesson, your daughter wants to know if you can take her shopping for the shoes she had to have yesterday, and the dog, in his eagerness to say hello, jumps up and gouges a scratch in your cheek with his paw?

Why is it that when you intend to be patient and understanding, you fly off the handle; when you want very much to say something delicate, you clam up instead; when you'd like to go fishing, you can never find the time; when you're geared up for an idyllic weekend getaway, you spoil it by getting into a dumb argument about a nasty remark uttered a week earlier?

When you're feeling especially fine, do you have any idea why you feel that way so you can keep the mood alive or recreate it? If you're filled with affection toward someone, do your actions show it? And after you've made a judgment, have you ever stopped to think how you arrived at such a conclusion?

Most people don't pay enough attention to what is happening inside themselves—what they are thinking, feeling, and wanting, and how that affects those around them. Everybody has access to this gold mine but too few tap it as a resource. Certainly you'd like to understand yourself better, yet you probably don't know where to begin. Or, you may think that you need someone to guide you. You don't. Just look in the mirror. You already possess all the skills you need to remove the veil from the inner you. What you've been lacking are the tools to assist you. We've developed a device called the Awareness Wheel to bring those hidden aspects to the surface.

The Awareness Wheel is the foundation for connecting with the one person who can guarantee your success as a communicator: yourself. How can you possibly communicate clearly and effectively if you are not aware of your motivating ideas and emotions? If you don't know what you want, it's difficult to make choices or settle on a plan of action. And if you don't know where you are coming from, you're likely to end up in a place you don't want to be. Limited self-awareness frequently catapults people into Control Talk because they are unaware of the intensity of their feelings or confused about their intentions. When you can identify your emotions they're less likely to boil over, and it's easier to avoid harmful outbursts. Furthermore, when you speak from a position of full awareness, you minimize the possibilities of misinterpretation that can lead to conflict.

With the Awareness Wheel you gain access to the inner information you need to match style to content. When you understand yourself, you are able to choose the best style to express yourself. You can switch into Search Talk when an ordinary Small Talk exchange with a repairman escalates into a serious argument. You can move into Straight Talk when your Awareness Wheel tells you that you are getting nowhere in Search Talk. The Awareness Wheel is the basis for connecting in Straight Talk, but it's more than that. It's a means to connect in the style you choose at the level you choose with everyone you encounter: your mate, your family, your friends, your colleagues. But first and foremost, you must connect with the source—yourself.

Who are you? Red hair, green eyes, flat feet, skinny arms. That may be the physical you. What you look like and how you behave are visible to the outside world, and those aspects may be all that others will ever see. The other you, the inner parts that psychologists label "the self," is invisible and often hidden—not only from the outside world, but sometimes from you, too. You may not know *how* to reach inside or, as we discussed in Chapter 1, you may be *afraid*—afraid of losing control, risking intimacy, becoming vulnerable. To become a good communicator and make connections, you must understand those intangible elements that define you: the things that stimulate your senses, the myriad interpretations floating inside your head, your feelings or emotions; the wishes and wants that add up to your intentions; your actions or behavior.

The Awareness Wheel is a mental camera that you can activate at any given time to bring the information you need for a detailed portrait of your inner self into focus. The Wheel has six parts: a hub and five spokes. At the hub you place any issue or event that you'd like to examine:

- Your relationship to a person you're dating.
- An irritating patient at the hospital where you work.
- Your responsibility to Uncle George now that Aunt Martha is dead.
- Your weight.
- The fun you had soaking in a hot tub with your partner.
- Why you and your teenager are suddenly getting along better.
- The promotion you expected and lost.

Although it's common to put some disturbing element or concern in the hub, you can see by the list that you might also want to explore something pleasurable to understand how to reproduce or prolong it.

Whatever you put in the center of your Wheel, five essential kinds of information feed into it like wires hooked to a central switchboard. These are the sensations, interpretations, feelings, intentions, and actions that together create the sum of your experience, and often, you aren't plugged in to every part. That's why experiences frequently overwhelm or confuse us. Something happens and we don't know why. Or we mull over a problem for days, even weeks, and can't seem to think our way out of it. The Awareness Wheel helps break down the unwieldy whole of an experience into the parts that cause it. You examine each part separately and suddenly the whole takes on a new coloration. What didn't make sense before makes sense now. Aspects you hadn't considered fall into place.

This sorting-out process sounds disarmingly simple. And it is. You jump in at any spoke of the Wheel and work your way around it. But before you can use the Awareness Wheel, you'll want to understand how we define the five spokes. Since people tend to be most aware of their thoughts, let's begin with interpretations.

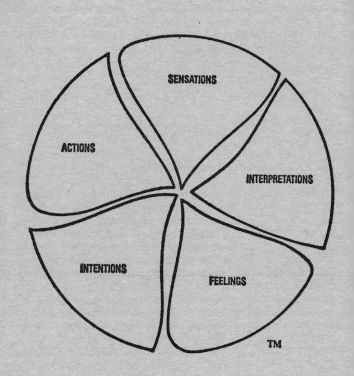

SENSATIONS

ACTIONS

INTERPRETATIONS

INTENTIONS

FEELINGS

TM

THE AWARENESS WHEEL

THE MUDDY WATERS
OF INTERPRETATION

Interpretations, meaning our thoughts, impressions, conclusions, opinions, beliefs, and attitudes, present one of the major obstacles to effective communication because two people rarely interpret the same thing in the same way. Each of us constantly gathers information through thousands of receptors and we get far more data than we can possibly deal with. To prevent a shutdown from information overload, we try to make sense of the input by assigning meaning to it. Since we construct meaning out of the combination of personal history and immediate experience, different people's interpretations of the same data vary considerably.

The differences stem from several sources. First of all, your interpretation of any event depends on the interplay between thoughts you've already formed and what your eyes, ears, and nose add to it. Suppose you are playing bridge and you trump too soon. Your partner mutters, "You dingbat." But because he says it with a broad smile, you interpret it as a joke. If, however, your head had been turned and you didn't see the smile, you could just as easily have interpreted the remark as an insult. And if you're feeling somewhat guilty because you've goofed, you're likely to interpret the insult as deserved criticism. You might also read your partner's smiling taunt as a way to make a feeble joke and avoid acknowledging your ineptness at cards. The possibilities for interpreting any single act are endless.

Let's go a step further. Your interpretations are also influenced by the bundle of beliefs and assumptions embedded in your memory bank. If you were raised to believe that people do not call each other names in public, even jokingly, you'd be hurt by your partner's remark no matter how broad a smile accompanied the word *dingbat*. But if affectionate name-calling was an acceptable pattern in your family, you'd laugh at the comment and interpret it as an endearment.

Your interpretations are also colored by the way you see yourself. If you have a low self-image, you may interpret even the most innocuous comment as a put-down, while an inflated self-image might block you from considering any meaning but your own.

Expectations affect your interpretations as well. If lighthearted bantering is part of your style as a couple, you might expect to be called a dingbat, a klutz, or a scatterbrain once in a while and you're likely to interpret those labels as affectionate teasing. But if your partner name-calls only in anger you won't find anything amusing in such a remark.

The same principle operates in all situations. Expectations develop from memories of past encounters and our hopes for the present. Thus, when a supervisor with whom you've had a harmonious relationship calls you into her office, you'd expect good news based on past history. But if you've had rocky times with this supervisor, when the summons comes—despite the fact that you may crave a kind word—you'll walk in expecting the worst.

Avoiding the Trap of Misinterpretation

In short, the interpretations you make are based more on your reading of a situation than on what "really happened." John and Mary, a couple in their thirties who came from different backgrounds, frequently clashed because they drew opposing conclusions from the same event. In an exercise one night, Mary gave us an excellent example of the way in which different points of view develop.

"We were leaving a Broadway theater after a matinee and a bearded young man in a thin coat was playing the violin under the marquee. By his feet was a cigar box with a penciled sign: *Please help me pay for my music lessons.* It was a chilly afternoon and my heart went out to him. I didn't have my wallet so I turned to John and asked him to drop some change in the box. He refused and I became furious. I thought he was hard-hearted and mean. Here was this poor, talented boy who needed help and John, who could easily afford a dollar, would do nothing." John had a very different version. "We left the theater and this scruffy kid was begging out front. He looked healthy to me and, though I sympathized with his plight, I felt that if he wanted music lessons, he should get a job to pay for them. I was raised with a strong work ethic and I believe that if you want something, you work for it—even if that means a job you don't like. I'm against supporting begging when my company advertises for unskilled labor all the time and can't begin to fill the positions."

It's just that easy for two people to look at the same scene and arrive at dissimilar interpretations. That's why you'll want to keep your interpretations flexible. Mold them in Jell-O instead of carving them in granite and remember these points:

- There is rarely one right and one wrong interpretation of any situation.
- You may not have sufficient sense data to draw a firm conclusion.
- When you can't make sense out of something because it's entirely new, don't jump to conclusions too quickly. An instant interpretation may prevent you from looking at alternatives or seeing something in an exciting, fresh perspective.
- What you see and hear can conflict with what you think or expect. If you force a conclusion you may be shutting out the other parts of your awareness that could add clarity.

MAKING SENSE OUT OF YOUR SENSES

We live in a world of impressions, but most of us pay very little attention to input from our senses. Pause for a moment—wherever you are—and try to become aware of what you are *seeing, hearing, tasting, smelling, and touching.* Maybe you'll become conscious of the hum of an air conditioner or heater or the noise of traffic outside. You may *see* patterns of sunlight you hadn't noticed or *hear* the noise of raindrops, wind rattling the windows, sounds that go bump in the night. *Feel* the texture of your pants, your shirt, the smoothness of your fingers against the skin of your cheek or the jaggedness of nails that need filing. Can you *taste* the cup of coffee you just finished or the staleness of a recent cigarette? Can you *smell* shaving lotion or onions frying?

Our senses tell us a great deal about what we're experiencing, and they provide the background for our interpretations. Usually, we tend to rely on one of our senses at the expense of the other four and that has an effect on our interpretations. You may be one of those persons who can walk into a room after six months' absence and notice that two ashtrays have been removed from the coffee table. Or you may be the type who'd barely notice that an office had red walls and a screaming purple sofa, yet you'd recall verbatim all the details of a conversation you had there. There is nothing wrong with being strongly visual or strongly aural. Nearly everyone leans toward one or the other, but too dominant a preference can become a self-imposed handicap.

Normally, we don't isolate our senses into neat compartments. We walk through life scanning images, almost automatically combining what we see, hear, and smell into a fast interpretation. Rarely do we record everything strictly in terms of sensory input. If we did, we might absorb information in this sterile manner:

> Jane came home from school today at 3:30. She wearing jeans, a green sweater, a plaid shirt and boots, and she smelled of stale perfume. She put down her books, ate a peanut butter sandwich, drank a glass of milk, and turned on the TV.

That's a detached scientific way to observe a situation and, on the basis of this sense data, we would then logically form some possible conclusions. However, most of us don't function that way. We link interpretations to sense data automatically, weaving a more complete picture of the same scene:

> Jane came home from school today at 3:30. She was wearders sagging as though she were carrying the weight of the world on her frail body. She'd dressed in a hurry that morning and thrown on the first things she could find: jeans, a sweater, and a plaid shirt. She didn't have time to shower and splashed herself with extra perfume, because the flowery scent was still strong. She threw her books on the nearest chair and, obviously starving, wolfed down a peanut butter sandwich and a glass of milk. She was reluctant to start her homework and flopped instead in front of the TV, figuring she had so much to do that she'd do nothing at all.

Don't Confuse What You See with What You Think

Because we all need to make sense out of what our physical senses tell us, it's natural to blend our interpretations with observations. But it can muddy the waters, and sometimes it's important to clarify a situation by sorting out impressions from sensations. In one of our group exercises we ask members to turn to their partners and, using only sense data, describe what they take in. Rarely does anyone respond with pure sensory information. Inevitably we hear comments like this:

"I think you have a lot of energy tonight." That's purely an interpretation. Sense data leading to the assumption of high energy might be, "I see you sitting on the edge of your chair . . . you respond quickly to my questions . . . your eyes are darting and dancing."

"I see you making nervous movements with your foot." Which of the senses registers "nervous"? Can you smell nervous or hear it? Nervous is the way the observer has interpreted a rapid, jerky foot movement.

"You look cheerful." Cheerful is an interpretation. What is the sense data that describes cheerfulness? A gay smile, bright eyes, relaxed facial muscles?

Although making such picky distinctions between sensations and interpretations may seem trivial, it's important to do so at times. As we saw in the earlier story about John and Mary, two people can witness the same event and arrive at very different interpretations. Moreover, these differences can stem simply from which data one chooses to emphasize. Mary was quite affected by the beautiful violin music she *heard*. John based his interpretation on what he *saw:* a seemingly healthy young man begging for money. And, since we usually don't separate our sense data from our interpretations—or, if we do, we rarely verbalize the distinction—we often misinterpret each other.

Unaware of what John sees, Mary thinks he's heartless. Unaware of what Mary hears and how moved she is, John thinks she's a bleeding heart and resents her inability to understand him. One way to cut through the hostility is to specifically review the sense data that each one used to draw his or her conclusion. The basic information often clarifies the origin of the interpretation, the reason it was made, and forms a basis for their discussion. When Mary and John replayed their exchange for us and separated their sensations from their interpretations, the reasons for their diverse reactions became clear. Remember, what you see isn't necessarily what you get.

GET IN TOUCH WITH YOUR FEELINGS

Feelings are our spontaneous emotional reactions to everything we experience in life. If you are unaccustomed to centering on what you feel, there are all sorts of clues to guide you. There are physiological signs: when you're nervous you may begin to sweat; when you're excited, your heart beats rapidly; when you're embarrassed, you blush. There are behavioral signs, too: you may raise or lower your voice if you're angry; giggle when you're scared; avert your eyes when you're uncomfortable; reach for someone's hand when you're unhappy; turn your cheek to avoid a kiss when you're displeased. There are indirect expressions of feelings as well, such as buying a gift when you feel appreciative or putting someone down when you're hurt. Whether you're intensely emotional or rather stoic, *all* your feelings—the best and the worst, the highs and the lows, the rage and the passion—are an integral part of the inner you.

Our language is rich with words to describe your emotions, and we don't always take advantage of them. Here are just a few that may reflect your emotions at any given moment:

pleased	elated	cautious
calm	uneasy	confident
comfortable	silly	uncomfortable
satisfied	hesitant	anxious
bored	surprised	discontented
jubilant	eager	solemn
fearful	angry	apathetic
daring	weary	hopeful
confused	glad	sad
lonely	grieved	proud
excited	contented	relieved

Although most of us are aware of our feelings—or at least certain ones—we don't always bother to assess *why* we're experiencing certain emotions. In fact, feelings are an excellent barometer to your reactions to both internal and external experiences. By getting in touch with your feelings you can use them as a resource to more accurately understand what you expect, what you're thinking, and what you want. In turn, you can use this greater awareness to improve your communication with others. Instead of lashing out in anger, you might tune in to that anger and discover it's motivated by strong disappointment. By sharing your disappointment instead of your anger with someone else, your conversation is likely to be very different—deeper, most honest, and more intimate. In addition, this kind of understanding can help you work through some of your more negative emotions.

For example, Mike is a twenty-eight-year-old lawyer who'd

been seeing a woman for six months. He liked her more than he was willing to admit and looked forward to weekends when he'd leave his office and drive eighty miles to be with her. When she told him one Sunday night that she was going into isolation to study for her doctoral examination and would not be able to see him for six weeks, he was crushed. She explained that their relationship was very intense and that she couldn't handle any distraction that might weaken her concentration. Her reasons were valid. Mike remembered how tough it had been to study for his bar exam. And he liked to think of himself as an understanding and accepting person.

Yet, as he tuned in to his feelings, all he saw was anger. His face was hot, his heart was pounding, and his nails dug into his palms. But as he paused to understand his feelings, he became aware of an underlying sadness too. Concentrating on the sadness, he realized how important this woman had become to him and that being without her for several weeks was going to be painful. His anger dissipated and he worked toward dealing with his disappointment.

Where Do Feelings Come From?

Your feelings stem from several sources, one of which is your expectations. Often what you expect doesn't jibe with what you experience and you aren't prepared for the resultant emotions.

You expect to be elected president of your organization. Nobody has said anything about opposing you. Then on election night, a dark horse appears on the ballot and beats you by four votes. You had expected to feel jubilant that night. Now you're stunned and hurt.

You're home alone reading, anticipating a dull evening, when a friend calls unexpectedly with an extra ticket for a show. Suddenly you're flattered and happy.

You want to repaper the kitchen. It's a tedious and messy job. You expect your partner to offer an excuse to avoid helping you, but you ask anyway. To your surprise, the response is, "Sure. When do you want to start?" Having expected to be turned down, you're delighted.

You rack your brains for a special anniversary gift for your parents and finally settle on concert tickets. When you give them the envelope, they thank you wanly and tell you they normally don't drive into the city after dark. You expected approval and now you're feeling hurt and disappointed.

When, as in these examples, your feelings sneak up from left field and surprise you, check out your original expectations and you'll have greater insight into your emotional response.

Your interpretations also have a tremendous impact on your feelings. Recall how you feel when you're waiting for someone in front of a movie or a restaurant and, as time goes by, the person doesn't arrive. All sorts of emotions begin to churn inside you. First, you may worry something has happened. Then, you may become angry at that person's thoughtlessness. Or, you may feel confused about misunderstanding the arrangements. Multiple feelings like these are quite common, and they usually indicate that you're making several interpretations at the same time.

Why We Deny Feelings

When our feelings are unpleasant, we may try to deny or repress them. Although it's easy to see why one might refuse to face negative feelings, there are people who hide positive feelings, too. For some, emotions like loving and caring are seen as a sign of weakness or dependency. However, ignoring feelings will not make them disappear. In fact, when you close yourself to emotion you lose control, and your feelings take over and manage you in indirect ways. One way to stay in charge is simply to allow yourself to feel. If you are sad, immerse yourself in sadness. Don't fight it. The same goes for joy. Take it as high as you can.

How to Change Feelings

Feelings change most dramatically when people look at them in the context of other parts of the Awareness Wheel. Barbara told us how angry she was one night when she'd been given a big promotion at work and Todd refused to go out and celebrate. He wanted to hold off until the weekend. "I was crushed at first," she said. "Then I got upset because I thought my promotion wasn't important enough to him. But I saw that he looked very washed-out, and I realized that while I'd been in an air-conditioned office all day, he'd been sweltering in hundred-degree heat in the greenhouse where he works. His lack of interest in my promotion wasn't the reason he wanted to postpone a celebration. He was just dead tired. I still felt let down, but I wasn't upset any more."

Elusive, slippery, painful, or exultant—latch on to your feelings, accept them, and live with them.

SIR, WHAT ARE YOUR INTENTIONS?

Everybody wants something. An infant bawls for milk. A schoolboy prays for a scholarship. A young couple dreams of moving out of an apartment to a home of their own. An ailing man hopes his heart will hold out long enough for him to witness the birth of his first grandchild. Sometimes your wants are quite apparent and, just as often, they are either unspoken or unacknowledged. And complicating the issue is the fact that there are many different kinds of intentions:

- *Simple Short-Range Intentions:* I want to go skiing to-morrow.
- *Long-Range Intentions:* Someday I'd like to buy a boat and cruise the inland waterway to Florida.
- *Goals:* After college, I want to attend law school.
- *Objectives:* Within six months I'd like to be jogging two miles a day.
- *Desires:* I want Jeff to appreciate my intellect. I'd like to go out with the new receptionist in our building.
- *Wishes:* I wish my hair were straight and silky. I wish we'd get snowed in so we could extend our vacation.

Although we frequently gloss over our intentions, there are many words we could use to admit them to ourselves:

to approach	to praise	to conceal
to reject	to defend	to play
to support	to hurt	to explore
to persuade	to be friendly	to be caring
to be funny	to ponder	to listen
to ignore	to help	to disregard
to clarify	to accept	to share
to avoid	to demand	to understand
to cooperate	to be honest	to be responsive

Whether you are aware of your intentions or not, they fit into two basic categories: ways you want to *be* and things you want to *do*. *Being Intentions* are held inside you and they tend to describe how you want to feel: you want to be

happy, to be accepted, to be charming; you don't want to be
ignored, rejected, seen as a failure. *Doing Intentions* are more
visible and resemble a list of New Year's resolutions: I want
to give Jane more help with the household chores; I want to
exercise and firm up; I want to quit smoking; I want to
change my job.

Being Intentions are the catalyst for Doing Intentions. If
you want to be respected, successful, or chic, you will have to
take certain steps to achieve your goals. Yet frequently, Being
Intentions are great unknowns. We don't think about how we
want *to be* in a particular situation; we plunge in at the *doing*
level without making a distinction between the two. When
you can say to yourself: "Now that wasn't what I wanted at
all," it's a good bet you weren't aware of your Being Intentions.

To avoid this trap, be careful not to put the cart before the
horse. Before you make plans or impulsively jump into doing,
get in the habit of stopping and asking yourself, "What do I
want?"

Let's say you are home on a Saturday afternoon, feeling
restless and out of sorts, so you impulsively reach for the
phone and invite two old friends for dinner. As soon as they
accept, you hang up with a sinking feeling. "Now why did I
do that? I'll have to shop, plan a menu, straighten the apartment, and cook dinner. That's not what I wanted." Before di-
aling you should have checked out your Being Intentions.
You might have discovered that you wanted some excitement
to relieve your boredom, and instead of having company
you'd have made plans to go to a roller disco or baseball
game.

Unmasking Hidden Intentions

Because our intentions may be ornery, mean, embarrassing,
or simply repressed, they are frequently difficult to identify.
When you aren't aware of your intentions or have trouble
pinning them down, look at these two clues for guidance:

1. *What does your behavior tell you:* Imagine that you are
chatting with someone about the new female president of the
City Council. Your companion takes the stance that her children must be neglected as a result of her public life. You
discover your voice rising in defense of the president and, in
a flash, you are railing at your companion, telling her she's
old-fashioned, stubborn, and needs her consciousness raised.

Your intensity comes as a surprise to both of you. Your spontaneous reaction tells you how much you had *wanted* to change your friend's mind.

2. *What do your feelings tell you:* Cheryl remembers the Mother's Day long ago when her children sent her an arrangement of spring flowers. As she read the card the florist tucked inside, she was aware that she felt disappointment rather than pleased. The flowers were certainly pretty enough. That wasn't it. Examining her letdown, Cheryl realized that she wanted a more personal demonstration of affection than a phone call to a flower shop. Not that she was ungrateful, but she would have preferred even a hand-scribbled poem or a homemade candle that would have shown her that the kids had taken the time and trouble to put themselves out on her behalf. By tuning in to her feelings, Cheryl uncovered her intentions.

How to Handle Conflicting Intentions

We've all experienced those frustrating moments when we want several things at once; we want to have our cake and eat it, too. In order to reach a decision at such times, it's important to sort out each intention, examine its merits, and try to establish priorities. This "rating" procedure is particularly useful when:

Intentions are at odds with each other: "I want to study for my exam but I also want to attend the swim meet tonight." "I'm so furious with my foreman that I'd like to tell him where to shove his job and his factory, but I want to keep my job."

Long-range intentions clash with short-range desires: "Tomorrow I have to take college board exams at eight, but tonight I'm dying to see my favorite rock group in a one-night-only midnight special."

Long-range intentions are themselves conflicting: You are mapping out a family vacation trip from your home in Connecticut to the Colorado Rockies. On the one hand, you want to fly so you'll have more time to spend in the mountains. On the other hand, you want to drive so the kids can see something of the country.

Nobody likes making choices, but you'll find that dividing intentions eliminates guesswork and sets goals. We'll explain how to use the Awareness Wheel to make decisions in the next chapter.

What I'd Like for You; What I'd Like from You

Thus far we've discussed only the intentions you hold for yourself. In a relationship you are also going to have Being and Doing Intentions for the other person. The intentions you have exclusively *for* someone else are Being Intentions, and they encompass all the rich and wonderful things you want your partner to achieve and experience. You might want your partner to be more confident, to become self-reliant, to be less tense, to have more time to pursue leisure activity, to get pleasure from his or her work, to be less restless, and so on.

Unless couples are in deep trouble we've found that the Being Intentions they hold for each other are consistent and generally positive. No happy wife wants her husband to be miserable, and vice-versa. But problems can develop when partners disagree on the way they want each other to pursue these Being Intentions. Sue wants Jake to be healthy. Jake also wants to be healthy. Sue thinks Jake should take vitamins and start an exercise program. Jake isn't interested in either of these routes and he thinks he'll remain healthy as long as he watches his diet. In Chapter 5, we'll show you how you can work out such differences with Style IV, Straight Talk.

Quite apart from what you want *for* someone are those things you want *from* a partner. "Froms" are related to Doing Intentions and encompass the things you want your partner to do to improve the quality of your life. Perhaps you'd like your partner to be more cordial to your family; to stop poking fun at your clumsiness; to take turns paying the bills. It's perfectly natural to want *from* your partner as well as *for* your partner, but too often in a relationship, people voice only the "froms." They demand more help, more patience, more attention, and reasonable intentions may translate into Control Talk demands.

What's missing is a balance of "for" and "from." While most of us have only good intentions for our mates, we make the mistake of assuming that they know what these are. Conflicts arise because only the somewhat demanding "what I want from you" intentions are verbalized. Once couples share what they'd like *for* each other in addition to *from* each other, the atmosphere changes and Straight Talk replaces Control Talk.

The ultimate purpose of examining all your intentions is to provide you with the opportunity to consider alternatives. If you know what you want or don't want, you are more likely to choose a satisfying course of action. Your wants are a very significant part of you, hard to suppress, and too often overlooked.

WATCH YOUR ACTIONS

Do you slam doors when you're frustrated? Do you whistle or sing in the shower when you're feeling terrific? Do you twist your hair when you're anxious or chew your nails when you're frightened? Actions like these are the visible signs of what you are experiencing internally. We are not usually aware of the little things we do—the pauses, foot-tappings, blinking, fingerpointing—that punctuate our conversation. Yet all this output becomes sense data that influences how others perceive us. We tend to be aware chiefly of what we say, while ignoring the accompanying gestures and expressions. But our listeners take in far more than our words. They note the tone of our voice, the way we hold our bodies, the look on our faces. And these body signs may say as much or more than our words. In short, both our verbal and nonverbal actions send messages, and unless you are conscious of both, you can't assess the impact you have on others.

When Claude described himself as a reasonably contented person at one of our group sessions, his wife looked surprised. "I don't see you smile very much lately and you've been shutting yourself up in your den more than ever." It was Claude's turn to be taken aback. "I had no idea I was so transparent. The truth is I have been down-in-the-dumps—the old male midlife crisis, I guess. But I thought I was hiding it pretty well."

Actions include not only what we say and how we say it, but the kinds of things we do as well:

dieting	frowning	listening
eating	talking	thinking
walking	pausing	yelling
laughing	nodding	avoiding
sighing	touching	smiling
smoking	interrupting	rushing
whining	watching	crying

Actions include what you are doing right now—reading this book—and they also describe your behavior in the past—yesterday, last month, last year. You can even look at actions in terms of the future—what you'll be doing tomorrow, next week, next year.

Although it's hard to step outside yourself and be a participant and an observer simultaneously, it's particularly useful to become aware of repetitive behavior patterns. For example, one of the co-authors of this book drops his voice to a near whisper at the end of a sentence when he's not confident about what he's saying. Another has a son who gets a silly grin on his face when he's embroidering on the truth, and that's how he gets caught in white lies. Maybe you holler more than you realize, or assume a supercilious tone with salespeople that affects the quality of the service you receive. Keeping tabs on all your actions would rob you of spontaneity, but some awareness is vital in order to understand the reactions others have to you.

To see yourself as others see you, don't look in the mirror. Take a look at your actions instead.

THE PITFALLS OF
LIMITED AWARENESS

While you cannot expect to be aware of your senses, thoughts, feelings, wants, and actions all the time—the very idea is exhausting—you probably have a pattern that habitually ignores some parts of the Wheel. Perhaps you live in your head and ignore your heart. Perhaps you barrel into action and ignore your intentions. You are unfair to yourself if you systematically exclude one or more spokes of the Awareness Wheel. The one aspect you bypass may throw a whole situation out of kilter.

What Happens When You
Ignore Interpretations

Few of us are unaware of what we think. Interpretations seem to leap into our heads automatically. A dysfunction in this dimension can occur in two ways. One, you may omit the documentation that explains your thoughts:

You say, "You must not care much about me," but you neglect to point out why you've reached that conclusion. Instead, say, "You haven't called me all week so I thought I wasn't very important in your life," to clarify the statement.

Two, you may not allow yourself to acknowledge certain thoughts:

Ann, a second-grade teacher, had a headache every day after school for a year but she never dared consider leaving the security of teaching for another career. Instead of thinking the unthinkable, she reached for an aspirin bottle because as a child she'd been taught that once you make up your mind about something, you stick with it. By censoring her thoughts, she limited her range of possibilities.

What Happens When You
Ignore Sense Data

Sometimes you see but you don't hear, or you jump to conclusions without asking for more information. The result is usually some kind of outburst that hurts someone's feelings or causes problems.

Albert was sitting in his office checking various company reports when he came to the current inventory sheet. Two weeks ago there had been 495 boxes of stuffed teddy bears in stock. But according to the sheet in front of him, there were only 94 boxes left. He stormed out of his office into the shipping department and growled at the man in charge, "How can we be so low on teddy bears. It's holiday time. You know how heavy our demand is now. You're supposed to keep up on these things. If we run out, your job's on the line." The clerk gulped hard and stammered, "Sir, if you look there in the corner, you'll see that I just filled an unexpected order for 200 boxes. That's why the inventory is suddenly so low, and I've already called the supplier for replacements." Sheepishly, Albert looked in the corner and saw a large stack waiting to be loaded on the truck. Because he hadn't bothered to check his sense data (what did he see and what information did he need), he jumped to conclusions, insulted and embarrassed the clerk, and made a fool of himself.

What Happens When You
Ignore Feelings

If you don't express your feelings, your actions can easily be misunderstood.

Maxine was a young psychologist who landed a consulting job with a large city school board. Each week she had to file

reports on special educational programs as a requirement of
the federal grant that funded them. She wrote the reports
and turned them over to the superintendent for approval.
The reports always came back with petty corrections. "Ands"
were changed to "buts." "Howevers" were deleted. Para-
graphs were recorded. Maxine wallowed in frustration. She
felt she could not please the superintendent no matter how
hard she tried, and she finally summoned the courage to
tell him she was resigning because her writing obviously
did not suit him. He was floored. "I think your work is fabulous. I couldn't be more pleased and satisfied. The only
reason I make changes on your reports is so that you know
I've been reading them."

What Happens When You
Ignore Intentions

When you don't check out your intentions, you may do something impulsive or unpredictable that doesn't reflect what you
really want. We saw this very clearly in an earlier example
when a young woman who was bored invited friends to dinner and was then angry with herself because she really
wanted to go out and paint the town.

What Happens When You
Ignore Actions

If you are unaware of your actions—especially your nonverbal ones—you can easily be misunderstood. You and your
mate are deciding whether to hire a gardener to landscape the
patio or try it yourselves. In the middle of the conversation,
you get up and go into the kitchen for a soda, but you don't
tell your partner where you are going—you just leave. Because your action is undefined, your partner may assume you
have no interest in the discussion. Had you said, "I'm listening. I just want to get a drink," you'd have indicated that you
were aware your action could be misinterpreted.

Unmagnificent Obsessions

Obsessing on one aspect of the Wheel and skimming past the
rest limits awareness as severely as omitting one or two dimensions. When you're overwhelmed by feelings, thoughts, or
intentions you can develop tunnel vision.

Tom was an auto mechanic with an artistic bent. He began
to dabble in welding with the tools around the shop and
eventually became a competent sculptor. When friends of his

moved into a new home, Tom made them what he considered a special and wonderful house gift: a welded sculpture for their garden. When he delivered it, his friends were not at home and he left the piece with their children. A week went by. No comment. Two weeks. Still nothing. By the third week Tom was seething. He was insulted, hurt, and furious at their neglect to say thank you. They were, he decided, rude, thoughtless, and not worth having as friends. By the time he received a warm thank-you note—with an apology for the delay—his feelings were at such a peak that he tore it up. He had been so preoccupied with his feelings that they had, in effect, done him in. Had he tuned in to the other parts of his awareness—his intentions, in particular—he might have called them, expressed his hurt, and saved this bruising attack on their friendship.

OVERCOMING LIMITED AWARENESS

When people are introduced to the concept of limited awareness, they ask us if it isn't natural to be stronger in some areas than others and therefore useless to try to change ingrained patterns. Everybody does have strengths and weaknesses, and this isn't a problem until your strengths become restraints and your stronger dimensions overpower your weaker ones. Full awareness doesn't mean that you have to place equal importance on all parts, but it does mean that you should at least try to touch upon all of them. Be aware that you have at least five dimensions, and try to tune into them.

- Keep the idea of the Awareness Wheel alive inside you.
- Recognize your pattern of reacting.
- If it's a limited one, take note of the parts you typically ignore.

We recognize that change is difficult. Think of overcoming limited awareness as a branching out—a stretching exercise in which you bend and pull existing muscles to new capabilities. What parts do you normally miss in your typical response pattern? Where do you start on the Wheel? Do you move beyond that part? Does the dimension you regularly choose eclipse all the others?

In the next chapter we will show you how to fill in and check out the five dimensions of your Awareness Wheel so you can communicate fully and clearly. Expanding your awareness by using the Wheel will help you gain control over your life and increase your chances of making effective, reasoned choices. And once you've learned how to use the Awareness Wheel, you'll be able to apply it in countless ways to improve your communication: to solve personal problems; to send clear messages; to listen attentively; to communicate with others from a position of mutual respect; to tackle issues and develop mutually acceptable solutions to joint problems. In short, the Awareness Wheel is the foundation for all the skills you'll learn in this book.

QUIZ: CHECKING OUT
YOUR AWARENESS

Look over the following statements and link each one to an appropriate dimension of the Awareness Wheel: interpretation, sense data, feeling, intention, action.

1. I wish you'd let me help.   _____

2. I'm glad.   _____

3. It's much too far to travel for a weekend.   _____

4. I'm sorry that we can't visit.   _____

5. I telephoned her six times last week.   _____

6. She called me once.   _____

7. I haven't been home one night this week.   _____

8. I'm going to sew these buttons while we talk.   _____

9. I want to do something about our relationship.   _____

10. Lately, she's seemed disinterested.   _____

11. Sometimes I feel lonely when we're together.   _____

12. There's a ring around the moon tonight.   _____

13. This means a change in weather.   _____

14. But the weatherman said no change.   _____

15. I hope he's mistaken.   _____

Answers: 1. intention; 2. feeling; 3. interpretation; 4. feeling; 5. action; 6. sense data; 7. action; 8. action; 9. intention; 10. interpretation; 11. feeling; 12. sense data; 13. interpretation; 14. sense data; 15. intention.

4

Acting on Your Awareness

When we teach the Awareness Wheel to our groups, participants invariably react in one of two ways. Some respond like
a ten-year-old with a new bike: they can't wait to hop on and
go for a ride. The others see the Wheel as a burden that will
inhibit spontaneity and slow normal interaction. "I can just
see myself," said one skeptic. "I dock my secretary for taking
extra vacation time; then I pause to consider the sense data
I'm receiving from her reaction and the way I'm interpreting
it, as well as my feelings and my intentions. That's ridiculous.
I wouldn't get any work done."

The Awareness Wheel wasn't designed as a straitjacket, or
a tool for people to use *all* of the time. You'd bore your
friends to tears trying to size up every situation, and pretty
soon you'd bore yourself as well. Although you may be the
most fascinating person you know, there is a limit to the
amount of time you could focus on your own consciousness
without losing interest. Constant self-evaluation isn't the purpose of the Awareness Wheel. Trying to be fully aware of
your experience moment by moment is not only impossible,
it's tiring, artificial, and inappropriate.

You wouldn't carry a screwdriver in your pocket every day
just in case you stumbled on something that needed repair.
But when your eyeglasses need tightening or a knob falls off
a drawer, it's important to know where the screwdriver is and
how to use it. Think of the Awareness Wheel in the same
way. It's a tool, a device, to help you understand an experience—be it troubling or pleasurable—that you'd like to appreciate in greater depth and breadth. Since the dimensions
of your Awareness Wheel are always active at some level,
you can bring them to the surface at will. Be selective. Don't

abuse the Wheel and don't fall into the trap of constant or unnecessary introspection.

After you use the Awareness Wheel several times, it becomes a natural procedure. Initially, however, it takes some practice and you might want to approach it on a step-by-step basis. Take a breather when you have some spare time and reflect on your life. What's been bothering you at work or at home? Are you satisfied with your relationships with your children, your friends, your parents? Are there some aspects of your behavior or your life that you'd like to change? Several concerns probably will float into your mind. Consider them the current issues in your life. Some may be very clear and precise while others may be fuzzy: I'm not happy but I don't know why. Things aren't right at the office, but I can't pinpoint the problem. I wanted so much to be president of my organization but now that I am, it's not very gratifying. Despite my intentions to bank more money, I never seem to have anything left after I pay my bills. Think of this uneasiness or irritability as a creative tension that you can focus on and utilize with the help of your Awareness Wheel. Most of us aren't logical thinkers. When we have a problem we circle it or try to solve it by bombarding ourselves with ideas from a million sources. The Awareness Wheel will help you structure all this input in an organized fashion.

EXAMINING ISSUES

People sometimes come to our groups complaining that they've been ruminating on a personal issue for a long time, yet can't seem to think it through. "I can't get a handle on it," is the phrase we hear. The Awareness Wheel is that handle—first, because it gives you a system for examining issues, and second, because it draws on good, solid subjective information. The best way to familiarize yourself with the Wheel is to use it on a major issue that's been troubling you. Here is a detailed example of how that works.

Over a period of several months Tim began to feel increasingly dissatisfied with his life. He was forty-two and, like many men his age, he felt a need for change, but he wasn't sure in what direction. His sixteen-year marriage was solid and still interesting, and his two children were a responsibility he welcomed. Taking them out on weekends to a farm they

owned, teaching the seven-year-old how to ride horseback
and the three-year-old to plant seeds, was often the high
point of his week. But it wasn't enough. One rainy afternoon
after a Couple Communication session, Tim sat down and
made a list of the aspects of his life that seemed troubling:

- My role in my company.
- Time with my family.
- Meeting my financial commitments.
- Time for reading, gardening, and photography.

His role in the company stood out as the most prickly
thorn among his issues, so he put that at the hub of his
Awareness Wheel (See diagram on page 78.) Tim was a
partner in a consulting and publishing firm. The company
was five years old, and its growth had created a heavy load
of administrative work that he found oppressive. He was a
mercurial type, quick with ideas and great with people, but
paperwork left him cold.

He began by considering how he was acting at work and
what he'd been doing both currently and in the past. Under
the Action dimension he wrote:

- Late going to the office.
- No longer working on long-range projects.
- Haven't created anything new in quite a while.
- Doing the same kind of work for two and a half years.
- Not bringing creative energy to the company as I did in
  the past.

Then he thought about what he'd seen and heard in relation to his work and, under Sense Data, he wrote:

- Schedules are not being met.
- Sales have dropped slightly.
- Inflation is worsening.
- My wife has been encouraging me to take some risks and
  experiment with different ideas on the job.

Next, he listed some random thoughts under the Interpretation dimension:

- No one is taking care of long-range development.
- I can't be concerned with day-to-day management and also
  give adequate attention to long-range objectives.
- The current division of duties isn't working; I'm neither
  managing well nor planning enough. Some changes must
  be made.

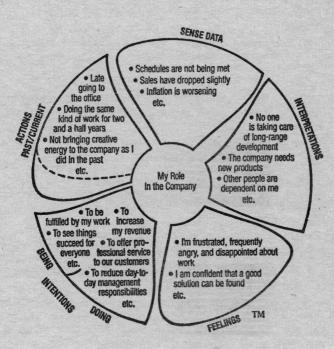

SENSE DATA
- Schedules are not being met
- Sales have dropped slightly
- Inflation is worsening
etc.

ACTIONS PAST/CURRENT
- Late going to the office
- Doing the same kind of work for two and a half years
- Not bringing creative energy to the company as I did in the past
etc.

My Role In the Company

INTERPRETATIONS
- No one is taking care of long-range development
- The company needs new products
- Other people are dependent on me
etc.

BEING
- To be fulfilled by my work
- To see things succeed for everyone
etc.

INTENTIONS

DOING
- To increase my revenue
- To offer professional service to our customers
- To reduce day-to-day management responsibilities
etc.

FEELINGS ™
- I'm frustrated, frequently angry, and disappointed about work
- I am confident that a good solution can be found
etc.

HANDLING AN ISSUE WITH THE AWARENESS WHEEL

- I'm not as much fun to be around these days at home or at work.
- The company needs new products.
- Other people are dependent on me.

Moving on to his feelings, he focused on the following emotions:

- I'm frustrated, frequently angry, and disappointed at the way things are going at the office.
- I feel no enthusiasm for my work.
- I do feel confident that a good solution can be found.

Finally, Tim considered his intentions and isolated what he wanted to be and what he wanted to do. As Being Intentions, he wanted:

- To be fulfilled by my work.
- To be more efficient and creative.
- To enjoy the business.
- To see things succeed for everyone involved.

For his Doing Intentions, he included:

- To increase my revenue.
- To offer professional service to our customers.
- To reorder and reduce my day-to-day management responsibilities.
- To shift more effort into creating new materials, promotion, and sales.

After reviewing the completed spokes of the Wheel, Tim moved to the blank spot under future actions and concluded that he would talk to his partner and share these thoughts and feelings. He'd propose shifting some of the management duties from his shoulders to his partner's to free him to do more travel, promotion, and sales. Those were areas where he thought he could both get more and give more. Tim folded the paper, feeling more optimistic than he had in months. By using the Awareness Wheel he'd cut through the vagueness and confusion that had been dragging him down. No longer mired in uncertainty, he did in fact discuss these ideas and proposals with his partner and, within a short time, made a major change in his role at the office.

PRACTICE MAKES PERFECT

Now that you've seen the Wheel in action, you're ready to try it yourself. Choose a major concern or problem, but since this is your first attempt, don't choose your most pressing issue. Next, on a piece of paper, draw a diagram of the Awareness Wheel and give yourself enough space to fill out each dimension. (Use the one on page 52 as a model.)

Place your issue in the hub of the Wheel and let your awareness flow as you fill out each spoke. Be natural. Don't suppress anything that pops into your mind. Let everything surface and write a word or phrase in the appropriate spoke. Try to fill out each dimension and don't rush. The newer you are at connecting with yourself, the longer it may take. But you aren't fishing in barren waters. The information you need is somewhere inside you.

Now your Wheel is full. Have you discovered anything: thoughts that were previously fuzzy? feelings you'd overlooked or resisted? wants you have ignored? You may want to ask yourself the following questions to see how completely you've fleshed out each spoke:

Sensations: Could you list what you've seen others say or do that led to your interpretations? Did you include data from more than one sense?

Interpretations: Were you able to list several thoughts? Were some of them old thoughts based on beliefs, assumptions, or expectations that you applied to the issue? Were some of them new thoughts that developed out of what you saw and heard? Can you tell the difference?

Feelings: How many different emotions were you able to list? Are they mixed, both pleasant and unpleasant? How intense are they?

Intentions: If you have both long- and short-range intentions, have you included both? Did you separate Being Intentions from Doing Intentions? Do you have only one or the other? Are any of your intentions in conflict? Of those intentions that involve other people, have you noted what you want *for* them as well as *from* them?

Actions: How many things could you identify that you've said or done in relation to the issue? Did you include both successful and unworkable actions? Were you able to formulate some plans for the future?

Because this process is unfamiliar, initially it may seem complicated and a bit tedious. We've presented it in such detail simply because it is new, and our graduates assure us that what first seems awkward and imposed later becomes spontaneous. In certain circumstances, the Awareness Wheel is supposed to slow you down so that when you do take action on a major issue it isn't blind action. One of the reasons people can't resolve issues or resolve them poorly is because they skip this processing step. Before you cross a street you check the light and look both ways. Yet we often charge through life without checking the information we need to direct us.

LOOK FOR RECURRING PATTERNS

As you dissect an issue in detail you may discover a pattern: a series of similar incidents or events that crop up in certain kinds of situations. This kind of information can become sense data that you can then apply to larger issues. Look for a common thread in recurrent or similar situations. For example, the last few times you've been bowling, you've had some sharp exchanges with your teammates. You were accused of being overly aggressive in the neighborhood basketball game. You brought a Scrabble set to the office this week but no one accepted your offer of a game during lunch. You could use your Awareness Wheel to deal with each of these situations, but you might also want to consider them as symptoms of a larger issue: is your super-competitive nature turning people off?

Reality is such that all our experiences do not fit into a neat little package of issues we want to consider or situations we must immediately resolve. Many experiences develop over time; therefore, *all* the relevant information *can't* be gathered at once. At other times, a quick decision simply isn't productive. When you go out to buy a new car or a new home, you may want to sleep on your decision. If you are looking at colleges, you'd want to visit several before choosing one. If you and your partner have separated and you both want custody of your child, you might benefit from a cooling-off period before you instigate a court battle. When you have plenty of information but not quite enough to act from full awareness, or when you are unsure of the right path to follow, leave the action dimension of your Awareness Wheel open-ended for a while. Live with the awareness of your feelings, thoughts, and intentions over a period of time. See if they change at all. Then formulate your action plan. You may even want to jot down some notes on your awareness as it progresses or changes.

Remember, *you* are the undisputed authority on the dimensions of your wheel. What you uncover is neither right nor wrong. It simply is. And knowing what *is* connects you with yourself. It dissipates the fog and gives you the confidence to work on issues with clarity and purpose.

SIZING UP SITUATIONS

Reflecting on major issues is one special use of the Awareness Wheel. It requires time and patience, both of which are in short supply in daily life. However, you can use the Awareness Wheel on a regular basis—and reap great benefits—for the many troublesome, irritating situations that crop up every day: when you and your partner disagree about intentions or actions; when you've blown up, or are about to, in an argument with a colleague, your boss, or your kids.

For example, it's the first hot, sunny Sunday in June and your teenagers barrel into your bedroom just after you've awakened, complaining that they have nowhere to go swimming. You're furious. "For five years we belonged to a swim club and you hardly ever went because you said you didn't like the people. I quit because I got tired of throwing my money away. Now you've got the nerve to come whining in here. Too bad. Sit in the bathtub." Stung by your angry outburst, the kids sulk off into their bedrooms. Your wife pulls the covers over her head and groans. Once again your hot temper has plunged the family into hot water. This is an ideal time to borrow a tactic from football, call a personal time-out, and use your Awareness Wheel to assess your overreaction.

It may seem awkward and artificial to stop in the midst of eddying currents and ask: What is the sense data? What do I think? What am I feeling? What do I want? What action can

I take? You may even think that you aren't capable of such a rational approach. But don't underestimate yourself. At first, these time-outs will require some extra concentration, but the more you use the Wheel, the more natural and internalized the process will become. Eventually, it will be second nature to hopscotch mentally around the Wheel whenever you sense that you need more information or clarification. Rest assured that a quick mental run through the Awareness Wheel in sticky situations will get easier and easier with practice.

Unfortunately, when people want to get a grasp on a situation, they look everywhere but in the most logical place: inside themselves. They wonder what precipitated the event. They watch what others are doing and listen to what others are saying. They pull in global generalities. Or, they spring into action with no forethought at all. We believe that the key to understanding any situation is to tune directly in to what's happening inside you. Ask yourself: At this very moment what do I perceive, think, feel and want? Then you can choose a course of action.

Consider the following ordinary situation, typical of the petty annoyances that can escalate into major arguments and needlessly fracture our daily lives. Watch how a quick turn of the Awareness Wheel can change the outcome and tone. Notice how:

- Your awareness moves fluidly around the Wheel in no particular order.
- Any part of the Wheel can spring into your mind as you process a situation.
- You use the Wheel to make choices.

The kids have been kissed goodnight and tucked in bed. The baby-sitter is squared away in front of the television and you and your wife, Penny, are walking out the front door on the way to a movie.

Your *senses* tell you: I hear Penny say "Just a second," and I see her turn back and go into the house.

You *think:* We'll be late and miss the beginning of the film.

You *feel:* Annoyed, confused, tense.

You *think:* What the heck is she going back for? She's always forgetting something.

You examine your *intentions:* I don't want to be late. I don't like guessing what I've missed in a movie. I want to leave now. I don't want to hassle Penny.

You *think:* Maybe I should follow her into the house and holler so she'll hustle.

You pause, tune in to yourself, and ask: What do I want to do? What *action* do I want to take?

You examine your *feelings:* I've been hassled and pressured all day at the office and I was looking forward to a fun and relaxing night with Penny.

You *think:* If I go in and yell, it will increase my tension and throw a wrench between us. Is missing the start of the movie worth the increased tension? I could start relaxing while I wait.

You choose an *action:* You sit down on the front step, take a couple of deep breaths, and begin to unwind and take in the beauty of the early evening as the first stars appear in a not yet inky sky.

You *feel* your tension subside.

You acquire new *sense data:* Penny comes bounding out of the house five minutes later carrying a sweater.

You *decide* to remain silent, walk to the car, and get on with the evening in a relaxed frame of mind.

You *think* to yourself: I will talk to Penny about her habit of running back at a more appropriate time.

Most daily activities don't require this kind of quick self-inspection, but it *is* important to have a tool to use—if and when you want it. However, there are certain kinds of situations where a look at your Awareness Wheel is always productive.

HANDLING INTENSE FEELINGS

When strong feelings well up inside you and you aren't sure what's causing them or what to do about them turn to your Wheel. Pat gave us this example:

"I was talking on the phone with a woman about a project for our church group, and I felt the hairs on my neck bristle when she told me she expected me to arrange for the speaker. I wasn't prepared to do that. When I hung up I was very irritated and I thought, Aha, now I have a tool to analyze this situation. I noted that I didn't know this woman very well and I responded with irritation to her tone of voice. She sounded pushy. Since it's risky to make judgments on the basis of what you hear, I concluded that I didn't have enough information to know if it were just her voice that was causing my annoyance or something else. Then I thought, What do I want here? I recognized that I wanted to have a good relationship with this woman because we'd be working together. I decided that since I had some very iffy pieces of information I'd give her the benefit of the doubt and wait until we could talk again.

"That's exactly what I did and, as it turned out, there was no basis for my original reaction. By using the Wheel to examine my feelings, I came to the conclusion that I was jumping to conclusions. That helped me temporarily table my irritation. I put it aside until we had a chance to meet and we resolved things beautifully. I think we were able to get together because I hadn't allowed these bad feelings to build until I had a chip on my shoulder."

CLEARING UP CONFUSION

Occasionally, you may be vaguely irritated or confused by a situation but find it difficult to isolate the problem. Perhaps you had some prior expectations that you weren't aware of, which aren't being met. But all you know is that something is wrong.

Renee signed up for a training seminar with high hopes of a stimulating weekend. By the end of the first day's session she came back to her hotel with steam pouring out of her ears.

"The guy who was running the workshop was just awful. I didn't like him one bit. His content was fine, but his attitude was dictatorial. He had all the answers, and we knew nothing. I had some really hostile exchanges with him, typical Style II stuff. I was all set to go back the next day and tell him off. This was just no way for a leader to act."

Renee knew what she was feeling; she knew what she thought; and she had a clear picture of the sense data. So she concentrated on what she wanted to accomplish.

"Usually I'm not that aware of what I want to do. I just act. I really gave this one some thought. Did I want to get this guy? The answer was yes. I wanted to crush him. I wanted to put him in his place. Then I asked myself what that would accomplish and I realized the answer was 'nothing.' There was no value in getting worked up over this guy and no purpose in alienating him. As a result I didn't act as I might have. I went back the next day in a calmer frame of mind, determined to ignore his attitude and concentrate on what he had to teach me."

CURBING IMPULSIVENESS

Parents often find that the Awareness Wheel is particularly helpful in certain interactions with their kids. They need to act decisively, but they aren't sure what to do, so they fall back on a routine response.

Your son says something sassy or disrespectful. Impulsively you smack him.

Instead of sweeping the garage as she was told to do, your daughter goes bike riding. The minute she returns you cancel her television watching for the remainder of the week.

In situations where you tend to react automatically, and later regret your behavior or face results you hadn't anticipated, the Awareness Wheel can freeze you momentarily, sending you inside for information that may lead to alternative actions.

Certainly you are frustrated when a child is fresh. Stop and ask yourself, What do I want here? If your intention is to be respected, will you gain it with the back of your hand? You don't want to ignore disobedience, but it's possible you and your daughter interpreted your instructions differently. Think back to your actions. What did you say? Did you tell her you wanted the chore done immediately? Is your interpretation of her disobedience justified?

BOLSTERING CONFIDENCE

At other times, you may lack sufficient confidence to take any action. Mired in what-ifs and yes-buts, you can't work your way out of a paper bag.

An ex-employee of yours, who was such a hard worker that it required two men to replace him, turns up one day asking for his old job. He tells you he's served six months in jail for assault, but he's turned over a new leaf and would like you to help him make a fresh start. You are torn. Part of you wants him back, part of you is leery, part is afraid.

Tune in to your Awareness Wheel to help you make your decision. Examine your feelings and consider the interpretations they may be based on. Do you believe, for instance, that all felons are hardened criminals incapable of change? If this is your assumption, does your sense data about this man support it?

WHEN YOU HAVE TO ACT FAST

You may have noticed that the Awareness Wheel is particularly useful in situations that have several common characteristics:

1. They crop up suddenly.
2. You need to make a decision that requires additional information.
3. The focus is in the here-and-now rather than in the past or the future.

For practice, pick a recent situation that has these characteristics. Imagine yourself back in that situation and quickly run through your Awareness Wheel. Try to identify:

• Your actions: how you acted and what you finally did
• Your sense data: what you saw and heard
• Your thoughts
• Your feelings
• Your intentions

Were you able to zero in on one or two bits of information for each category? Is there a dimension that's difficult to fill in? Perhaps that's a problem area you may want to concentrate on developing more fully. Possibly the dimensions you don't use could supply you with the information you're missing. In contrast, if one dimension stands out like a champagne drinker at a neighborhood bar—you are strongly aware of your feelings but little else—that may be a clue that you are not harnessing your *full* awareness. And finally, if this exercise has increased your understanding of a previous situation, would you play it differently if you had a second chance?

WHAT YOU DON'T KNOW
CAN HURT YOU

Have you ever sat down to help a child with arithmetic homework? You go over the problem. He complains that he doesn't understand. You explain it another way. He still doesn't get it. By now you're gritting your teeth and losing patience. "Now look," you say, "you're not paying attention." Your voice rises and you impatiently cover the point a third time. Suddenly the child is in tears. "Now what's the matter?" you ask in exasperation. "You're mad at me," he sobs. "I am not mad at you," you reply. But he keeps crying. You throw the pencil on the table and stomp out of the room.

We've all faced situations that spiral out of control, whether it's with a child, a boss, or a partner. Frequently, the reason is limited awareness. In this case, the parent is conscious of the intention to help, but out of touch with his or her feelings of frustration and the actions that manifest these feelings. Although the spoken words deny anger, tone of voice and facial expression say just the opposite. That's how limited awareness foments confusion. It occurs when you don't take the time to tune in to each dimension of the Awareness Wheel, or pay so much attention to some parts of yourself that others are obliterated.

Limited Awareness is a habit that develops into a pattern from years of unconscious use. Perhaps you are an intellectual who worships thoughts but denigrates feelings. You may be an activist who moves first and thinks later, or an all-talk-and-no-action type. You may be a sensitive soul who believes that feelings are the center of the universe. If you overwork any of these propensities you create a chronic reaction pattern that locks you into a rigid mold and interferes with your ability to connect.

When Darlene took Couple Communication, she discovered that she habitually omitted her intentions.

"Periodically, our basement needs cleaning. My typical pattern is to think and to do. I'd say to myself, 'The basement's dirty again,' and I'd clean it. Then I'd be annoyed that nobody offered to help me and angry at myself for not asking anyone. Now I use my Awareness Wheel and the outcome is quite different. I say, 'Okay, the basement is a mess. I think it's time to clean it. That depresses me. I don't want to clean all that junk so I'll ask the kids to do it instead.' For so many years I've been so quick to think and do that I never considered what I wanted. I've got nine kids and inevitably I was angry or disappointed with somebody because I'd do things for them when I wanted them to do something for me."

Suppressing intentions has traditionally been a female characteristic. According to the stereotype that's molded the female image for centuries, women are sensitive and supportive. Intuitive by nature, they concentrate on sensations and feelings and have the knack of picking up their family's mood and empathizing accordingly. "Poor dear has had a hard day; I'll fix him a drink." "My baby has a terrible cold. I can't bear to see her so uncomfortable." Noble as such emotions are, they've conditioned women to bury their own intentions, since strong personal desires are likely to interfere with their eternal sensitivity to others. When women *are* able to tune in to what they want, they usually feel guilty about going after it. "How can I take a job that requires travel and some night work? I'd be neglecting my family."

The male stereotype has been very different. Men are supposed to be thinkers and doers. They rely on their interpretations, intentions, and actions as the key to success. They interpret a situation, decide what they want, and move into action. Since a man is conditioned to be decisive, he often bypasses sense data because it may slow him down, force him to ask questions, or appear wishy-washy. Feelings are equally insignificant in the male stereotype because too much emotion is considered a sign of weakness.

Of course, today these myths are fading. Men can cry and wear aprons, women can head corporations and install telephone lines and hardly a head turns. But for millions these old stereotypes still exert a subtle influence that causes limited awareness. Men must make an effort to recognize their feelings and count them as part of their experience. Women must try to ask themselves what they want and use the information more actively to direct their behavior. Otherwise both sexes will be crippled by a limited awareness that impedes connecting.

FROM SELF TO OTHERS

In a world where information processing has become a top-level industry, most of us have no systematic organized way to sort out the vital information that connects us with ourselves and others. The Awareness Wheel fills that void. It breaks issues and situations into manageable pieces and realigns them in more complete and sometimes new shapes. It forms a basis for making changes, if you choose to do so. And, perhaps, most important, it gives you the courage to accept and act upon your convictions. Cathy, a forty-five-year-old active housewife, mother, and volunteer, is typical of the many people who take our course and, as a result of using the Awareness Wheel to connect with themselves, develop a stronger self-image. She told us:

> "I've never been very sure of myself and, because I was somewhat insecure, I hid my feelings and wouldn't say what I wanted. Either I wasn't confident that I was right or I was afraid of appearing selfish. Going through the process of the Awareness Wheel gives me the confidence to accept my conclusions on their own merit. I don't need outside reassurance. I force myself to come at something from the many directions of the Wheel. That helps me recognize that my viewpoint didn't appear out of thin air and that it's just as good as anybody else's. When I've come to grips with something that way, I'm able to stand up for myself. And you know what, I find I'm getting more of what I want."

Although good communication begins within, its ultimate purpose is conveying information to others. When that information is delicate, touchy, critical, personal, harmful—anything beyond Small Talk—we find ourselves at a loss for a style to say it without hurting or violating someone else. Now we'd like to introduce you to that style: Straight Talk. Once you have connected with yourself via the Awareness Wheel, you are ready to connect with others through Straight Talk.

5
Straight Talk

Straight Talk begins in a place where the other styles never venture. Instead of going outside to other people and events, you burrow inside yourself for a look at what you are experiencing at this very moment. Small Talk, Control Talk, and Search Talk never touch on the present. Small Talk typically reports on what happened earlier or what you plan to do later: "Boy, I had a rough day at the plant." "Let's go to look for carpet tonight." The nearest Small Talk comes to the present is an innocuous comment like, "Isn't this a gorgeous day?" Control Talk is locked into "you dids" or "you shoulds," and Search Talk studies the whys of yesterday and the maybes of tomorrow. Straight Talk, however, is centered very much on the here-and-now, involving the past or future only as it's relevant to the moment.

Although it isn't easy to lower our defenses and expose the normally concealed inner you. Straight Talk makes such openness possible because it's a dimilitarized zone where all attacks are outlawed. No matter how furious or hurt you may be, you promise to focus only on the issue at hand and your inner response to it. No unfair tactics are allowed, such as dragging in what Aunt Martha said, what your friends at work advised you to do, or why you think it's all the other person's fault.

Obviously, Style IV isn't the one to trot out when you're buying fish. You'll find it effective when you have something personal and special to share or, more commonly, when you've got an issue to wrestle with: quitting your job, asking for a raise, taking separate vacations, sending the children to camp. With Straight Talk you bore to the core of an issue and handle differences without blaming, demanding, defending, or deceiving. Your aim is to build, not to destroy. Here's an example:

Martha, thirty-five-years old, has been offered a chance to return from part-time occasional nursing to a responsible full-time position as head nurse on the cardiac care unit of a major city hospital. Although she's excited about the prospect, she's also worried about the conflicts she anticipates between home, family, and career. Her husband Jim, an insurance agent, has his own doubts about the effect of this change on their life-style. Watch how they talk about trading the security of a fifteen-year routine for the uncertainties of an unpredictable future.

MARTHA: If I read another one of those women's lib articles about lovely Mrs. So-and-So with four children who just opened her own bank, leaves home every morning at seven, entertains with gourmet buffets, and plays softball with the PTA, I think I'll throw in the towel or stick my head in the oven. It can't be that easy. I'd like to read about women like me. We were taught to see ourselves as wives and mothers and it's hard to chuck that stereotype for a career. I want my new career. I love nursing. But I also want the freedom to care for you and the house and Jeffrey and Dana. I liked being Brownie leader and room mother for their classes.

JIM: You sound like you're the rope in a tug of war.

MARTHA: I really am torn. Part of me is looking forward to this job. Then I start to worry. Suppose you have a seminar in Chicago or Las Vegas and I can't get away to join you as I always have. Or suppose you want me to entertain business contacts and I'm too pooped. I'll think I've failed you. I'm caught in the middle of wanting the best of both worlds.

JIM: As you're talking I can feel my stomach tightening. If you get overcommitted at work, it's going to put pressure on me. This is a pretty important time for me, too. I just received that promotion and I've got to deliver on the job and suddenly I'm going to have to direct a lot of my energy here to fill in for you. It could be hard for both of us. Frankly, it's a little scary.

MARTHA: The fact is, our life is about to change, and we aren't sure exactly how. I'm scared, too. Not just about the changes but how we're going to handle them.

JIM: I can see us having less time for Jeff and Dana, less time to be with each other, and less time for the things we like to do.

MARTHA: That's probably true, but I expect to be compensated for time pressures by the rewards I'll get from my job—just as you get satisfaction from yours. I wonder if we could set up some kind of balanced schedule beforehand.

JIM: What did you have in mind?

MARTHA: Well, I'd like to sit down in advance and plan things out as much as possible. Look at the calendar and set aside time to be together, so we don't get lost to each other. And I'd like to know just what you expect from me. How available do you expect me to be? I'm worried that when I'm no longer Johnny-on-the-spot, you'll be annoyed.

JIM: I'm not really sure what I expect from you. I'll have to think about that. I do know what I'd like *for* you, and that's for you to be able to do all the things you want. But I won't like it if you're overextended so that when we're together it's rush-rush and hassle-hassle. I imagine I'll get pretty frustrated if I want to go out some evening and you're on late duty.

MARTHA: That will take adjusting for both of us. We'll just have to be more organized and less spontaneous.

JIM: Well, let's try to plan ahead as much as possible and talk about snafus when they happen, instead of burying the anger.

MARTHA: You mean we won't leave things to chance as we do now because I'm generally here and available?

JIM: Right.

MARTHA: I feel better now. I think you'll be supporting me in making these adjustments and I'm really glad about that.

The group that watched this Straight Talk dialogue in action saw two people sitting on the floor, facing each other, listening earnestly, nodding, obviously involved in what they were saying, how they were saying it, and how they responded to each other. History wasn't being made. The earth didn't move. Yet the air was filled with the sparks of connecting. Normally, Straight Talk conversations take place privately between two people who have something important to discuss. If your parents used Style IV, it was probably in the seclusion of their bedroom and that's why it's one of the least familiar models we have.

Yet many of us have experienced the glow of Straight Talk connecting: a truly honest interchange of thoughts and feeling with another person. You and your partner both had the comfortable sense of understanding and being understood, and when it ended, regardless of the content, you both experienced the exhilarating essence of human contact. However, for many of us, such conversations seem to occur almost randomly and, much as we may want to, we don't always know how to initiate or recreate such Straight Talk exchanges. This chapter will help you recognize what's going on when you're connecting, and show you how you can set the stage for Straight Talk and connect deliberately rather than accidentally.

You can connect at some level in every style, but connecting in Style IV is the difference between floating pleasantly on the surface of the waves or diving deep and discovering buried treasure. It's more complete than the other styles. There's no attempt to maintain the calm superficiality of Small Talk; to blame, compete, or attack as in Control Talk; to ponder in an uncommitted fashion with Search Talk. With Straight Talk you rely on your full awareness and communicate your thoughts, feelings, and wants in order to select a course of action.

Straight Talk is the most committed style because it is oriented toward resolution of an issue. However, the commitment to an outcome is very different from Style II where outcomes are thrust upon us like orders. You do this; I'll do that. You give up smoking and I'll go on a diet. Somebody tells you what to do and your only choice is acceptance or refusal. In Straight Talk, commitments are mutual decisions that evolve from a sharing of information. Each of you hooks up to your internal data-processing machine—your Awareness Wheel—and moves beyond the facts to the impressions, feelings, and desires which, once exchanged, create genuine solutions rather than imposing arbitrary ones.

THE THREE A'S: A NEW KIND OF SCHOOLING

At the heart of Straight Talk is a process we call the Three A's: Acknowledge, Accept, and Act. You don't need a classroom or a teacher to learn to acknowledge, to accept, and to act upon your experience. You can do it yourself with the help of the Awareness Wheel and graduate to a higher level in all your relationships.

To Acknowledge

To acknowledge you need only become aware of what's happening both in your inner and outer world. You cannot be so preoccupied with your personal thoughts and feelings that you shut out others, nor so caught up with life around you that you're unconscious of your contribution or responses to it. In Straight Talk you neither stifle, ignore, nor avoid any experience. You embrace it. You don't chew your nails and agonize over what should be. You take your experience as a statement of what is.

By experience we mean thoughts, feelings, desires, and action—in short, all the spokes of the Awareness Wheel. And this includes your partner's Wheel as well as your own. You run through your Wheel, then you encourage your partner to reveal what he or she sees and hears, thinks, wants, and feels. Unlike the other styles, Style IV is especially sensitive to all kinds of feelings: anger, joy, sadness. It's alert to issues hiding under the surface as well as tension crackling in the air.

Because it's focused on the here-and-now, Style IV acknowledges whatever may be currently alive and kicking for you and a partner. Acknowledging present experience doesn't mean that the past is sealed or the future is off-limits. What's bothering or pleasing you at any given time could very well be the memory of an event that happened three days or three months ago, the anger of an altercation an hour earlier, or the anticipation of an encounter tomorrow. We aren't suggesting that you block out yesterday or tomorrow, only that you acknowledge the past and future in terms of their effect on your thoughts and feelings at the moment.

In the opening dialogue between Martha and Jim, Martha gets into Straight Talk by looking at her intentions as the key to acknowledging her inner struggle: "I want my new career. I love nursing. But I also want the freedom to care for you and the house and Jeffrey and Dana. I liked being Brownie leader and room mother for their classes." Had Jim chosen to back off from her disclosure or deny her feelings, he might have responded in Small Talk: "Oh, it's not as bad as you make it sound." Or in Control Talk: "You have to take a stand. You never can make decisions." Or in Search Talk: "Perhaps you've had too much on your mind lately. Maybe you need to take a breather."

But he acknowledged her conflict with Straight Talk: "You sound like you're the rope in a tug of war." Martha, at this point, could have slipped back to Style I by saying: "Oh well, it's not that important. Would you like to go to a movie tonight?" Or, she would have blamed Jim for her troubles with a Style II retort, "You think you could do better? You go off to work and that's all you have to worry about. You wouldn't be so complacent if you had to manage two careers." Or, she might have dodged the issue by putting it under the glass lid of Style III. "Maybe I'm just tired. It's possible I've had too much on my mind lately."

But she stayed in Style IV by *acknowledging* that Jim's comment was on target and admitting more about her *feelings:* "I really am torn. Part of me is looking forward to this job. Then I start to worry. Suppose you have a seminar in Chicago or Las Vegas and I can't get away to join you. Or suppose you want to entertain business contacts and I'm too pooped. I'll think I've failed you. I'm caught in the middle of wanting the best of both worlds."

Jim then followed suit by *acknowledging* some of his own feelings about the issue. He's worried about being pressured; he's scared about the proposed changes in their lives. Now that they've both shared their Awareness Wheels by acknowledging what they are experiencing, their next step is to move toward an acceptance of their thoughts, their feelings, and their wants.

To Accept

What each of us experiences at any given moment is personal and highly individualized. We may like or dislike what we're thinking or feeling and others may disagree with us, yet none of that changes the reality of what is. And because our experience exists for us, it does not have to be justified. It need only be accepted.

Many view acceptance as a kind of resignation, giving in to something that can't be changed. We see acceptance through an optimist's lens. We believe that once you are able to say, "There is where I am," you free yourself to look for ways to change, should you want them. Acceptance is not surrender; it's liberation.

When you refuse to accept your experience, you condemn yourself to tread water interminably. It's impossible to see alternatives or forage for choices unless you first accept the reality of what is. Yet, for many, acceptance is a snake in the grass. We don't like what we see when our eyes are opened, so we run for cover and pretend it isn't there. That's understandable. It's difficult to confront an experience that's painful, embarrassing, or frightening. Thus, we lie to ourselves: "I didn't mean that." "I don't really feel that way." "I don't want that to happen."

Sometimes, the pressure to distort experience is generated by our fear of what others would think if they could read our minds. Afraid of being judged, we pre-judge ourselves: "I must be awfully selfish to have spent that whole check on myself." I don't really want to do this; I'm so lazy." At other times, a particular thought or feeling seems so evil that we assume no decent, normal human being ever harbored such a shocking idea.

One night, during a group discussion about accepting the unacceptable, a young executive who had married a divorced man told us that she'd been plagued by the wish that her three fractious stepdaughters "would fall off a mountain or something." She was surprised and relieved when a friend in similar circumstances confided to her, "Sometimes I have this shameful dream that Mike's kids have dropped off the face of the earth, and our lives are smooth as silk without them."

Finally, we may squelch our experience because we believe we have no right to it; we don't deserve it. We say to ourselves, "How can I be jealous? He's so good to me." "I'm wrong to expect consideration." "How dare I look a gift horse in the mouth." "I'm so successful, yet I still worry about failing. What's the matter with me?" The more disturbing our experience, the harder it is to accept.

Acceptance builds on Acknowledgment. First, you recognize through the use of the Awareness Wheel that what is, *is*. Second, you affirm it by accepting your responsibility—your part in it—by focusing initially on yourself rather than on other people and outside influences. Taking responsibility is much more than a currently fashionable buzz word. By accepting ownership of your contributions and your responses, you make a major shift in consciousness that will have a remarkable impact on your communication and your relationships.

The acceptance of self-responsibility can be the turning point in any exchange. Suppose your teenage granddaughter has gone away to summer camp for two months. After four weeks you haven't received so much as a postcard. Your daughter calls one day and you unload on her. "That thoughtless kid of yours. She hasn't written to me yet. When she was younger I always got a card. She can't be so busy she doesn't have five minutes to think about her grandmother. All my friends have heard from *their* grandchildren. I bet she writes to you every week, but I'm not important enough to her." By now your daughter is feeling uncomfortable and becoming angry with her daughter for provoking this attack from you. Squirming, she says, "What's the big deal if you wrote to her first. Must you always stand on ceremony?" You snap, "The issue isn't ceremony. It's respect. I'm the grandparent and she should show her respect for me by writing first. Now that she's a big-shot thirteen-year-old she no longer has any manners."

Now, let's consider how this conversation might have differed had you, as the grandparent, acknowledged your feelings and wants and accepted your responsibility in the relationship. You might have said, "I'm so disappointed I haven't heard from Jill. Now that she's getting older she doesn't seem to have the time or interest in me that I enjoyed so much when she was younger. I guess teenagers are different and if I want us to have a relationship, I'm going to have to take the initiative. Frankly, it goes against my grain to write to her first. I think it shows a lack of respect for me that she hasn't written. I think I'll put some of what I'm feeling in a letter."

Acknowledgment and acceptance have a point-counterpoint relationship. Looking back to the opening dialogue, note how Martha and Jim follow the acknowledgment of their experience with several comments that demonstrate acceptance. "I am torn." "The fact is, our life is about to change." "It could be hard for both of us." These are Straight Talk responses.

Had they shifted to Small Talk, Jim might have said, things have a way of working themselves out." Or, he could have turned to Control Talk: "You're a worry wart. You never look at the bright side of anything." And Martha, instead of accepting her experience, might have retreated to the speculation of Search Talk: "I wonder what would happen if I didn't take the job?"

Acceptance demonstrates that you are accountable for what happens in your own life, and it removes the blaming "you make me . . ." implication from relationships. Rather than being dependent on others for your well-being and satisfaction, you relate to people with the interdependence of two equals. Furthermore, when you are responsible for yourself, you tend to be more responsive to others. Rather than react, you can accept their experience in a receptive mood, knowing full well that it may be vastly different from yours. Differences are less threatening in Straight Talk because the intention shifts from controlling to understanding. Accepting differences is a learning experience that leads to growth.

To Act

Sometimes, you aren't aware of how excited, upset, or nervous you are until you start to talk about it. Talking helps formulate ideas. In Straight Talk, if understanding isn't an end itself, the exchange of ideas usually leads to some kind of action. Or, in some cases, the decision not to take any action at all. (The promise of action gives hope to Style IV and conveys a sense that two people can cope together to find successful solutions.)

Acting is not reacting. You do not *act out* with the blaming, labeling, or accusing of Control Talk; rather, you *act on* mutually shared information. Energies are focused and flowing; both parties are participants in *creating* a solution rather than *superimposing* one.

The discussion between Jim and Martha sets the stage for action. They commit themselves to looking at their calendars and figuring out ways to adapt to change. Martha concludes by saying, "I think you'll be supporting me in making these adjustments and I'm really glad about that." With those words she highlights the positive feelings that arise from acting on ideas developed through Straight Talk.

STRAIGHT TALK IS THE AWARENESS WHEEL IN ACTION

In contrast to the limited disclosures that characterize the other three styles, Straight Talk consciously touches on each spoke of the Awareness Wheel. Actions grow from the expression, inspection, and appreciation of sense data, thoughts, feelings, and wants. If any dimension is missing, the speaker is not being completely straight.

As a consequence of full disclosure, people using Style IV are noticeably balanced, alert to their inner and outer world in a state we call *centered-self*. In contrast, the self-centered speaker of Style II is off-balance, scattered, and often desperately pushing for his own ends. His Control Talk is marked by a focus on only one or two parts of the Wheel: his feelings or his intentions. His vision is narrowed. He cannot read a situation accurately, and consequently, he lashes out. Thus, your style is influenced, to a large degree, by how completely you use the Wheel.

Straight Talk, inextricably bound to the Awareness Wheel, is strong, dynamic, frequently intense, and based on a sense of mutual esteem. As you talk, there are no phony fronts, and you'll find that people generally respond quite favorably to authentic, honest disclosures. On the other hand, when there's a discrepancy between your words and your actions, your listeners will usually spot it, and the resulting distrust can damage your relationships.

People committed to Straight Talk promise to see an issue to its resolution—to act on it. That promise may take considerable time and may involve many painful or difficult conversations, but the process does generate a sense of confidence because progress *is* being made—a new reality *is* evolving. There are no Control Talk demands; there are only *choices*. They are not necessarily easy ones nor the right ones, but at least they are your own; they are not forced upon you.

In a nutshell, Straight Talk involves:

- Exploring and expressing *each* spoke of the Awareness Wheel.
- Paying attention to what is happening now.
- Taking responsibility for self, rather than foisting it on others.
- Acting *on* information rather than acting *out* feelings.
- Creating and discovering solutions together.

PUTTING THE THREE A'S TO WORK

Cal and Ali came to Couple Communication when they'd been married to each other less than a year. He was a veterinarian whose first wife had left him. She was a divorced elementary school teacher with three children. Both were determined that their love would be better the second time around because they were going to improve their communication. We recorded the following dialogue between them because it shows how well they understand and utilize the principles of Straight Talk.

CAL: Something's going on between us that's pushing me into a corner. Either it's the way I grew up or the circumstances of my divorce, but I have a real problem dealing with a woman's anger. Because you're so much more expressive than I am, as soon as I do something to offend you, you really let me know it. And that really upsets me and makes me feel uncomfortable, too. Now no way in the world do I want to deny you the right to express yourself. But, by the same token, I don't like being upset as often as I am. I'm uptight with this bad feeling when you react in anger.

ALI: Let me check that out. You feel trapped because on the one hand you want me to be able to express my feelings and, on the other, if I do express them, at least the way I do now, it makes you upset and uncomfortable.

CAL: Essentially that's right. In fact I'm so uncomfortable and I feel so bad that I sense I'm withdrawing and that's a block to our communication. We're bogged down and I wonder where we can go.

ALI: Maybe it's just my style. Could you handle the anger if I found another way to express it?

CAL: Yes. I wish there were some way you could be angry without being sarcastic, or jumping on me, or getting that tight look around your mouth. And I wish you could throw in some reassurance that you loved me despite the fact that we get this way.

Note the way Cal, in this last comment, expressed his Being Intention *for* Ali (to be angry without being sarcastic) as well as his Doing Intention *from* her (some reassurance that you love me). If their talk ended here, they would have *acknowledged* and *accepted*, but they would not have reached the third important plateau of *acting* on their insights. As they move on to appraise the possible solutions, note how they ask each other for changes. Had they been in Control Talk, changes would have been demanded even before choices had been discussed. But in Straight Talk, actions *evolve*.

ALI: That's a point well taken. I'd like to cool it, but it's hard for me. Boy, am I having a bunch of feelings right now. I'm down on myself because I've always had this problem of being too sharp and too reactive and other people have told me about it. I've been struggling with it, trying to temper it. I don't think I'm always aware when I come across sharply. I think I could change if, instead of pulling away from me, which makes me feel shut out and mad, you could say, "Hey, Ali, you're getting sharp." Give me some feedback. I know that would help me tone it down because I really don't want to hurt you. I do love you and I want you to know that all the time, even when we have our differences.

CAL: I could do that for sure, and I've got to work on letting more of my anger out in the open. I was raised to be very slow to anger. I go to such great lengths to suppress things and brush them off that I actually have trouble knowing when I am mad. But when I blow, I really blow. I'm committed to helping you soften your anger and expressing more of my own.

Powerful, isn't it? Here is a couple revealing deeply held thoughts and feelings—not necessarily pleasant ones—and nobody is shouting, nobody is withholding, nobody is victimized. That's the beauty of Straight Talk. It lets you loosen all kinds of pressure valves with the assurance that no one will be disfigured by unexpected bursts of steam. That doesn't mean there won't be occasional pain, even anguish, inflicted by words singeing sensitive places. But the cooperative spirit makes it possible to voice things you didn't dare say aloud before or didn't know how to broach because they were so potentially hurtful.

NOW IS THE TIME FOR STRAIGHT TALK

When people in Couple Communication courses first latch on to Straight Talk, they think it's a style to be reserved for heavy matters. Quite the contrary. Straight Talk is extremely useful in any number of common situations where it's advantageous to be up front and committed.

It's a Positive Style for Dealing with Negatives

When we are upset, disturbed, or guilty; when everybody is carousing and we're in a bah-humbug mood; when we've behaved rashly or rudely—in short, whenever our feelings, thoughts, or intentions have a negative cast, our typical response is repression or aggression. We either ignore our inner messages or vent them in Control Talk. But Straight Talk can clear the air and disperse these negative feelings. Note how it's used in the following dialogue.

A. *Handling Tension.* Diane walked into the party, delighted to see her friend Lynn who'd recently had gallbladder surgery. Though somewhat thinner, Lynn looked cheerful and peppy. Diane ran to hug her to say hello and felt her friend's body stiffen with rejection. Puzzled, she glossed over her feeling and began chatting. Within two minutes Lynn cut her short and walked off to get a drink. Diane mentally clicked on her Awareness Wheel. Lynn's stiffening body was the *sense data* that led her to *think* Lynn was angry. Diane *felt* bad about this and *wanted* to patch things up. As a result, she followed Lynn and launched into some Straight Talk: "Lynn, I think you must be angry with me. I was so glad to see you just now but you seemed so aloof." Had Diane not used her full awareness, she might have acted out feelings of rejection or guilt and, instead of Straight Talk, she might have tried to smooth things over with Small Talk or to counterattack with Control Talk.

B. *Expressing Feelings of Dissatisfaction.* Lynn, in touch with only the feeling dimension of her Wheel—her anger— responded sarcastically in Control Talk: "Not in the least. Why would I let you bother me?" Diane persisted in Straight Talk, noting her feelings and her sense data. "Well, I felt rejected by you just now and I'm concerned that I may have upset you. You don't normally walk off in the middle of our conversations."

C. *Resolving Broken Expectations.* Still fixated on her feelings, Lynn exploded in Control Talk: "Upset me? Hah! That's putting it mildly. You hurt me terribly. Not once did you come to see me while I was sick. Big deal. You picked up the phone a few times. I expect more from my friends." Diane stuck to Straight Talk, now adding her intentions and some sense data to clarify Lynn's interpretations. "I wasn't aware of your expectations. I *wish* you had said something on the phone. That was a very pressured time for me. I had three weddings to cater and I also had to bake and freeze cakes to fill the orders that were due during my vacation. I didn't know you'd be so hurt."

D. *Saying "I'm Hurt" without Laying on a Guilt Trip.* Lynn was unimpressed. In pure Control Talk she retorted, "Friends are supposed to show they care. If you were the kind of friend I thought you were, you'd have found the time to visit me." If Lynn had been in Style IV, she might have said, "I was truly disappointed that you didn't come. Our friendship is important to me and I got the impression that it must not matter quite as much to you."

E. *Getting Beyond Anger to Deeper Thought, Feelings, and*

Intentions. Diane, hit by Lynn's Control Talk blast, struggled to stay in Straight Talk and not to play follow-the-leader. She acknowledged the underlying thoughts and feelings that produced her friend's anger, and added her own intentions and feelings. "I can see you're furious. You were thinking I don't give a damn about our friendship. I can imagine you lying in bed, feeling kind of abandoned and uncared-for. I never intended for that to happen. I'm much too fond of you to hurt you knowingly."

F. *Asking Forgiveness*. Diane continued, "I'm feeling awful that I hurt you. I'm really sorry about it. I have to admit I kept telling myself I should get over to see you, but I guess I didn't push hard enough to do it."

G. *Sharing Vulnerability*. By this time Lynn was much calmer. She'd ventilated most of her anger in Style II and was able to join Diane with some Straight Talk acknowledging of her own. "I was going to tell you how I felt, but I'm always scared to put my feelings on the line. I don't like to let people know how sensitive I am, so I try to play tough."

H. *Recognizing a Harmful Pattern*. Diane listened thoughtfully and replied: "You know this isn't the first time you've hidden your feelings about something I've done. Remember when I forgot to tell you I was going to the rally? You later told Joan that I was thoughtless, but you never said a word to me." She finished the conversation by suggesting an *action*. "I think our relationship would be smoother if I knew when I was doing things that bothered you." Lynn nodded. Diane put her hand on her friend's arm and squeezed gently. This time Lynn did not back away. She smiled.

Straight Talk Is a Style for Facing Changes

Whether we fear change or embrace it eagerly, even the most welcome changes can stir up uncertainties that may need clarification. And that's when Straight Talk can be especially productive. Use it the following three ways.

A. *To Recognize Impending Change*. In the opening dialogue, when Martha said, "The fact is, our life is about to change and we aren't sure exactly how," Jim and Martha were using this kind of Straight Talk to acknowledge that they were moving into a transition phase.

B. *To Anticipate Future Uncertainties*. She continued, "Suppose you have a seminar in Chicago or Las Vegas and I can't get away to join you as I always have? Or suppose you want me to entertain business contacts and I'm too pooped. . . . I'm not scared about the changes, but how we're going to handle them." Although this exchange actually begins with Search Talk, as soon as Martha acknowledges her feelings and asks for future action, she moves into Straight Talk.

C. *To Request Change without Demanding It.* Martha doesn't tell him that he must adjust to her new way of life. She never demands he accept her career on certain conditions or else. Those would be Control Talk tactics. In Straight Talk she asks, "Could we set up some kind of balanced schedule beforehand?"

Straight Talk Is a Style for Sharing

Although people typically turn to Straight Talk to handle stress or conflict, it is an ideal style for verbalizing joy, exuberance, and appreciation. We've already discussed the destructive nature of that prevalent myth: "If my partner really loves me, he or she will know what I'm feeling and what I want." You can bury that myth completely and share the private you by disclosing the thoughts and feelings that you have assumed are understood or have been reluctant to reveal. Couples draw closer together when they use Straight Talk to:

A. *Affirm Yourself, Your Partner, and your Relationship.* Martin and Ellen were sipping their after-dinner coffee and chatting about the day. The kids had gone off to do homework. The mood was tranquil when Martin paused a moment, grinned like a bashful suitor, and said, "Remember the other day I was weeding in the garden. You come out and kneeled beside me and we weeded together for half an hour. I felt very close to you then. It was quiet out there and I didn't have to worry about the phone ringing. I couldn't hear the kids. There was just the two of us, talking softly, and there was a feeling of real warmth. It was neat, you know."

Ellen looked surprised. "I can see by the smile on your face that you really enjoyed it. You've hardly ever mentioned anything like this before. I didn't think it meant anything to you."

Martin nodded. "Well, it seems like everything is so hectic for us and here we had this little interlude, soaking up the sun, being together. I liked sharing it with you."

B. *Thank Your Partner for Thinking of You.* To Ellen, that time in the garden had been rather ordinary. But that didn't diminish her pleasure in hearing Martin's reaction and she let him know it. "To me it was just working in the garden. But I really feel nice to hear that it was special for you. Thanks for telling me." When somebody does something for you or gives you a verbal bear hug by saying something nice, respond with a Straight Talk thank you that lets them know their gesture was noticed and appreciated.

C. *Use Your Partner as a Consultant.* When you are wrestling with a personal issue, don't tackle it alone; turn to your partner for help. Pete had agreed to run the charity bazaar for his church, a mammoth undertaking that was beginning to require far more time than he anticipated and was aggravating him far more than he'd suspected possible. He was seriously considering resigning and turning the project over to his co-chairman.

He asked Barb if she'd help him think out loud, which she was very willing to do. As she listened, Pete went around his Awareness Wheel and Barb added her observations without giving any advice. First, Pete focused on his feelings of frustration and irritation and some thoughts those feelings produced—that he wasn't well organized, that he had trouble dealing with uncooperative people. Next, he looked at what he had initially wanted from the project—the satisfaction of raising lots of money. Barb suggested he might also have wanted the gratitude of the congregation. Then Pete talked about what he wanted now—more free time, relief from pressure.

Barb mentioned that he might like to think about how he'd feel if he resigned. She helped him get in touch with his awareness mainly by raising questions and reflecting back on his comments with some Search Talk maybes and what-ifs. Aided by Barb, Pete's Style IV exploration of this personal issue helped him reach the decision to stay at the helm and also find some ways to handle his current frustration.

STRAIGHT TALK SCARES PEOPLE

While the frank openness of Style IV appeals to many, it can also seem terribly threatening. It is, in fact, a risky style. You become vulnerable when you confide your weaknesses along with your strengths and let someone else peek at the inner you. Straight Talk also introduces new ideas and experiences into your life that may be unsettling. Moreover, it requires you to assume responsibility for yourself and your behavior and you may not be ready for that giant step. Keep in mind, however, that the possible risks involved in self-disclosure are balanced by the opportunity to create more intimate and satisfying relationships.

People often steer away from Straight Talk because they're locked into certain assumptions about the possible outcome.

They believe in a long line of clichés based on the idea that you're likely to drown when you rock the boat:

If I say something, I'll stir up trouble and increase tension.

If I open my mouth, things could backfire and I'll be worse off than I am already.

Talking has never helped in the past. We never reach a good solution.

There's no hope that saying anything will improve this mess.

These assumptions are based on the mistaken concept that nothing changes, when in reality nothing is forever. Situations change; people change; you *can* change events by changing your approach to them. Of course, there is no guarantee that a change will improve a situation. You must weigh the potential benefits against the predictable losses in every situation.

Many people also believe that they won't get what they want if they ask for it, so they avoid Style IV because its outcomes are negotiable. Owen told a group that he was in the habit of keeping things from his wife when he thought she wouldn't go along with his plans.

"I had arranged this fishing trip with some guys in the office and I didn't tell Mary Beth about it until a couple of nights before we were leaving. It wasn't that I feared her. I now know it was because I felt guilty and didn't want to face it. I'd been spending a lot of time at the office and not as much at home as I should have. Here I was going on this fishing trip, which I really wanted to do. So I kept it hidden from Mary Beth until the last minute. When I told her, she really was upset. One of the things I learned in the course was that if I'd acknowledged why I wanted to go and my guilt about it and I'd explained all that to Mary Beth we might have avoided a big hassle. Instead I risked an ugly scene at the last minute because I wanted to be sure I got my way."

You may be among the people who avoid Straight Talk because they tried it once and nothing happened so they conclude that it doesn't work. Check whether your intention was to seek change subtly without being up front about it—without saying what you really wanted. If it was, you probably weren't really using Straight Talk. You might have been sophistically manipulating with Control Talk and wondering why you weren't more successful. On the other hand, you may very well have been in Style IV, expecting miracles on your first attempt. It takes time, effort, and consistent practice to alter patterns of communication. One or two stabs at Straight Talk may only lead your partner to suspect that you're experimenting with a new weapon to wheedle the changes you want.

People also avoid Straight Talk because it frightens them. Once you let someone know the location of your soft spots, you're opening yourself to the risk that they'll use the information against you. We've probably all been nailed now and then by revealing something we regretted later, so this fear isn't unfounded. However, we've found that it *is* often exaggerated, even irrational.

Many of the fears about Straight Talk involve imagined loss. You hide yourself because you worry that if others discover you're incompetent, lazy, anxious, and so on, they won't like you as much. Or, you have such crazy thoughts in your head that you can't believe anybody would accept or approve of them, so you keep them tightly under wraps. To be sure, intimate disclosure can be embarrassing, but we've found that this fear is also overplayed. Can you think of a time when you've disclosed something weak or cowardly only to receive the respect and admiration of others for your honesty?

Perhaps the greatest fear many people have is that they'll be seen as unlovable if they share what is really going on inside them with others, and their relationships will suffer. These poor souls really believe that it pays to keep silent. While a smokescreen may maintain certain kinds of relationships, it won't let them flower on an intimate level.

And finally, there is the oh-so-real fear of change and the uncertainties it brings that prevent some of us from making

Straight Talk commitments. We all know people who are locked into an insufferable situation because, as bad as it is, at least they know what to expect. For such people, fear of the unknown is the warden of a self-imposed prison, sadly preferred to the uncharted waters of change.

SHOULD YOU OPEN PANDORA'S BOX

The fears and risks stirred up by Style IV are genuine. We don't minimize them, and we understand why people might retreat from a style that could potentially hurt them. Nor do we offer Straight Talk as a panacea for righting the wrongs of troubled relationships. Severely impaired alliances cannot be cured merely by improving communication. However, we do believe that you have much to gain by acknowledging the risks of Straight Talk, by accepting your fears of disclosure, and by refusing to let them intimidate you.

It's fine to begin slowly, in small ways. When you sense the timing is right, begin with small disclosures to those you trust and see what kind of responses you get. We think you'll be surprised by the results.

Obviously, we're pretty excited about Straight Talk. We believe it adds an invaluable dimension to your repertoire, although we certainly don't recommend it for every situation. A steady diet of Straight Talk robs ordinary conversations of zest and spontaneity. It's inefficient for handling everyday decisions because it requires time and energy. Would you want to lunch regularly with someone who plows through Style IV to choose between a tuna sandwich and a cheese omelette? Yet nothing compares with Straight Talk when you're in a stalemate, when you have to confront a sensitive issue, or when you just want to share yourself in an intimate way. It's a reach-out style and, for connecting to occur, somebody must extend a hand.

Despite its low-keyed nature, Style IV is extremely potent simply because it isn't pushy. Its fair-handed openness, its "I'll-tell-you-my-side-then-you'll-tell-me-yours" has a magnetism that draws people into your inner circle when other attempts have failed. Some couples who enroll in our course report incredible gains in their relationship from mastering this style to handle conflict.

HOW TO STRAIGHT TALK WITH
SOMEONE WHO DOESN'T KNOW HOW

About now you're probably itching to Straight Talk with someone and wondering how it's possible if your partner, your friends, or your colleagues haven't read this book. Rest assured, it is possible. Since Straight Talk combines the best of head and heart, you will begin to engage people with your warmth and directness. Accepting self-responsibility gives you the confidence to take charge of your life and makes it more difficult for others to manipulate you with Control Talk. As you reveal more of the inner you to others, you *will* find yourself being understood in a clearer and more reasonable light. However, there *are* several conscious actions you can take to help you involve others in Straight Talk:

Look at your intentions. Is your goal to connect or to control? If you turn to Straight Talk as a sophisticated ploy to get your own way, people will probably see through your veneer of authenticity and you'll meet with little success. In addition, remember that there is a tendency to slip into Control Talk to force connecting, and that won't work either. Also consider your Being Intentions *for* and *from* your partner. Do they clash or mesh with your own?

If the other person clearly does not want to Straight Talk, drop your effort and try another time. Ask them directly, "Would you be willing to talk now? If not, how about later?" And don't be shy about stating the seriousness of your intention to have a heart-to-heart. "Could I talk to you for a while about something that's really important to me?" In this way, you are giving others choices, and choice is central to connecting.

Tune in to other people by checking out their awareness for them with open questions that explore their sense data, their thoughts, their feelings, their intentions, and the actions they'd like to take. Listen carefully to what they tell you and accept what you hear without being judgmental or censorious. Listening is as crucial to Straight Talk as sharing.

Stay in the present by limiting your observations to the thoughts, feelings, and intentions you and your partner are experiencing at the moment. If your partner strays into yesterday or tomorrow, bring him or her back with a comment such as "I think we could handle this better if we stuck to what's happening right now."

Don't announce that you've got a new gimmick called the Awareness Wheel that you're going to test. This will put people on guard or frighten them off.

Be patient. There are no guarantees that people will always join you in Straight Talk or respond as you'd hoped. If you're not successful, try again, perhaps with a less threatening issue. And don't judge the other person by his failure to participate. It takes time for people to develop trust and open themselves to others.

Don't start to Straight Talk with your toughest customer. Hone your skills with somebody who is fairly sensitive and would be willing to experiment with you in learning a new style.

Remember that you don't have to follow the leader. You can be the leader and people will follow you into Straight Talk. You will then connect as a result of exchanging that most generous of gifts—the gift of self.

QUIZ: WHAT'S YOUR PREDOMINANT STYLE

In each of the following situations, choose the response that would most resemble your own.

1. Your partner had more alcohol than desirable last night and you were embarrassed by the way s/he acted. The next day you say to your partner:

   a) There were a lot of interesting people at the party last night.
   b) Before we go out again we've got to have a clear understanding about how much you will drink.
   c) You acted in a way last night that's just not like you at all. I'm wondering if the alcohol was behind it.
   d) I felt embarrassed last night when you told Marge that her teeth are crooked. I don't think you would have said that to her if you hadn't had several drinks.
   e) (nothing at all)

2. Your partner has not kissed, hugged, or touched you affec-

tionately for several days. When you initiate an affectionate gesture s/he seems much less responsive than usual. You say to your partner:

a) (nothing)
b) Something seems to be happening between us. Do you think we are less affectionate lately?
c) Why are you always so distant lately? You never show any affection.
d) I'm worried. I haven't had a good kiss from you in a week. When I tried to snuggle up to you just now you began to talk about getting the kids to Sunday School tomorrow. I don't like the distance between us. Can we talk about it?
e) Would you like to go out for a walk?

3. Your partner's most recent purchase has exceeded the holiday budget—seriously so, in your opinion. You say:

a) You've really done it this time! It'll take us six months to get out of hock.
b) I'm really getting uptight about our holiday spending. We're about $80 over budget now. I don't want to be a wet blanket for you, and at the same time I want to be able to enjoy the holidays, too, without worrying about consequences.
c) I think our Christmas spending may stress our budget too much. Can we plan a way to deal with this?
d) Maybe we should ask Santa to bring us a nice poorhouse.

4. Your partner is enthusiastically planning to go to a new Mexican restaurant while you've had it "up to here" with ethnic foods lately. You say:

a) What I'd really like is some plain, simple eating like meat loaf and potatoes. I feel bad telling you this when you sounded so eager for tacos and enchiladas. On a scale of 1 to 10 how much do you want Mexican food?
b) Don't you ever get tired of ethnic dishes? Can't you enjoy plain, simple American food?
c) Somehow. I don't think I'm in the mood for that.

Maybe it's because I've eaten so much ethnic food lately.

d) Another ethnic restaurant! Are we searching for somebody's roots or something?

e) Nothing; take an antacid and think tacos.

5. You've had a major change in your job, and you want your partner to assume more responsibility for housework and child care in the home. You say:

a) Nothing; you shoulder the extra burden, seething silently.

b) Nothing; you decrease your work around the house and wait for your partner to pick up the slack.

c) What the two of us need is a good old-fashioned housewife. Let's advertise for one—male or female.

d) I'm feeling pressured and over-tired since taking on my new job. I'd like to redesign our plan for home chores because I think I'm attempting too much. Would you work on it with me?

e) Either shape up or ship out—I can't do it all!

f) I wonder if I'm feeling pressured because we haven't made any shifts in home chores that take my new job into account?

Now, look at your answers and decide whether each one is Small Talk, Control Talk, Search Talk, or Straight Talk. And, just for practice, identify the style of each of the other responses as well. (The correct answers appear below.) Do you favor one style more than the others? Is Straight Talk missing from your repertoire too often? Do you want to make any changes in your pattern of style usage?

Answers:

1. *a*) Style I; *b*) Style II; *c*) Style III; *d*) Style IV; *e*) Style II (you are passively discounting your own wants)

2. *a*) Style II (a self put-down); *b*) Style III; *c*) Style II; *d*) Style IV; *e*) Style I

3. *a*) Style II; *b*) Style IV; *c*) Style III; *d*) Style I

4. *a*) Style IV; *b*) Style II; *c*) Style III; *d*) Style I; *e*) Style II (a self put-down)

5. *a*) Style II (a self put-down); *b*) Style II [a nonverbal manipulation of partner]; *c*) Style I; *d*) Style IV; *e*) Style II; *f*) Style III

6

Matching Style to Situation

The rumble of Dick's snoring awakened Sally from her light sleep. "Too much Saturday night partying," she thought and gently pushed him from his back to his side. Her eyes fell on the clock dial, gleaming in the dark: 3 A.M. With a shock, Sally realized she hadn't heard their daughter, Amy, come in. Amy, a bubbly high school sophomore, had been swept up in a social whirl all spring. For the last several weekends she had been coming home from dates or parties well after midnight. Torn between their pleasure at her sudden popularity and their concern about her tardiness, Sally and Dick had treated the matter rather casually. At breakfast the next morning they'd say something like, "Came in rather late, didn't you? How about paying more attention to the clock?" "After all," they told us ruefully when this incident was later aired in a group, "we didn't want to seem like old-fashioned parents."

Now Sally panicked. She checked Amy's bed. Empty. Her imagination went wild. She envisioned her daughter lying in the wreckage of a car, arrested for drunken driving, mutilated by a rapist. Her hand was on the phone to call the police when she heard Amy's key in the door and her fears came tumbling out in a barrage of Control Talk anger. Now the family had a genuine problem that might have been avoided had they initially treated it in a style more appropriate than Small Talk.

This is typical of the way a situation can escalate when you don't take the time to match your style to the situation. Even if your repertoire includes all four styles, if you don't use them appropriately your communication will suffer. Frequently, you can avoid a mixup, a blowup, or a foul-up by pausing a moment to choose the style that fits the circumstances instead of blundering in with your habitual response.

Matching style to situation is always desirable for clarity. And it is absolutely essential when you're dealing with conflict or in the midst of an exchange with the potential for conflict. In some cases you will find that the wrong style—an irritating Control Talk comment or a too casual Small Talk remark—can actually generate misunderstanding and create confusion. In this chapter we will present some guidelines for meshing style and situation and some techniques for keeping out of trouble.

NEVER SMALL TALK BIG ISSUES

As Sally and Dick sadly learned, Small Talk has serious limitations for handling issues and disputes. Unfortunately, too many people develop a pattern of sloughing off conflict with Small Talk. Instead of boring to the nitty-gritty and facing facts, they concentrate on being nice, avoiding what they think, feel, or want, glossing over major differences, pretending problems will disappear when the sun comes out. These are the types who prattle, "Things could be worse." "Let's look on the bright side." "It'll work itself out, you'll see." You wouldn't carve a turkey with a butter knife and you shouldn't use Small Talk for serious business.

That's what Sally and Dick did. And when Amy waltzed in at 3 A.M., Sally experienced a whole gamut of intense emotions—fury, worry, betrayal, relief—which triggered her into a Control Talk attack she later regretted. Small Talk offered Sally and Dick no way to express the multiplicity of their initial concerns or the changes they wanted Amy to make in her behavior.

Possibly the most common inappropriate usage of Small Talk is the casual jesting that many people hide behind when they can't or don't know how to deal with reality head-on. Janice thought she was being witty when she repeatedly joked at dinner parties that she knew just what it meant to be a liberated woman. "In my bedroom, it's my husband who always has the headache." Her husband never laughed at that remark. This kind of "lighthearted" humor has the greatest potential for abuse when it's turned into a barb that builds up tension instead of relieving it.

Many people who can't express their feelings honestly rely on sarcastic humor to vent frustration, anger, dissatisfaction, and so on. But, in fact, each bad joke becomes less and less funny, and friends flinch because it's too painful to laugh. Janice and her husband obviously had a sexual issue to wrestle with, and Janice's hostile Small Talk joking only made it worse.

LIGHT CONTROL WHEN IT'S NECESSARY TO TAKE COMMAND

Light Control Talk is perfectly appropriate when situations call for some leadership, or when there's a minor conflict that involves no strong emotions or only slight differences of opinion. Sally and Dick could have nipped their developing problem in the bud if they'd immediately issued a Light Control directive: "From now on, you're to be in by midnight. No later."

Parents, teachers, and bosses need Light Control Talk. Business would grind to a halt if supervisors and managers had no appropriate style for giving directions or issuing orders. However, because these messages are woefully short on background information, the asking and persuading of Light Control frequently mushrooms into the demands and blames of Heavy Control Talk. When you're using Light Control Talk without apparent results, it's important to assess the situation carefully and consciously switch to another style. If a student doesn't respond to a teacher's directive, and the teacher notices that he seems somewhat discouraged or confused, another Light Control order won't help. Perhaps the student didn't understand the assignment or instructions; perhaps he's troubled by some personal concern. A teacher who's on top of the situation might dig for more information in Search Talk or discuss the matter in Straight Talk. Similarly, when a normally efficient worker repeatedly ignores a boss's order, the boss may decide that a Straight Talk private discussion would be more fitting than another Light Control directive or a casual Small Talk comment.

In order to avoid crossing the very fine line between Light and Heavy Control Talk, be alert to the situation and choose the most appropriate style.

HEAVY CONTROL TALK NEVER WORKS

Unfortunately, in the many irritating situations, that crop up in our daily lives, it's all too easy for many people to automatically pick up the bludgeon of Heavy Control Talk. Perhaps, like Amy's parents, they fall into the Heavy Control trap because they used an inappropriate style earlier. Perhaps Heavy Control has simply become a habitual response to any kind of conflict or problem. There are even those who are exhilarated by the screaming and shouting of Heavy Control. People who get high on the uncontrolled wrath of Control Talk become addicted to anger. Invariably, after their fury subsides, they feel awful for the terrible things they've said and done.

No matter what kind of situation you're facing, Heavy Control Talk won't ease the tension or solve the problem. So it's very important to learn how to avoid Heavy Control Talk, and that's basically a matter of recognizing when you're there and switching to another style. Since Control Talk has a language all its own, you can use its key phrases as a clue. Watch for these signs in yourself as well as in others, and use the signals to shut off Heavy Control and switch to a more appropriate style.

DON'T BLAME ME

Statements that begin with "you" are almost always intended to tell others what to do or how to act, and they invariably make people feel trapped.

You'd better type that over. The boss doesn't like errors.

You can never make up your mind.

You wouldn't be depressed if you didn't let little things bother you.

You have to run the meeting for me.

If you don't sober up, I'll take the kids and move in with my parents.

You need a haircut.

A second kind of "you" statement places the responsibility for your feelings on others:

> You make me nervous.
> You make me crazy.
> You get me furious.

Remember that self-responsibility is a basic tenet of Straight Talk. It's unfair to hold others responsible for your feelings. Keep the focus on yourself, back your feelings up with precise explanations, and you'll avoid Control Talk. *Instead of saying,*

> "You make me so mad."

Say:

> "I get mad when I think you are accusing me of something I don't think I did."

Instead of saying,

> "You make me happy."

Say:

> "I feel good when you notice my effort to be less critical."

Instead of saying,

> "You know you secretly like it when I stand up to you."

Say:

> "I got the impression that you were pleased when I stood up for what I believed yesterday and didn't back down to you."

Tacking the prefix like "I think" or "I feel" on a sentence, or simply avoiding the word "you" won't remove the blaming quality from your messages unless the shift from *you* to *I* is accompanied by a shift in tone and emphasis. It must be clear that the phrases "I think" or "I feel" are a *true* report on your personal reaction, not a way to couch an attack on your partner. Identify what your reaction is—a thought, a feeling, an intention—as well as the remark or action that triggered it.

Bart was in the kitchen doing the dishes when Louise came in and began to dry them. After a moment of silence, Bart said, "When I'm working and you walk over to help me, I feel you're checking up on me and I don't like that." Louise might have tossed the towel in his face and offered a Control Talk retort: "Then do it yourself. If you don't need me, that's your loss." Instead, she focused on her reaction to his remark and answered, "It's not my intention to make you feel ill-at-ease, or as though I'm looking over your shoulder. It's more my intention to let you know I want to help and I enjoy doing things together. I'm saying that I want to be with you, not that I want to check on how well you've scrubbed the pots."

YOU SHOULDN'T HAVE DONE IT

There's another type of Control Talk command that implies you *must,* you *should,* you *ought to,* you *have to,* even though the "you" isn't always verbalized. These "shoulds, oughts, and have tos" raise hackles because no one likes to be backed against a wall without options. If we comply with these directives, we feel powerless. If we don't, we feel guilty.

Have your personal phone conversations after five.
Don't leave the light on again.
You shouldn't complain so much.
Just stick to the facts.
You must make a doctor's appointment.

Again, the key way to banish these demands from your messages is to focus on yourself. What do *you* want?

Don't say: "You've got to give me examples."

Say: "I'm having difficulty knowing what you mean when you say that I don't reason well. I'd like you to give me some specific examples so I can understand what you're talking about."

Don't say: "Stop calling me a child. I'm as mature as you are."

Say: "When you call me a child I really get ticked off. I can't even answer you I'm so mad. I'd really like you to try to stop saying that kind of thing."

In both the above examples notice that in addition to focusing on your own response, you are not *demanding* change, you are *asking* for it. Requests beget choices, while demands are a one-way street. We bristle when, as adults, we're treated like children under the thumb of parents who tell us we must do this or that. When we *were* children, we had little freedom in choosing how to respond to the demands of grown-ups. We did as we were told. Now that we're the adults, we seize the chance to get even. Nobody is going to push us around. That's why we're likely to resist even a reasonable order out of sheer obstinacy as soon as we hear "you should," "you ought," or "you must." Yet, rephrased as a request, we might be perfectly willing to comply.

Instead of:

"You must change your pants or I won't take you with me."

Try:

"I'd like you to change your pants." Or, "Could you change your pants. I don't think torn jeans would go well at Grandma's."

Instead of:

"You ought to stand up straight."

Try:

"I notice that you seem to slouch. I think you'd look a lot better if you tried to stand up straight."

CUT OUT THE LABELS

Always and *never* are two commonly used and extremely unfair Control Talk labels. We all have faults, but we don't repeat them with the regularity of the morning alarm. When the grand generalizations of Control Talk—always, sometimes, never—are sprinkled in a conversation, the speaker comes across as the unquestionable authority on other people's behavior—and it's very unlikely that he or she will be well received by others.

"You have such a pessimistic outlook about everything." "That's ridiculous. I'm an upbeat person."

"You don't ever give me the benefit of the doubt." "That's not so. Yesterday you said the movie was playing at the Eric and I knew you were wrong, but I kept quiet."

"You never listen to me." "Okay, say something. I'll listen."

"Every time we're out somewhere, you lose something." "I do not."

Since few of us act the same way in every situation, we resent being labeled as "always late," "never thoughtful," or "generally sarcastic," since a single label cannot possibly capture the totality of us as individuals. Similarly, people don't like being informed that they are good or bad, right or wrong because they are certainly capable of judging their own mistakes and successes. Thus, we all tend to react adversely when labels, judgments, and evaluations are pinned on us.

"Sometimes you say the most terrible things."

"That's the wrong way to ask."

"You don't have the nerve to demand what's coming to you."

"It's your fault we fight so much. You're impossible to please."

Understandably, we seek to defend ourselves against global evaluations and unreasonable judgments, and an argument ensues over who is right. Replace this kind of Control Talk with responses that focus on what is happening in the present —at that moment. Limit your remarks to a particular action rather than someone's overall behavior, and don't imply that the action occurs continuously. When you confine yourself to specifics, your comments are easier to hear and accept. And people will be less likely to dismiss a remark as an unwarranted exaggeration.

Don't say: "You're always crying about something."

Say: "Today, when you started to cry after I called you an air-head, I felt guilty, but I also thought your crying was a way to manipulate me."

Don't say: "You have a negative attitude about all my suggestions."

Say: "When I tell you that I'm going to do something and you tell me that it's wrong or that I won't do it right, I get very upset and I begin to think you don't see me as having much sense."

DON'T ASK CLOSED QUESTIONS

Be on the lookout for statements disguised as questions. Although they seem to be asking for information, they are worded in such a way that you can only respond by agreeing or disagreeing with the speaker. These mock queries are called *closed questions* because they control your response and preclude the expression of feelings or intentions.

Don't you think that was a dumb idea?

Wouldn't it be more fun if they came along, too?

We sure have a good time together, don't we?

Isn't it sweet the way he stands up when she leaves the table?

Wouldn't you be better off if you ordered it today instead of waiting?

The unanswerable demands of the "why" question are a particularly lethal variety of closed questions.

Why shouldn't I think of myself?

Why do you always say no before you say yes?

Why must you worry him with such trivia?

Why can't you remember a simple thing like a phone call?

Why must you be so close-mouthed?

Whys don't work. They are little darts that rip the fabric of our well-being by stirring up shame because they imply that we've done something wrong and demand that we justify or alter our behavior. They either lay blame or probe for motives that we usually can't identify, and they tend to generate a defensive response because they are so hard to answer. Often, we don't know why we slammed on the brakes, why we had seconds on dessert, why we hate to ask for help, why we acted like Simon Legree when we had intended to be as sweet as Mary Poppins. And, when we *do* know why, it may be no one's business but our own. Inevitably, why questions generate self-doubt, so we respond in one of two negative ways: with guilt, or with some Control Talk of our own.

The antidote to the closed questions of Control Talk are the open questions of Search Talk. Whenever you hear yourself asking a "why" or closed question, follow the guidelines below and choose a more appropriate style.

OPEN COMMUNICATION USES OPEN QUESTIONS

Search Talk is essentially a fishing expedition in which you bait the hook with open questions that raise all kinds of possibilities. Open questions don't impugn other's motives with demanding "whys," and they encourage expanded, thoughtful responses rather than a narrower "yes" or "no" answer.

Open questions begin with "Who," "What," "Where," "When," and "How."

Where did you hear that I'd already made up my mind?

Would you like to talk about that outburst at the water fountain?

How often do you have trouble falling asleep?

What do you want to know about my reaction to the offer?

What's that grin on your face about?

Who do you think is responsible?

Closed questions box you in a corner; open questions invite you to join the hunt. Note the difference:

Closed: Didn't you love the show?
Open: What do you think of the show?
Closed: Could you believe the nerve of her?
Open: How did you react to what she just said?
Closed: Don't you think you should drive to town with us?
Open: Where would you like to go?
Closed: Isn't this the worst food you've ever eaten?
Open: What do you think about dinner?

The closed questions above seek agreement; the open questions solicit opinions. Open questions also look for input:

What would you like to do to celebrate your birthday?

Closed questions don't:

Wouldn't you like me to take you to that swanky place for dinner to celebrate your birthday?

Open questions clear up confusion:

What was the problem with buying that necklace?

Closed questions don't:

Did you decide not to buy the necklace because the salesman was so obnoxious?

Open questions consider the suitability of a proposed solution and, in the process, prevent spontaneous decisions that you may later regret.

I can't make up my mind whether to work this summer or take extra credits so I can graduate early. If I work I could use the money toward tuition. What do you think makes sense?

Closed questions don't:

Why wouldn't you work this summer? You need the money for tuition, don't you?

Open questions can sound snoopy because they are traditionally the ammunition of news reporters who are taught to ferret out the facts with the Five W's: Who, What, Where, When, and Why. But you can avoid the interrogative nature of open questions if you refrain from using them as a one-way street to gain information about others without giving some about yourself. Don't interview people unless it's your job. Use the questioning words of journalists to initiate sharing. You'll discover that the inclusion of self-information can make the difference between a conversation and a connection.

DON'T GET STUCK IN SEARCH TALK

While Search Talk is an appropriate style for exploring disturbing situations, it is the wrong style to use when you need to resolve conflict. Cautious types are likely to mistakenly attempt to handle problems in the tentative mode of Search Talk. They'll look at the "cause" of the dilemma—anything from a mean streak in the family to recurrent headaches. They'll examine the "contributing factors"—anything from nuclear radiation to job pressures to a generation of disrespectful kids. However, they will *not* examine their feelings or intentions and, without these two crucial elements, it's impossible to arrive at a resolution.

Talky-talk is the danger of relying on Search Talk for anything more than background information. It's a style easily misused as a sophisticated means of intellectualizing. By searching endlessly with no real intent to find, you manage to dodge the very issue you're pursuing. There are pitfalls to malingering in Search Talk:

- Prolonged exploration of past and future events often prevents examination of important information about present feelings.
- Because it eschews commitment to a plan of action, decisions and solutions are left dangling, and partners become confused about what to expect from each other.
- Too much procrastination frustrates people.

However, Search Talk is an appropriate mode for examining issues that affect us only indirectly. Since our lives are intertwined with friends and family, we often become involved with conflicts that don't relate to us directly but are tangential to our lives because we care about the people they affect.

Cousin John and Mary were called to the police station where their son had been booked for shoplifting. Joe's been in a serious depression since he was fired. At fifty, he feels he's over-the-hill and won't get a decent job. Your grandmother isn't speaking to Aunt Sally because she didn't invite Uncle Moe to her daughter's wedding after he got drunk and insulted her at the last family picnic. Although none of these conflicts requires your intervention, you are concerned about their outcome and need a style to analyze them. Search Talk is the one.

At times, talking about other people's problems in the vacuum of Search Talk permits you to discuss issues in your own relationship that might be too touchy to raise independently. Cora and Roger told a Couple Communication group how they'd used Search Talk to take a revealing look at extra-marital relations by reflecting their views about a friend's affair. Cora said:

"I brought up the subject as a way to get Roger to talk without moralizing. First, I told him the details of the story about our friends. It seems the affair had been going on for several months when she found a letter from his lover that he'd carelessly left among a pile of bills. Ordinarily, he paid all the bills and she never touched the checkbook. This particular afternoon she'd had a repairman in to fix the dryer and didn't have the cash to pay him. When she picked up the checkbook, the bills and the letter fell out. In a rage she drove straight to his office. There was a stormy confrontation; ugly labels hurled back and forth. They even visited a lawyer. But when the initial fury subsided and they were calm enough to talk, they decided they had too much invested in each other to split. Now, they're trying to pick up the pieces and start all over. 'What would you do in that situation, Rog?' I asked him. 'Would you leave me if you discovered I'd had an affair?' He had quite a bit to say. I did too. We agreed on some points and violently disagreed on others. And because it was all in the framework of an issue that wasn't ours, Search Talk freed us to air some sensitive things we'd never talked about before."

DON'T STRAIGHT TALK SMALL ISSUES

While Straight Talk is the best style for resolving conflict or sharing personal intimacies, there are times when it can do more harm than good. Sometimes, people who discover themselves through the Awareness Wheel mistakenly think that they must share their inner being all the time. However, very often it is totally unnecessary for others to know what you are thinking or feeling. Such information may be puzzling, embarrassing, or just plain tedious.

The butcher does not need to know you are only buying a small steak for yourself because you recently had a medical examination and the doctor discovered your arteries are clogged and suggested you cut down on meat. Your children do not need a recitation of your concern for their health when you tell them to douse the lights and go to sleep.

Suppose you get a call from a persistent and persuasive insurance agent who wants to make an appointment. Is there any reason for a definitive Straight Talk response: "I'm sorry that I can't meet with you because I can imagine your disappointment. At the same time, I don't want to use my time for something unproductive and I simply can't imagine switching agents. I'd like to get off the phone now because I'm expecting another call."

Use Straight Talk to reveal inner information only when it's appropriate. Don't abuse it.

STYLES AND SKILLS

In this first section of *Straight Talk*, we've described the four very different conversational styles you have at your disposal and the enormous impact your choice of style has on the way you communicate. But that's only the first step on the road to building and enhancing your connections with others. In the next section, we'll be teaching you specific communication skills—skills to say what you really mean and use each style appropriately.

PART II

Skills to Say What You Really Mean

7

Sending Straight
Talk Messages

Whether you want to connect with the most important person in your life or an interesting stranger, you cannot assume that they'll know what's going on inside your head. We've already discussed how misleading this myth is. Connecting comes from understanding, which, in turn, results from the exchange of clear and accurate messages. You build existing relationships and initiate new ones by translating your inner experience into words so that people do not have to guess or assume. Guesswork, in any form, is a major roadblock to connecting. Even when you know someone well enough to interpret certain private signs—a frown, a shrug of the shoulders, a particular facial expression—judging nonverbal clues is a risky business.

There are many ways, both verbal and nonverbal, to express your inner consciousness accurately and fully, but the simplest is to connect with your Awareness Wheel. This is the bridge that leads you to others through the disclosure of personal information. And there are six basic skills that you can use to share your full awareness with someone else.

How much you choose to share is always up to you.

1. SPEAKING FOR SELF

The first and most important step in connecting with others is to begin by speaking for yourself. Whatever personal pronoun you use—I, me, my, or mine—your intention is to claim ownership of your perceptions and your actions. There should be no question that you're describing any experience other than your own.

It's important to me.
I want more time to think about it.
My impression is different.
I'll call you before Thursday.
I'm delighted with your progress.
I saw the most beautiful sunset yesterday.
I wanted to stop time and capture it forever.
I wonder if I'd have the nerve to refuse.

You can speak for yourself in the reporting of Small Talk, the wondering of Search Talk, or the acknowledging of Straight Talk. Control Talk, however, is usually directed away from self and earmarked by the manipulative speaking-for-other. And if you do speak for self in Control Talk, it's generally only to bark an order or make a demand.

Speaking-for-self establishes you as the sole authority on your awareness, and it declares that your thoughts, feelings, and intentions have a great value. Most of us were raised to consider such I-statements improper because they seem ego-centric, vain, even imperious. We don't believe that speaking-for-self is at all selfish as long as your intention is accuracy and clarity. However, if you only want to draw attention to yourself, you're misusing the skill and perverting its aim. Henry's conversations are filled with I-statements, but he speaks mostly *about* himself, not *for* himself:

"Last week I was in the mayor's office and I told him, 'Joe,' I said—we're on a first-name basis—'you've got to do something about better police protection for businessmen, or I'll take things in my own hands.' I let him know I mean business. After all, I'm president of the merchants' association. I've got lots of people expecting me to solve this problem, and, of course, I will. When I set my mind to something, I do it. Say, did I tell you I got those front-row seats for the Sinatra concert?"

The goal of speaking-for-self is not to entertain people with your accomplishments à la Henry. It is intended to identify you as the source and originator of your messages. Self statements tell others that you are responsible for your thoughts, feelings, and deeds, that you speak from personal awareness and allow others to do the same. And this willingness to accept personal responsibility is, you will recall, an integral aspect of Straight Talk.

Too often, though, we are not as direct as we could be. Held back by fear, timidity, or lack of confidence, we couch our feelings or intentions in generalities to avoid revealing our true selves. We use cover words, such as "people," "some folks," "it," "one," and we make *under-responsible* statements that belong to nobody:

> *Most people* would be mad if this happened to them, don't you think?

> *It* might help if Jane didn't yell at her class so much.

> There are *those* who believe in mandatory retirement.

> *One* needs eight hours of sleep to stay healthy.

Much of Small Talk is under-responsible, but when your conversation is casual or marked by light chitchat such statements are relatively harmless. However, when you want to connect, it's very important to be upfront and committed. Under-responsible statements force your listeners to guess at the source of "your" opinions. And *over-responsible* statements that smack of Control Talk convey an authoritative tone that's equally destructive to meaningful conversation. Like edicts issued from the director's chair, over-responsible statements rely on words that imply universal power—"we," "everybody," "all"—and frequently link these omnipotent pronouns with "should" and "ought" directives.

> You couldn't understand how I'm suffering.

> You'd like this movie. It's got lots of shooting and you always enjoy the good guys against the baddies.

> Everybody says the fashion color this season is red.

> All men know women want to be romanced.

> We shouldn't spend so much money on food.

By submerging your opinions in general but powerful "yous," "alls," and "everybodies," you establish yourself as the authority on someone else's experience. Nobody likes to be told what they are thinking or feeling, or what they ought to do, and their tendency is to fight back. If you find yourself arguing frequently, you may be relying on too many over-responsible Control Talk statements in your conversation.

The element of control in over-responsible statements belittles others by denying them real choices. Suppose your kids are outside playing and you walk over to them and whisper, "Your father would really like it if you asked him to join your basketball game." You have robbed your husband of the chance to speak for himself and you've manipulated your children. To avoid being the captain of everybody's ship, use first-person Straight Talk pronouns—I, me, my, or mine. Then, there can be no conflicts over who is responsible for whom.

WIFE TO HUSBAND: I'd like you to play ball with the kids because you haven't spent much time with them this week.

HUSBAND TO WIFE: Not a bad idea. I will as soon as I finish reading the sports page.

There are times when it's appropriate to be *indirect* and times when it's necessary to be *directive*. But most of the time you'll get the best results by being direct, which simply means speaking-for-self.

2. SAY WHAT YOU SEE AND HEAR

Speaking for yourself becomes second nature when you use the spokes of your Awareness Wheel as a foundation. Let's begin with sense statements, clear reports of what you see, hear, smell, taste, or touch:

I see you have dark circles under your eyes this morning.

I hear a lilt in your voice right now.

I see you staring off into space and not responding to my questions.

Your hands feel rough to me.

I smell a new perfume on you.

Although sense statements may seem like an unnecessary comment on the obvious, they are quite important in providing a frame of reference so that people understand exactly what you mean. They may describe past events or present activities, and the more specific you can be, the more effective your statement becomes.

GENERAL STATEMENT: I guess you don't like my fancy cooking.

SPECIFIC STATEMENT: Tonight I made a gourmet veal dish and you didn't eat much and didn't comment on it. How did you like my fancy cooking?

Be as specific as possible about:

TIME: This morning when you left for work . . .

PLACE: I was in Miller's Pharmacy yesterday and I saw . . .

ORDER: Just before you started to answer my question, I saw you hesitate, bite your lip, and look away from me before you began to speak.

Good sense statements offer precise and helpful information about where, when, what, who, and how. Note, though, that "when" by itself is rather vague. Don't say:

"When you forgot to pick up the cleaning . . ."

Pinpoint the exact time by saying:

"When you forgot to pick up the cleaning last Thursday and again yesterday . . ."

Sense statements by themselves do not supply the "whys" for any situation or comment. Explaining "why" requires reasons and meanings—in other words, interpretations—and while sense statements give data, they do not interpret it. However, they do provide necessary background for your listeners, making it easier for them to understand your ensuing interpretations accurately.

3. SAY WHAT YOU THINK

Your ideas are valuable simply because they are yours and you are important. If you don't express them, you deny your self-worth. You can present your view of the world with interpretative statements. By using first-person pronouns, you demonstrate very clearly that you are not out to make authoritative pronouncements but rather to offer your *personal* view of things.

I think you'd enjoy this ballet.

It seems possible to me.

I think that's the wrong approach for this problem.

I don't think you've caught my drift; I think you've missed my point.

I think Sharon was a fool to let Joe out of her life.

I think the only way to stop inflation is mandatory price controls.

Although interpretative statements do, in fact, stereotype, categorize, and evaluate people and events, that doesn't negate them as an expression of your experience. Moreover, values and opinions are not etched in stone. The very concept of thinking implies an on-going process, and your current interpretation of any event is always subject to change. Over time, you may perpetuate, modify, and even destroy your current interpretations and perhaps create new ones. But most important, when you take ownership of interpretations by speaking-for-self, you make it obvious that you don't necessarily expect others to agree with you.

4. SAY WHAT YOU FEEL

American florists have built a booming business around the slogan, "Say It with Flowers," because some savvy advertising man recognized that many people are uncomfortable about expressing their feelings verbally. It's very common to express emotions indirectly or symbolically by buying gifts to convey affection, by speeding on the freeway to vent frustration, by yelling at the kids to dispel anger at a spouse. There are also numerous nonverbal ways to be direct about feelings:

- Kissing
- Hugging
- Sneering
- Laughing
- Crying
- Slamming doors
- Banging on tables

There's nothing inherently wrong with such nonverbal demonstrations of emotions. Actions can speak louder than words and they often have high impact. But if your actions aren't supported by feeling statements, they can be extremely ambiguous. Crying, for instance, can express joy, sadness, disappointment, anger, or relief. If you've ever been around a mother who can't seem to comfort a bawling baby, you know how important words are. "How I wish he could talk and tell me what's the matter," says the mother. And that's what feeling statements do. Simply and explicitly, they put your emotions into words.

I am thrilled at the way this project is working out.

I'm discouraged by this cold and cough.

Boy, am I relieved you called.

I hate spinach.

I'm nervous about this job interview tomorrow.

Right now I feel so relaxed and contented.

I'm angry that you didn't find time to get the tickets and I'm disappointed that we won't see the game.

Direct statements of feeling are quite powerful. When you say flat out, "I'm really upset" or "I feel fabulous," people generally perk up and respond. But there are those who wallow in feeling statements mainly to draw attention to themselves and, like the boy who cried wolf, after a while their chronic complaining or unnatural cheeriness turns people off. Then, when a genuine statement of feeling comes along, nobody notices it.

In recent years, as a result of the ME decade, feelings have been elevated to the center of the universe. Certainly, life is bland and devoid of excitement without them. But they should be the salt and pepper that season conversations, not the whole meal. Don't overemphasize what you feel. You'll become boring, and you'll fall into a very common and insidious trap of language pollution: substituting the term *I feel* to describe thoughts and interpretations.

"I feel that my life is meaningless." That's what you *think*. What you may *feel* is bored, lonely, or unhappy.

"The Big Z Company feels its customers should be treated with kid gloves." That's what the company *thinks*. Companies can't *feel*.

"The President feels Americans should tighten their belts." That's his *opinion*. What he may *feel* is scared that he can't control the economy.

The point we're making is that there *is* a distinction between your interpretations and your emotions, and the two aren't interchangeable. Most people choose the word "feel" for emphasis. Especially when they want to express a strongly held moral principle, they'll substitute "I feel" for "I believe." For example, "I feel that mercy killing is a crime." That is not a feeling. The speaker really means: "I don't believe in euthanasia."

When you want to differentiate your thoughts from your feelings, try this simple trick. If you can follow the words "I feel" with the word "that," you are probably expressing an idea not an emotion.

I feel *that* you don't pay attention to me. (an opinion)

I feel rejected.

I feel *that* I'll never be a decent bridge player. (a judgment)

I feel discouraged about the way I play bridge.

You can describe your emotions without ever using the phrase "I feel." If you feel excited, simply say "I'm excited." If you're hurt, say "I'm crushed." If you're feeling confused, say "I'm perplexed." Check the list of feeling words on page 59 to expand your emotional vocabulary.

Initially, verbal expressions of emotions may be difficult. Many of us were raised to lock up our emotions behind a closed door marked "Private." And we're further hampered by cultural beliefs about appropriate and inappropriate displays of emotion. For example, until recently men weren't supposed to feel silly and women believed that the verbalization of anger wasn't ladylike. Moreover, it *is* difficult to acknowledge negative feelings of envy, greed, or jealousy even to ourselves—let alone to voice such feelings aloud.

Finally, many of us have developed the habit of substituting the opinions, evaluations, or closed questions of Control Talk for feeling statements.

"You have no right to tell me what to do." (Control Talk)

"I'm resentful when you give me an order like you just did." (Straight Talk)

"You're married to your job." (Control Talk)

"I felt hurt when I didn't get a birthday card from you.

Sometimes I think you are so involved in work that your friends don't matter. (Straight Talk)

"You're always tired. You never want to go anywhere." (Control Talk)

"I feel sad that we don't do as much together as we used to." (Straight Talk)

Notice that in the above examples, the harsh, jarring phrases open with the pronoun "you." These, of course, are the same blaming "yous" of Control Talk that speak for someone else and put the responsibility for your feelings on someone else's shoulders.

One sure-fire way to avoid this kind of Control Talk is to consistently express your feelings in I-statements. As soon as you say "I feel," the picture changes. The accusatory quality disappears and a potential Control Talk attack becomes a Straight Talk shared awareness.

5. SAY WHAT YOU WANT

"Sir, what are your intentions toward my daughter?" asks the protective father as the innocent heroine blushes demurely. The villain, twirling his mustache, says, "Strictly honorable, I assure you." Then he turns to the audience, snickering, "He'll never know what I really intend to do until it's too late." Hidden intentions are fine for increasing the suspense of a melodrama, but connecting requires full disclosure of your intentions. When you tell others what you do or don't want, they know what to expect and they can then act accordingly.

Why is it so difficult for us to make clear intention statements? When we were young, we were too innocent to be other than direct about what we wanted. But as we grew older, we were taught to keep our intentions to ourselves. We bought another set of assumptions: saying what we want is selfish, brash, presumptuous, it's nobody's business, it's easier to get what we want by operating underground than by being up front. In short, we learned that it was self-centered or impolite to be direct, so we discovered other ways to reach our goals.

The child says openly, "I hate cheese." The pre-teen slides the cheese in a sandwich to the dog.

The child says freely, "I don't want to go to bed now." The teenager dallies over homework until bedtime passes.

The child says directly, "Sally is a pig. She takes my toys. I don't want to play with her anymore." The adult doesn't return Sally's phone calls and snubs her at parties.

In competitive situations, it may not always be a good idea to reveal *all* your intentions. But most of your relations are not competitive ones (we hope), and buried intentions should not be a feature of your communication. As we've said before, whether or not you acknowledge your intentions, you have them and they are bound to surface. Unspoken intentions are the backbone of our hidden agendas. We are least likely to reveal what we want when we fear that our partner doesn't share that wish. And, when our intentions are exposed, as they're bound to be sooner or later, there's trouble. For example:

You invest a chunk of your savings in a stock deal but neglect to tell you wife because she wants to put that money in a vacation house. She finds out and the fur flies.

You like Joe and Susan. Your husband does not. You go ahead and invite them to dinner. Then you tell your husband and he blows up.

To avoid such unpleasant—and often unnecessary—confrontations, discuss differing intentions in Straight Talk. You may not get your own way, but together, you can search for a solution that satisfies both of you. Straight Talk can be quite valuable in forcing couples to look at clashing intentions and develop compromises.

By making intention statements, you will also avoid confusion and vagueness in your relationships. Imagine that a friend called to ask you to play tennis and this is how you responded:

"Well, I might be able to play tennis with you this afternoon. I suppose I could. If we don't play today, perhaps we can next week."

Do you or do you not want to play tennis? It's awfully hard to tell. Might, could, perhaps are spongy words that serve a purpose in Search Talk but have no bearing on intentions. Note the difference in this clear Straight Talk intention statement.

"Well, I'd like to play tennis with you this afternoon. I think I can, although I've got a lot of work to do. Please call me about three. If I can't play today, I want to next week."

Many people shy away from intention statements because, if they aren't stated judiciously, they can sound like Control Talk demands. Instead of coming out as "I want," the intention gets translated into "you should" and becomes a Control Talk command. Note the difference between the following Control Talk statements and intention statements, and learn to phrase your intentions accordingly.

You should have gone to the party with me. (Control Talk)

I wanted you to go to the party with me. (Intention statement)

Don't make so much noise. (Control Talk)

I'd like you to be quiet. (Intention statement)

You've got to help me fix this broken screen. (Control Talk)

I'd like you to help me fix this screen. (Intention statement)

You'd better not answer me like that. (Control Talk)

I don't want you to speak to me in that tone. (Intention statement)

Phrases such as "you must," "you have to," "you should/ought," are the red flags of Control Talk, confusing the "being" intentions you have for yourself ("what I want for me") with your "doing" intentions for someone else ("what I want from you"). The latter implies that your satisfaction depends solely on your partner's response. That's as heavy a burden as placing the responsibility for your feelings on someone else. Before you make intention statements, tune in to exactly what your intentions are and whether they are *for* or *from*. Ask not what your partner can do for you, but what you want for yourself. Then say it with an I-statement.

Perhaps you would like to spend more time hiking and camping with your partner. You could say:

"We should go camping next weekend." (No good: speaking for both)

or

"You never have any time to go camping anymore." (No good: speaking for other)

or

"I would really like to spend more time camping than we're doing now." (Ideal: speaking for self)

A less hostile but still manipulative method to express your wants is to intensify them into needs. There's an urgency about needs, and substituting the passion of "I need" for the simplicity of "I want" tends to overstate most intentions. If you really do need something, it's a good idea to explain why, and what might happen if your need isn't met. Otherwise, use "I need" sparingly as an intention statement and don't play with its power. Look how the impact changes when this relatively simple intention is stated in three different ways:

I'd like to go to bed early tonight. (weak)

I want to go to bed early tonight. (stronger)

I need to go to bed early tonight. I'm exhausted and I have an exam tomorrow. (strongest, and properly supported)

Most wants and desires can be negotiated if, by stating them, you invite your partner's help in making them a reality. Being direct about what you want or like doesn't guarantee that you'll get it, but it certainly improves your chances and minimizes the possibility of unpleasant surprises when hidden agendas emerge from the shadows.

6. DESCRIBE YOUR ACTIONS

Although you can disguise your intentions, you can't hide your actions. Often, they speak for themselves and they speak louder than words. But they still should be verbalized, because, without words, actions can be misunderstood. Action statements describe three states.

A. *What you did in the past:*
I tried to call you yesterday.
I was really harried when my in-laws arrived early for dinner and I hadn't finished cooking.
I jumped all over my secretary when she lost the address I needed this morning.

B. *What you are doing presently:*
I'm listening.
Sorry, I'm not paying attention. My mind is still on a problem I had at work.
Let me break in here because I think I have a solution.

C. *What you will do in the future:*
I will not be able to attend that meeting.
I will try to be less critical.
I will try not to say anything that cruel again.

Action statements focus on *your* behavior, not what you see others doing. They stem from tuning in to the action dimension of your Awareness Wheel, and they demonstrate that you are conscious of what you do:

I snubbed you yesterday.
I spoke harshly to you just now.
I know I've been unusually testy all morning.

By stating your awareness of your actions, you automatically invoke two of the Three A's of Straight Talk. You *acknowledge* that you know what you are doing and you show that you've *accepted responsibility* for your contribution to a situation.

Action statements are often necessary for sheer clarity. If you called a friend but no one answered, your friend would have no way of knowing what you did unless you mentioned it. At other times, an action may be questionable and thus subject to misinterpretation. For example, your partner sees you staring into space. She has no idea what that means. She could interpret it as a rebuff or an indication that you're depressed or puzzled. But an action statement can clear the air:

"I've been thinking all day about what you said at breakfast."

or

"I'm just daydreaming about being marooned on a desert island with Jane Fonda or Bo Derek."

Action statements can also be a way of satisfying intentions. When you must elicit a commitment from someone,
why not ask for it? The person who stated in an earlier example, "I'd like to spend more time camping," could have followed her intention statement by asking her partner for an
action on his part. "Would you be willing to set aside one
weekend a month?" You'll find people far more agreeable to
being asked than being told.

A crucial part of action statements involves verbalizing
your plans for the future. In effect, you lay out an agenda
and commit yourself to a defined course, completing the third
"A" of Straight Talk: Action. Many future action statements
concern ordinary matters, and although mundane, they are
important because they keep life running smoothly.

> I'll pick Rachael up on my way home.
> I'll make the appointment for tomorrow.
> I'll meet you in front of the arena.

Other future action statements involve serious commitments and they often remain unstated because they test your
ability to keep your word. There's a risk involved, for instance, when you promise out loud to change a habit:

> I'm going to quit smoking in bed.
> I'm going to cut down to one day of golf a week.
> I'm going to resist impulse buying and deposit part of my
> paycheck in a savings account.

And you put your reliability on the line when you announce a future action that promises a change in attitude:

> I'm going to be more affectionate.
> I'm going to be more attentive.
> I'm going to be more assertive.

People understandably shy away from future action statements because they're afraid they can't or won't follow
through. Fear of Commitment was one of the Four Fears we
outlined in Chapter 1, and it prevents many people from
completing this necessary aspect of Straight Talk. How will it
look if you renege on your promise? What will happen if you
want to change your mind? What if you fail to live up to the
commitment? Will you look like a phony who never really intended to change? Will your partner use your failure as a
weapon: "You said you'd start to come home on time for

dinner and you're late again, as usual. I knew you didn't mean it!"

Why, you're probably wondering, should you bother to make such statements since they're so potentially dangerous? Because if you don't, your partner has no way of knowing what to expect from you. At the start of the chapter we mentioned the weakness of partnerships based on guesswork and assumption. Strong relationships are built on trust, and trust develops when you demonstrate repeatedly that you can live up to your commitments. Certainly you will have lapses. To err is human and none of us is infallible. That's why erasers were invented. So word your future action statements carefully and, when you are uncertain, share your doubts with your partner explicitly. For example, you might say, "I'm uncertain. I'd like to make this promise, but right now, I'm not sure I can keep it. I want more time to figure it out." People who stick by their action statements are viewed as dependable and effective individuals, in touch with their behavior and willing to take responsibility for it. Fence-sitters who steer clear of action are seen as weak and wishy-washy.

HOW TO TURN YOUR
DIALOGUE AROUND

Getting into the habit of speaking for yourself to reveal the findings of your Awareness Wheel is a major step in connecting. But you'll soon find that statements pinpointing only one aspect of your awareness aren't sufficient to express all you have to say. If you were to look at a painting of two people on a blank canvas, you'd be puzzled about how to interpret it because the painter left out the background. Where are they? What are they supposed to be doing? Limited statements describing only one spoke of the Awareness Wheel—your feelings or your actions, for example—also leave us guessing about context and hungry for more information.

ONE IS NOT ENOUGH

About midway through every Couple Communication course, someone comes to class complaining that his or her partner seems fixated on sense statements, feeling statements, or intention statements. While the relationship has improved, something is still missing. John told us this typical story.

"Since we started this course, my wife has really tuned in to making feeling statements. While that's fine for her because she knows where her feelings come from, it's just confusing to me. For example, the other day I came back from jogging and she said to me, 'I'm really upset.' Bingo, the old bell went off in my head. What did I do this time? But it turned out I hadn't done anything. She was upset because she'd been figuring the bank statement while I was out running and she found she'd forgotten to enter several checks she'd written and she was overdrawn. It sure would have saved me an anxious moment if she'd said all of that at the beginning."

John's wife had given him what we call a one-part message—any simple statement that combines speaking-for-self with one element of your awareness:

I see you had a haircut. (Sense statement)

From what the doctor says, I think Dad is going to recover. (Interpretative statement)

I am bursting with joy. (Feeling statement)

I'd like to catch a movie this weekend. (Intention statement)

I've been snippy all day. (Action statement)

In many situations, one-part messages are all that's necessary. But, as John pointed out, they can be inadequate. As you become comfortable speaking for yourself, you'll find that it's helpful to combine your thoughts and feelings or your intentions and actions. Linking the parts of your Awareness Wheel provides your partner with the proper context to understand *all* that you are saying.

TWO ARE BETTER THAN ONE

Nothing is more boring than a conversation where someone drones on and on without adding any new information. If you listen closely, you'll soon realize that the speaker is stuck on one dimension of his or her awareness. You can easily avoid the trap of limited awareness and make your conversation clearer, more interesting, and more informative with two-part messages. Any statement that combines speaking-for-self with two elements of your Awareness Wheel is a two-part message. Not only do two-part messages spice up your delivery, they also define exactly what you mean.

Instead of her one-part message, "I'm upset," John's wife could have used a clearer two-part message:

I'm upset because I think I've overdrawn the bank account. (Combining feeling and thinking statements.)

There are several other combinations:

I'm so bored driving on the turnpike. I'd like to take the scenic route for a while. (Combining feeling and intention statements.)

I think John's grades are slipping and I'm going to make an appointment with his teacher. (Combining thinking and action statements.)

I've been such a grouch from this cold all week I'd like to take you to dinner to make up for it. (Combining action and intention statements.)

I've put off responding to the invitation for Jane's birthday party and I think it's because I really don't like Jane. (Combining action and thinking statements.)

You can say a great deal in a two-part message and, without increasing the quantity of your words, you can improve the quality and clarity.

A Special Two-Part Message

We've left out any combinations using sense statements because they are part of a special two-part message we call *documentation*. When you link sense data to thoughts, you give your partner the valuable information necessary to understand how you arrived at your particular interpretation. We'd like to make a banner that says "No interpretation without documentation." That's how important we believe this principle is. Countless times each day we make interpretations without explaining how what we've seen or heard leads us to our conclusions. A wife tells her husband, "You really don't understand me." A boss tells her secretary, "I don't think you appreciate the importance of this job." A brother tells his older sister, "You think you're my mother." A guy tells the gal he's seeing, "I admire you." In each and every instance, the listener has to *guess* what the speaker means. Notice how each statement changes when sense data is added.

> WIFE TO HUSBAND: When you came home from your business trip two days ago I told you that I missed being alone with you, and today you invited Joe and Harriet to join us for dinner. I don't think you understand me.

> BOSS TO SECRETARY: You've been late every day this week. Your typing is full of errors and yesterday you forgot to put an appointment in my book and I had two people at the same time. I don't think you appreciate the importance of this job.

> BROTHER TO OLDER SISTER: First you tell me to wash my hands before dinner. Now you tell me to get my elbows off the table. I saw you whisper to Dad when I got catsup on my shirt. Geez, you think you're my mother.

> GUY TO GAL: I really admire the way you can dig into your work, then walk away and forget it when you're relaxing.

Because we are constantly interpreting the world we live in, we tend to forget that others don't always make the same observations that we do. We neglect to support our impressions with sense data and then we wonder why we've been misunderstood. Without documentation there is no way for two people to be sure that they are reacting to the same information, and a common frame of reference is a prerequisite for understanding.

The key to effective documentation is being as specific as possible about what you saw and heard by citing the exact time and place. It may seem picayune to be so precise, but we find that anchoring your interpretations to specifics makes a tremendous difference. It can be so frustrating when someone says to you, "You always interrupt me," or "Whenever I try to talk to you, you walk away," or "You don't like the way I dress." These are the demeaning global generalities of Control Talk. What is the person referring to? When did you act that way? Now, consider what happens when these same statements are documented:

> "At dinner last night I said that I wanted to talk to you and you got up and left the table. I came in and started to say something while you were watching TV now and you went into the kitchen for a snack. So often when I try to talk to

you, it seems that you walk away. This is starting to bother me."

"When I tried on my new suit for you this morning, you grinned and asked me when baggy pants were coming back in style. I don't think you like the way I dress."

"We've been chatting for fifteen minutes and I haven't been able to finish one sentence. I even counted that you broke in on me ten different times. I'd really like you to be aware of how much you interrupt me and try to stop it."

Unfortunately, documentation is not always used to create understanding. Sometimes it's pulled out of the bag to prove a point. Carl was supposed to pick up Eric at the train station; he arrived a half hour late.

ERIC: What happened to you? I said 5:30 at the Westmont Station. It's 6:00. Where have you been?
CARL: I thought you said the Haddonfield Station. I was waiting there.
ERIC: This morning when I left for work I distinctly said Westmont at 5:30.
CARL: If you said Westmont, how could I have heard Haddonfield?

Did Eric say Westmont or Haddonfield? Is Carl right or wrong? Tune in next week and they'll still be arguing. No amount of documentation can settle a struggle with someone who has difficulty admitting he's made a mistake or someone who needs the ego satisfaction of being right. The real issue gets buried under a fruitless Control Talk contest to see who can come out on top. In a case like this, it's extremely important not to play follow-the-leader. Get out of the blaming and attacking of Control Talk and move into Straight Talk:

CARL: Well, it seems to me one of us was confused. What's important is that we found each other and we're both okay.

THE MORE THE MERRIER

If you've ever tried to fill out one of those contest forms that says, "Tell us in twenty-five words or less—————," you know that it can be difficult to compress a complicated idea. But with the Awareness Wheel, it can become surprisingly easy. Any statement that includes speaking-for-self with three

or more dimensions of the Awareness Wheel is a multipart
message. By multi we don't mean conflicting; multi-messages
don't confuse. They clarify by introducing as much helpful
information as possible.

You build a multi-message by adding on to a one- or two-
part message:

"I'm concerned." (One-part message; feeling statement)

"I'm concerned that I've overdrawn the checking account."
(Two-part message; feeling and action statements)

"I'd like to know if you write any checks without recording
them in the ledger because I'm concerned that I've overdrawn the account." (Multi-message; intention, feeling, and
action statements)

"I'm going to laze in bed all morning." (One-part message;
action statement)

"It's raining and the kids are in school and I'm caught up on
my housework, so I'll laze in bed all morning." (Two-part
message; sense data and action statements)

"I'm feeling lazy and I'm not going to feel guilty about it. I
think everybody is entitled to time off. It's raining, the kids
are in school, and I'm caught up on my housework. So I'm
going to goof off in bed all morning." (Multi-message;
feeling, interpretation, sense, and action statements)

You won't notice too many multi-messages in Small Talk
or even Control Talk. People wedded to these styles talk a
great deal but don't say much because they are locked in to
limited awareness. Small Talkers tend to chitchat about what
they saw or heard. Control Talk conversations hover around
what others should think or do. Even Search Talk, which
ranges further afield, relies mainly on interpretation statements—what might have caused thus-and-so to happen; what
might be done to alter the course for the future. Feelings are
purposely avoided.

Only Straight Talk seeks to combine the many dimensions
of awareness, and it is characterized by consistent references
to feelings and intentions. Using multi-messages is the way to
connect in Straight Talk and avoid the destructive Control
Talk undercurrents of blaming or demanding. Although
slightly more complicated, Straight Talk multi-messages are
worth the extra time and effort. During the next few days,

pay attention to how you express yourself to others. Do you offer enough variety of information to be clear and concise? Can you translate what you are experiencing into feelings, thoughts, intentions, and actions, and do you share those awarenesses with others?

Betty and Don were a delightful couple who'd been married nearly forty years when they took our course. Don had always been the strong, silent type and Betty had jogged merrily through their marriage, assuming that he agreed with her on almost everything. Whenever they'd have a fight, she was surprised to discover she'd misread him because he hadn't said anything to indicate his disagreement. On the last night of the course, she bustled in triumphantly. Don was grinning too. "I finally learned how to get him talking," she announced. "Now I say to him, 'Since you're silent and not answering me I'll have to *assume* you agree with me. As soon as I say 'assume,' he perks up. He'll say, 'No, I didn't mean that,' and then go around the Awareness Wheel. After all these years, we've finally discovered how to talk to each other."

8

Tuning in
to the Outer World:
Attentive Listening

The man who listens to the voice of a friend, or his wife, or his child, but does not catch the message in the tone of voice: "Notice me. Help me. Care about me," hears—but does not really listen.

The person who attends a concert with his mind on business, hears—but does not really listen. The person who walks among the songs of birds and thinks only of what's for supper, hears—but does not really listen.

The person who does not pay attention to his conscience, who turns away and thinks he has done enough already, hears—but does not really listen.

May we learn to listen to the music of the world, the infant's cry, the sighs of love.

May we listen to the call of help from the lonely.

May we listen for the sound of a heart breaking.

May we listen not only to the words of those we love, but for those things they don't say out loud.

May we begin to listen to the things inside ourselves that we did not have words for and find the words to say them.

Our world is woefully lacking in good listeners. If you have ever had the experience—and we hope you have—of being understood at a needy moment because someone really listened to you, then you know how treasured such moments are. Yet all of us want to be listened to whenever we speak, regardless of what we have to say.

Listening is as much a part of genuine communication—of connecting—as talking, and, in fact, you cannot succeed at Straight Talk if you are unable to listen. While most of us are born with the capacity to hear, we must learn how to listen, and there is a fine distinction between the two. The person who merely hears is a passive receiver who accepts and stores information like a tape recorder. But a good listener is an involved participant in an exchange. And whether that exchange is as breezy as a family trading news of their day at the dinner table or as momentous as a couple wrestling over the decision to have a child, the skills for listening are basically the same. It's the intensity that varies.

ARE YOU LISTENING

Have you ever noticed that when you are listening to someone you unconsciously being to compare how you would feel in a similar circumstance or what you'd do if you found yourself in their shoes. Gradually, as they talk, your thoughts drift away from what they're saying and focus on your reactions to it. You agree or disagree; you proffer advice; you pronounce judgments. While these are perfectly natural responses—and sometimes even appropriate—they are sure signs that you are not what we like to call an attentive listener. Because, while you may be terribly interested in the speaker, your focus is not on that person but on what you can offer.

People who equate a rapt audience with good listeners may be surprised to learn that the two are not synonymous. When you've got one ear tuned to a speaker and the other tuned to yourself, you're a pseudo-listener. You appear to be listening, but you are really waiting for your turn to talk.

There are different styles for listening as well as for speaking. When you're watching a football game or playing Monopoly, you wouldn't chat in Straight Talk and you wouldn't need the skills of attentive listening. How you listen depends on the situation and your intentions. Style I listening is appropriate when you're playful, bored, tired, or not terribly interested. You will listen lightly, indicating that you aren't in the mood to be serious or intense.

Style II listening, like Control Talk, is aggressive and judgmental, focused on giving advice. A Style II listener takes charge of a conversation and gradually shifts his or her emphasis away from the speaker to what he or she can do for the speaker. There are three common forms of Style II listening: the Rescuer, the Judge, and the Negator. In the dialogues that follow, note the differences between each of these forms and truly attentive listening.

The Rescuer. Many genuinely compassionate souls are so eager to correct problems that they make the poorest listeners. Rushing in like Mr. Fix-It with emotional BandAids, they are quick with advice and solutions that would work for them. But it's a general rule of thumb that when someone confides in you, the last thing they really want is answers. What they are looking for is understanding; someone to care about their troubles.

SPEAKER. I don't know why I can't pull myself together since our dog was hit by that car. I didn't think I was that attached to her. I always thought she was the kids' pet. Now I keep staring at the spot on the rug where she used to lie and I just want to cry.

RESCUER: Why don't you get a new dog?

ATTENTIVE LISTENER: You sound really unhappy—almost as if the depth of your feelings surprises you.

The Judge. Whenever you want to know if you made the right decision, used your best judgment, or said what you should have, it's easy to find someone who will gladly examine your behavior and evaluate your choices. Unfortunately, you'll learn nothing from this kind of listener. You'll only receive approval or disapproval based on his or her point of view.

SPEAKER: I thought it was crummy of Harvey to run for class treasurer when he knew I wanted the position. What kind of friend does that? I told him off, too. Don't you think I was right to do that?

JUDGE: Sure you were. People have every right to express their feelings.

ATTENTIVE LISTENER: I can see you were really sore at him. But you seem uncertain about whether it was a good idea to tell him off.

The Negator. There are some people who seem to find fault or take exception to everything they hear. They listen only in order to launch an attack on the speaker's credibility or judgment. And needless to say, people soon stop talking to such listeners.

SPEAKER: Sometimes I feel like I don't have any real friends. I know I'm busy and all that, but it seems to me that it's only because I call people to make arrangements. Nobody ever calls me.

NEGATOR: That is the silliest remark I ever heard. How could you let your imagination run on like that. Sometimes I really wonder about you.

ATTENTIVE LISTENER: I think I hear a mixed message there. You say your life is full of people, but at the same time you feel friendless. It seems you want more assurances that you're wanted.

Style II listeners hear only what they want and are usually more interested in responding than in listening.

Style III listeners are Fact Finders. They are eager to assist, but unlike the Rescuer, they don't give advice; instead they probe every aspect of the issue with you. When Fact Finders are not heavy-handed in their questioning and know when to back off, they can be genuinely helpful. However, the flip side of the coin is the kind of Style II listening that grinds you down with endless questions, and, in the process of gathering data, ignores feelings. Eventually the speaker believes that he or she has been interrogated instead of supported.

SPEAKER: I had such a weird dream last night. I came home from work and my boss was cooking dinner in my kitchen. The house was full of smoke, yet I calmly started to set the table.

FACT FINDER: What was she cooking? Has your boss ever been to your house before? How did it end?

ATTENTIVE LISTENER: What do you make of the dream?

The Rescuers, Judges, Negators, and Fact Finders of the world, although well intentioned, are misguided. You can't practice attentive listening when you are primarily interested in expressing your viewpoint or airing your opinion. Attentive listeners temporarily silence self in order to concentrate on other. Their intention is to understand, not to force agreement. Their eyes watch for nonverbal cues; their ears are keen; their hearts are open.

Because you are familiar with the Awareness Wheel you are already on the way to becoming an attentive listener. Just as you used the wheel to tune in to yourself, you can now use it to listen to others—to listen to understand, to listen accurately. Many people who teach listening skills emphasize only the feeling dimension of the Wheel. Although listening for feelings is certainly important, we've said before that feelings are not the only thing that matters. In addition to searching for feelings, an attentive listener is alert to sense data and looks for thoughts, intentions, and action statements as well.

Using the Awareness Wheel as a reference point, an attentive listener employs certain listening skills to round out his effectiveness in Straight Talk. You've already learned how to send Straight Talk messages. Now, in order to participate in that style as a listener as well, you must learn the following skills:

- To observe.
- To acknowledge.
- To encourage.
- To check out.
- To interpret.
- To share a meaning.

ATTENTIVE LISTENERS OBSERVE

As you listen, think about the dimensions of the Awareness Wheel and try to fill in as many parts as you can from what you see and hear.

1. *Listen for sense data:* Take special notice of nonverbal cues. Observe the speaker's facial expression. Do body movements—jerky motions or a relaxed stance—tell you anything? How about posture or breathing rate? All of these signs convey messages that influence the interpretations you make. Looking and listening for sense data can be particularly helpful when what you see doesn't jibe with what you hear. And that's an all too common occurrence in many of our daily exchanges. Suppose you meet a friend on the street and casually ask, "How's it going?" She replies, "Oh, fine. Great." But her voice is flat; her lips grim. You'd be confused because her words don't fit her demeanor. A sensitive observer of sense data would comment on it. "You say you're doing swell but you sure don't look like you mean it. Your voice sounds tired and your usual smile is missing."

2. *Listen for interpretation statements:* "My guess is the party will be canceled since her dad went into the hospital."

3. *Listen for feeling statements:* "Ever since the layoff notice was circulated I've been scared to death that my job will be axed."

4. Listen for intention statements: "I want to trade this gas-eater of mine for a smaller car."

5. Listen for action statements: "I'm going to audition for the new amateur theater group in town."

Because the Awareness Wheel channels you toward specific areas of information, you'll immediately find that you are aware not only of what is said but also what isn't. You might notice, for instance, that a speaker harps on her feelings but completely ignores her intentions. You, as the attentive listener, can either choose to keep the conversation on the feeling level or inquire about her missing intentions. In either case, your pointed response indicates that you are paying close attention.

In addition to engaging your attention, focusing on the five spokes of the Awareness Wheel can help you mentally organize and remember what you hear.

"I said he *thought* the pay was too low for the work involved."

"I *intend* to marry this guy despite my mother's opposition."

"I am *going* to be away the first week in July."

Recognizing and classifying different kinds of statements imprints them on your memory. Later, when you want to recall what you heard, you can touch base with the particular dimensions of the Wheel, and information retrieval will be that much easier.

ATTENTIVE LISTENERS ACKNOWLEDGE

To let someone know that you are really listening, learn to paraphrase what they've said.

SPEAKER: Before I pick up the steaks for dinner, I've got to stop by the studio, then sign some checks at the office, and drop a package at the express mail. There's a good chance I'll be running late.
ACKNOWLEDGER: You've got a slew of errands and you'll probably be late bringing dinner home.
SPEAKER: I've had a pounding headache since Phil went into the hospital. I don't know if it's nerves or something more serious.

ACKNOWLEDGER: Hmm, you're not sure whether you've got a tension headache or a physical problem.

Obviously, this technique is only appropriate in certain situations; otherwise you might sound like a parrot. But you can also reflect your interest nonverbally. Nods, smiles, concerned looks, comments such as "uh-huh," "that's interesting," "I'm with you" all indicate your absorption. Try to establish eye contact as well whenever you listen. It's awfully hard to believe that you have someone's ear when his or her eyes are glued to the floor or staring off in space.

ATTENTIVE LISTENERS ENCOURAGE

Frequently, you simply will not have enough information to interpret what you hear. Invite the speaker to tell you more with short encouraging statements:

I'd like to hear more about this.
Can you fill me in on what you were feeling then?

Encouraging words are far more potent than they seem. In contrast to the Fact Finder's probing questions which assume responsibility for the conversation, these brief statements shift the responsibility back to the speaker and they can be the turning point in a conversation. The listener, in effect, says to the speaker, "You're in charge here. You're the authority on your experience."

People in positions of authority often have difficulty taking a back seat while they gather information. They tend to lead you, rather than to follow your lead, and that's an intimidating tactic. Consider a typical consultation with a doctor.

The take-charge authority ushers you into the office and asks:

What's bothering you?
You reply: I have a pain in my chest.
He asks: How long have you had it?
You reply: A week.
He asks: Is it sharp or dull?
You reply: Dull.

And from that point on, you become the follower, expecting the doctor to ask the right questions while you furnish yes, no, or one-word replies. He may cure your pain, but you will leave the office feeling emotionally unsatisfied.

The doctor who has learned to be an encouraging listener begins with the same initial question: What's bothering you? But his second question is critically different: Can you tell me more about it?

Instead of taking charge as the expert on *your* experience, he allows you to be the guide and to spontaneously report your version of the details of your illness. The two physicians may be equally competent, but you may perceive one as a good doctor and the other as a poor one simply on the basis of their respective inability and ability to listen and to ask the right kinds of questions. When you find yourself in the listener's seat, don't try to steer the car.

ATTENTIVE LISTENERS CHECK OUT

As you construct meanings from what you hear, you may question your interpretations. "Does that make sense. Is it accurate? Maybe I'm jumping to conclusions." When you aren't sure if your interpretation is an accurate assessment of what you heard, it's wise to check out those dimensions of the speaker's Awareness Wheel that seem unclear. And you can do this by using the open questions we discussed in Chapter 6—the where, what, and how queries that invite elaborate responses and can't be answered by yes or no.

What did you *hear?*
What do you *think?*
How do you *feel?*
What do you *want* to happen?
What do you plan *to do* about it?

When we introduced the skill of checking out at a workshop in Philadelphia, a mother of eight commented, "When I get checked out, I usually feel it's because I've done something wrong. I think that goes back to my childhood. My mother would say, 'Marge, did you leave the third-floor light burning?' It seems to me that checking out can be awfully accusatory."

Indeed, checking out *can* be a subtle way to lay blame—if that is your intention. "Why" questions often aim for control rather than elucidation, so try to phrase your questions in a less accusatory fashion. Use the more open-ended "how" and "what" instead. And don't use a checkout only to gain information without sharing any of your own perceptions in return. That's Style II listening—an interrogation, not a conversation. We've all encountered people who ask a million questions. At first, it's flattering to think they are so interested in us. But after a while we start to feel uncomfortable because there isn't any exchange. They aren't checking their interpretations; they're using the checkout questions as a shield to avoid revealing anything personal.

The purpose of a checkout should be completeness and accuracy. It tells someone that you've been listening carefully, that you've made some interpretations and wish to test them. Here are some examples:

> "Half the time we've been together tonight you've been telling silly jokes, while the rest of the time you've been very quiet. I wonder if you're joking to cover up some sadness you're feeling."

> "When you didn't respond to any of my suggestions for soliciting that account, I got the idea that you didn't agree with me. Is that right?"

> "You don't seem to be giving me any help deciding what to do tonight. I have the impression you want to go out with me but you don't care where we go. Is that so?"

Checkout questions request access to missing information that the listener needs to support a conclusion. A checkout implies you're uncertain about something. You've got an idea but it's only tentative, so you are seeking confirmation on the speaker's home court, where it belongs.

ATTENTIVE LISTENERS INTERPRET

People often have difficulty making direct statements. But whether they talk in circles, make deliberate omissions, or simply can't find the right words, they still expect to be understood. And remarkably, they often are. We humans are quite adept at filling in gaps, at weaving meanings from threads of information. Thus, we all interpret to some degree, but the interpretative listener is especially thorough. He digs for missing parts by asking himself what dimensions of the

Awareness Wheel have been skipped, then he fills them in out loud.

Danny called his mother at work to ask if he could be excused from religious instruction later that afternoon. He said, "I have work to do in the yard. I don't really want to go. I can take the test next week anyway." His mother picked up the word *test* and interpreted his remarks by filling in what he hadn't expressed. She said, "I have an idea you don't want to go because you aren't prepared to take the test. That's really why you're calling." Danny hesitated, then admitted, "Yeh, you're right. I didn't study for it. Could I have an extra week?"

On one level, interpretative listening is a way to show complete understanding. On another level, the interpretative listener serves as a guide to lead the speaker to unexplored places that he might never travel to on his own. He assists the speaker in recognizing thoughts, feelings, or intentions that may have been overlooked accidentally or never even considered. Pay attention to whether a particular spoke of the Wheel seems to dominate a conversation as a clue to where the speaker might be stuck. Then with interpretative listening, you can help someone broaden their perspective to include missing parts of their Wheel. Watch how Danny's mother does this as their conversation continues.

"I'll let you off the hook with the test this time, but tonight I want to have a talk with you about your difficulty meeting your obligations." Danny agreed. "Nothing is going right for me these days. I was up until midnight two nights ago trying to finish a book report for the next day. Last Monday I nearly missed my saxophone lesson because I was playing basketball and forgot what time it was. And you know what happened today? That girl I liked started to go with somebody else." Recognizing Danny seemed locked into sense data, his mom asked, "What do you *think* is behind things turning sour for you?" "I think I'm a loser," Danny replied. "So you *feel* less confident about yourself?" she suggested. "Yeh. That's part of it, too." "Well, we'll talk later about what you might *do* to get some control over yourself," his mom said. Having used interpretative listening to move Danny from his concentration on sense data to a brief look at some other dimensions of his awareness, she said goodbye and hung up the phone.

The skill of supplying insight into missing bits and pieces is a powerful tool in communication. It can become dangerous if you use it as a weapon to manipulate someone toward a particular end through the power of suggestion. The purpose of interpretative listening isn't to prove the excellence of your point of view. When you tell someone, "I know exactly what you mean; now here's what you should do," you are exercising authority; you are not listening. To avoid such take-charge control, don't fall back on your experience as the basis for interpretation. Instead, check out carefully and don't be offended if you aren't on target with your interpretation. There's nothing wrong with somebody retorting to your questions by saying, "No, that isn't what I mean." Simply try again. Here's how the process should sound:

SPEAKER: Well, today's the day I find out if I passed the insurance physical (*laughs nervously*).

ATTENTIVE LISTENER: Sounds to me like you're worried about the outcome. (Fills in feelings)

SPEAKER: You better believe it. I've already had one heart attack and I need the coverage for my family.

ATTENTIVE LISTENER: You want to make sure your family won't have any financial problems if something happens to you. Is that it? (Fills in intentions; checks out)

SPEAKER: I guess that's really what's bothering me. What will happen if I can't get life insurance. I'm not a rich man and with my medical history it makes sense to be prepared for the worst.

ATTENTIVE LISTENER: Do you have any reason to believe you won't pass? (Fills in interpretations)

SPEAKER: Actually I'm doing very well on a cardiac rehabilitation program my doctor put me on. Still, I worry a lot about leaving my family without money.

ATTENTIVE LISTENER: So it isn't your health that's got you scared, it's your lack of financial planning. (Fills in interpretations)

SPEAKER: Right. It's money. What will they do for money if something happens to me?

ATTENTIVE LISTENER: Maybe you could consider some alternative plans in case this company refuses your application? There may be other kinds of insurance, like disability, or some investments you could make. (Fills in future action)

SPEAKER: Well, I've been so worried about being accepted that I hadn't thought about other ideas, but I bet I'll feel better if I do. It would certainly ease my mind to know about some alternatives.

STEPPING BACKWARD TO
MOVE AHEAD

Any of these attentive listening skills will increase your understanding and appreciation of what you hear. But there are special times when the threat of misunderstanding exists before a word is even uttered. You sense in advance that you could be misinterpreted and you're worried about it. Perhaps you want to talk about a touchy personal issue, or criticize an action, or vent an uncomfortable feeling. In order to risk skating on thin ice, it's essential that your meaning be perfectly clear. How do you wave the red flag? You do what we call *sharing a meaning*.

A shared meaning involves recycling a message back and forth until it's clear that the message sent by the speaker is *precisely* the same message received by the listener.

If the content of the message isn't emotionally charged, a slight disparity in meaning won't cause serious problems. But when the issue under discussion has strong feelings attached to it, an accurate meaning becomes terribly important. Have you ever found yourself saying, "I know what you're going to think about this, but hear me out before you make up your mind." Or have you gone round and round on an issue because you can't seem to make yourself understood. At such times, you'll want to ask your partner to share a meaning. Call for a time-out to step backward a moment and clear the path so you can move ahead.

Margo and Dave had been friends since high school. They lost touch when Dave left the country to work as a missionary in Africa, but when he returned they picked up as before. The first Christmas Dave was back in the United States he and his wife invited Margo and her family to spend Christmas Eve with them. Margo knew the invitation was Dave's way of showing her how much he valued their friendship and she didn't want to hurt his feelings when she refused. Thus, it was quite important to her that he understood why she said no. Here's how she did it:

MARGO: Dave, I'd like to share a meaning with you. It's about the invitation you extended for Christmas. We've always enjoyed being at your home, but Christmas Eve has long been a special time for us as a family. It's kind of a tradition for us to be together and exchange our gifts privately. We're going to decline but we'd like to come another time. What message do you hear?

DAVE: Well, Christmas Eve is a special night and you have a family tradition you don't want to break. But you'd like to get together at our house another time.

MARGO: You've understood me perfectly.

What did Margo accomplish by prefacing her remarks with the phrase, "I want to share a meaning with you." First it signaled Dave that she had something meaningful to say, something that he might be likely to misinterpret. Second, it put him on the alert to listen attentively and not to react spontaneously. Third, it prevented Dave from sailing off into left field with a crazy interpretation such as, "They're too lazy to drive all the way to our place in the country. This tradition thing is just an excuse."

Partners who take Couple Communication seem to like using the phrase, "I want to share a meaning with you" because it clearly signals that an important and possibly troublesome statement is forthcoming. If you find the phrase clumsy, merely substitute something like, "I'd like to clear the air a minute," or "There's something I'd like to check before we move on." And if you aren't comfortable asking for feedback by saying, "Can you tell me what you heard," simply say, "What does that mean to you?" or "Could you run that back for me?"

A shared meaning doesn't have to start with the speaker. Just as often a listener may respond to a statement with a rush of strong feelings and request a time-out before carrying on the discussion. Regardless of who does the initiating and how many times the message goes back and forth, a shared meaning has three basic parts.

Part I: Someone expresses an intention to share a meaning and asks the receiver to report back what was heard.

Part II: The receiver acknowledges the request by *putting into his or her own words* just what was heard.

Part III: The sender either confirms that the message has been accurately received or, if it has not, clarifies it and asks for another report.

A shared meaning can be as short and sweet as Margo's and Dave's, or it can be extended until both sides are satisfied that the meaning is clear and they're ready to move on. Pat and John were building a new home and Pat had been accumulating decorating tips, fabric swatches, wallpaper samples, and estimates for paneling, draperies, and so on in a big envelope. On Sunday evening John had been looking through the envelope; on Monday morning Pat couldn't find it. She was frantic, and she called his office and jumped on him for losing it. Later that day one of the children mentioned that they'd seen the envelope lying on the counter and put it in a drawer. When John came home for dinner he was still smarting from Pat's attack.

JOHN: I want to clarify my reaction to your phone call this morning.

PAT: Okay.

JOHN: I get frustrated when you call me at the office and unload on me, especially when there's nothing I can do about the situation at that moment.

PAT: I understand. You don't want me to call you at the office.

JOHN: No, I like it when you call me. I only object when you call to unload an emotional problem that I can't solve.

PAT: Oh, now I see. You don't like me to call and dump my anger or frustration on you at work when there's not much you can do to help me out.

JOHN: You've got it.

John kept the shared meaning process going until he was confident that the message he sent was the message Pat received. When an issue is more complicated and both partners want to clarify their point of view, a string of shared meanings may be required. Carl and Nancy used a series of shared meanings in class one night to resolve Carl's longstanding confusion about Nancy's attitude toward his Saturday golf game. For them, this weekly dispute had become a thorny issue.

CARL: I want to share several meanings with you. I enjoy playing golf and, by your statements, you seem to encourage me to play. But whenever it's time for me to leave, I sense that you resent it. What do you hear me saying?

NANCY: I hear you saying you really like to play golf and you think I support that. But although I encourage you to go verbally, when your particular golf date arrives, you think I resent it.

CARL: Yes. I'd like to continue. In the past, when I've called to your attention what I've just said, you inevitably dealt with the issue by saying you don't resent my golf in particular but you do resent the fact that I don't do certain chores around the house before I leave. What do you hear me saying?

NANCY: I hear you saying that when you tell me that I seem to resent your golf, I reply that it isn't so much the golf that bothers me as the fact that you haven't completed certain household tasks.

CARL: That's correct. And I think that though I have been slow in taking care of things around the house, I have vastly improved in the last few years, yet I still believe the issue is being brought home to me too often. What do you hear?

NANCY: You think you've improved in taking care of your responsibilities, but I haven't acknowledged that change and I keep harping on it.

CARL: Right.

NANCY: I'm glad we shared this meaning because sometimes I think you hear my words but you misinterpret them to mean it's the golfing I don't like, and I am honestly glad you have that interest and you pursue it. What do you hear?

CARL: I hear that I sometimes misinterpret your views about my golf. That it truly isn't the golf that bothers you but the fact that I may not complete things around the house before going golfing.

NANCY: I'm satisfied that we understand each other.

Notice that each of the sending messages was simple and to the point, and that the feedback was reworded just enough to assure clarification on the meaning without altering or augmenting the original message. Once Carl and Nancy understood each other, they were able to go home and resolve the issue in Straight Talk.

Obviously, shared meanings disrupt conversations and break the flow of natural dialogue. They are meant to be artificial and grab attention. Many people who take our course find that next to the Awareness Wheel, a shared meaning is the most valuable skill they learn. Kate, a high school science teacher, discovered that calling for a shared meaning made a world of difference in her relationship with her architect husband.

"I have to really listen to what he is saying and suspend my judgment. I'm one of those people who jumps right in with my interpretations and opinions, and it really slows me down to have to repeat his thoughts back to him. It's amazing how many times he didn't say or mean what I thought he said, and that was the cause of so many of our breakdowns in communication."

Admittedly, asking someone to share a meaning can be rather awesome. And, because the wording can be stilted and awkward, many people shy away from this skill at first. When Joe, a social worker who took our course, first learned this technique he said, "When you say to someone, 'Now tell me what you heard,' it seems as if you're treating them like a little kid." Yet, by the end of the course Joe was enthusiastic, too. He concluded that for him shared meanings should be reserved for important issues, and he came to class with this story.

"I wanted to talk to Doris about a sexuality issue between us and I was afraid of being misunderstood, so I said, 'Let's share a meaning.' If she hadn't agreed, I wouldn't even have started to talk. I wanted to make sure she listened to my whole statement. It was my way of making certain she delayed her reaction until she understood me, and that took away some of the risk. I didn't especially want to change her mind or solve the problem, I just wanted her to know how I felt. It was kind of like being at a dangerous crossing and saying whoops, wait a minute, let's make certain we both know what we're talking about and then we can proceed."

AGREEING TO DISAGREE

Some people see the world as black or white; others perceive it as a collage. If you belong to the either-or school, you will have difficulty training yourself to be an attentive listener because you will tend to tune in to only those parts of a conversation that match your way of thinking. And, when you don't agree with what you hear, you'll automatically try to persuade the speaker to accept your viewpoint. Either-or folks aren't necessarily hardheads or tyrants. They've been raised—as have most of us—to listen for agreement, which implies that there is a right and a wrong position, and only if two people can agree on a particular point of view can their relationship percolate. So, when a difference surfaces, two people tend to struggle over which one has the true view of reality. Until one party can be convinced to see the situation through the other's periscope, neither is satisfied.

We prefer a more complex view of reality. Picture any

relationship, situation, or issue as a giant puzzle with many pieces. As listeners, you hold some of these pieces and so does the speaker. And only when the two of you combine pieces will the puzzle start to fit together. Therefore, to become an attentive listener you must give up the idea of listening for agreement.

That may come as a shock to you. All your life you were probably told that the strength of a relationship depends on how much two people have in common and how frequently they concur. But, as we've pointed out, agreement is an unrealistic goal because each of us experiences reality in a different way. When you listen for agreement, differences become an affront to your judgement; you take things personally. You focus primarily on yourself and your reactions.

Imagine that you oppose abortion and your friend confides that her unmarried daughter is pregnant. If you listen for agreement, your antiabortion bias will keep you from hearing her dilemma and her pain.

Imagine that you own a small gas station and you discover that one of the high school boys who pumps gas for you part-time has been stealing. You confront him. He admits it, seems genuinely remorseful, and offers to pay you back from his earnings if you'll let him stay. Then he begs you not to tell his parents. You believe in swift punishment. Can you hear his shame and help him save face? Not if you listen for agreement.

The alternative is to listen for understanding. Instead of attempting to eliminate differences, make room for them. By dismantling the barrier of agreement, you will be able to include ideas and feelings you do not necessarily share or endorse but have no right to judge. Listening for understanding has a totally different orientation from listening for agreement.

- It shows that you value someone else's perceptions.
- It enables you to see differences and broaden your view of reality.
- It puts you in a holding pattern while you listen to learn how someone's experience affects him or her, *not* how it affects you.
- It indicates that differences are healthy.
- It awakens you to explore, to discover, and to grow.

The heart of attentive listening is listening to learn, not to force conformity. We think you'll find that listening for understanding in place of agreement greatly reduces conflict. Try it by choosing an experience that you and your partner have shared—a party, a film, a family squabble—and use the dimensions of the Awareness Wheel to sketch in what you saw and heard, how you felt, what you thought and, if appropriate, what your intentions and actions were. You will probably disagree on more points than you agree on. That's okay. Appreciate those differences. Try to understand them, and try not to change them. Then watch the tension evaporate as the need for false togetherness wanes.

It may take some time to substitute understanding for agreement because you've learned to feel comfortable with the latter. You will be surprised, however, at how much stronger your relationships will be when you abandon forced compliance and relax with the acceptance of differences. Eventually you will appreciate that being understood brings people closer together than any form of artificial agreement.

9

It's Not Just What You Say,
But How You Say It

Whenever people get together—at a party, in a meeting, on the telephone, or even in bed—conversation will unconsciously flow from one style to another. Each of the styles we've described represents a way of connecting at a particular level. If you add all four styles to your repertoire, you will have the ability not only to make superficial connections but to connect with your heart as well as your head.

Consider this typical encounter when Harry visited Warren in the hospital. Warren, a robust and high-powered forty-five-year-old restaurant owner, had suffered intense chest pains a week earlier and had been rushed to the hospital where his EKG showed that he'd had a rather severe heart attack. When Harry came by late one afternoon, he was out of danger, with an optimistic prognosis.

"Hi, Warren, old buddy. I sure am glad to see your big bucktoothed smile. How are you feeling?"

Warren grins weakly. "Well, I'm here and that's what counts."

Harry looks around the room. "Boy, you've got it made. Color TV, flowers, breakfast in bed. Are any of the nurses under thirty?"

"They give the pretty ones the night shift when I'm too tired to do anything but look."

The cheerful banter of Small Talk is perfect here for meeting and greeting and leads naturally to a shift into Search Talk. Harry sits by the bed and says:

"Hey, Warren, what do you think caused this? Too many late nights? Too many nightcaps? Maybe that crazy chef of yours who is always threatening to quit? I thought the way you go to the gym twice a week, you'd be in tough shape. Could be you overdid the exercise bit?"

"I don't think it's any of that," Warren says, following Harry into Style III. "It could be the rich food. You know I love chocolate icing and cream sauces. But we've got a history of heart trouble in our family and I guess I just inherited it."

Now Harry's concern propels him into Light Control Talk.

"Well, you'd better stick to the diet the doctor gives you. Take this as a warning and slow down. You ought to give up whiskey, too. Switch to white wine or something lighter."

Warren responds in Small Talk.

"Oh, I'm gonna be fine. I never was a carrot-and-celery man. Did you miss me on the golf course Sunday?"

Warren's comment triggers Harry into a Straight Talk answer.

"Sure did. I've been thinking a lot about you since Louise called me with the news that you were here. I was damn scared I might lose you and I realized how much our friendship means to me. We've been through some rock-bottom times together. You really helped me pick up the pieces after my divorce—calling me on the phone all the time, having me over to dinner."

Harry throws a mock jab at his friend's arm, a physical gesture typical of men who want to touch but don't quite know how, and moves back to the playfulness of Small Talk.

"Hey, I'm gonna starve if you don't get outta here soon. How can I impress my dates with the lousy table in the back that your headwaiter gives me when you're not around."

You can see how naturally a conversation juxtaposes styles. The way people talk to each other is a better index of their relationship than the content of their actual words. A stranger overhearing Harry and Warren could tell by the way they conversed that they were good friends with a history of caring and concern. And someone who'd read this book could tell that they evidently had a grasp of all four styles and were comfortable using them.

Combining and switching styles flexibly is a key to effective communication. It offers you a range of choices for expressing yourself, enabling you to connect on a variety of levels. But when you're wedded to one or two predominant modes of expression and have trouble switching gears when necessary, your range is limited. Had Harry been unable to shift styles after his initial Small Talk comment, Warren never would have learned about Harry's deeper feelings. Similarly, if Harry had been stuck in Light Control Talk during his visit, offering Warren various bits of advice about his health, Warren might have thought twice about asking Harry to stop by again.

Remember, variety is the spice of life. In one of our groups a man complained that the first time his wife packed a lunch for his hiking trip, she fixed a tuna and cheese sandwich. He told her that he enjoyed it and she's been packing the same sandwich for him ever since. "And that's the trouble with our communication," he said. "She can't get out of the tuna sandwich rut."

WHEN TO SWITCH STYLES

While some of us naturally glide from style to style, switching styles is a particularly useful tool whenever emotions heat up or communication breaks down. It can be especially beneficial when an issue is being avoided by a Small Talk coverup or pummeled with the iron fist of Heavy Control. And, at times, digressing from Straight Talk with a little Small Talk joking lightens tension.

Evan and Dick were in a serious Straight Talk discussion about Dick's fears that his business might not survive the current economic recession. At one point, Dick leaned his cheek against his hand, contorting his face into the hangdog look of a basset hound. Even joshed, "Hey, you look just like my old dog, Ginger," and he tossed Dick some peanuts from a bowl on the table. "Ginger always perked up when I gave her a treat."

Knowing when to switch styles is not difficult if you tune in to your inner awareness and observe the outside world carefully. The clues are readily available and easy to read.

Common *external signals:*

- One party banters in Small Talk while the other is deadly serious.
- An argument drags on and on, moving nowhere.
- Tone of voice, facial expression, or posture suggest rising emotions or feelings that are at odds with what is actually being said.
- A serious matter is getting a Small Talk treatment; a light issue is blown out of proportion in Straight Talk.
- Important decisions or actions are avoided because the parties are stuck in endless Search Talk ruminations.
- A situation is not progressing smoothly; what you expected or wanted isn't happening. At such times, beware of the tendency to dig in with the style you're using or slide into Control Talk to apply pressure.

Common *internal signals:*

- You feel bored.
- You regret something you just said.
- You feel anxious or vulnerable. When this happens, be very careful about switching styles. It's all too easy at such times to jump into Small Talk to escape facing feelings, or slip into Control Talk to counterattack. Consider Search Talk or Straight Talk, so you can acknowledge and accept these disturbing emotions.

Although switching styles is a very useful method for handling conflict or stress, it is *not* a skill to hold in reserve and pull out only during troubled times. Skipping from one style to another can relieve the tedium of cocktail party chatter and inject vitality and sparkle into all your conversations. However, it should not be used to manipulate others in an attempt to get what you want. Changing a Control Talk demand: "Get this typed immediately," to a direct but polite request: "I need this report for a meeting later. Could you type it right away?" doesn't necessarily mean that you'll get an affirmative response. You may be told: "I'd like to help but I'm swamped." Shifting styles is not a magic wand that will turn a situation in your favor. Its purpose is to establish a common ground so you can express yourself clearly and connect through understanding, not forced agreement.

HOW TO SWITCH STYLES

The basic tool for switching styles is the Awareness Wheel. Once you've determined that a change of style might improve a situation, instigate the transition with a comment that zeros in on some aspect of your awareness. Any direct statement of feeling will steer you toward Straight Talk. Any statement using speculative words—"maybe," "what if," "I wonder," "perhaps"—will direct you toward Search Talk.

"I'd like to get serious for a moment." (Intention statement)

"We're going round and round on this. Maybe we can talk about it another way." (Interpretation statement)

"I'm disappointed that you won't join me." (Feeling statement)

"I'm not ready to get in this deeply." (Action statement)

"I'm wondering if you're angry at what I just said." (Checking out interpretations)

"I see you fidgeting. Are you bored?" (Sense statement)

Whenever possible—especially in pressured situations—expand your awareness into a two- or three-part message encompassing several dimensions of your Awareness Wheel.

"I see you toying with the Kleenex in your hands and chewing on your lip." (Sense data) "I think this discussion is upsetting you." (Interpretation) "I'd like to continue." (Intentions) "Is that all right?" (Checking out)

As we mentioned earlier, switching styles is an important way to exercise choice. When you become adept at using all four styles and integrating them in your life, you'll have a variety of alternatives for handling any situation. The following series of vignettes clearly illustrate the benefits of style shifts. In each case, consider the possible shifts and note the effect each one has on the tone and possible outcome of the exchange.

Joan and Dick were sitting in their library sipping after-dinner coffee. For some reason, instead of a pleasant recap of their day's activities, they began bickering back and forth in petty Heavy Control Talk. If they stay in Control Talk, tension probably will escalate:

Control Talk: "All you've done is pick-pick-pick tonight. Just get off my back."

However, either one of them could break the pattern by shifting into another style:

Small Talk: "I hear there's a great special on TV tonight. Let's put it on."

Search Talk: "I'm wondering if there's something going on under the surface between us?"

Straight Talk: "I'm aware that I'm picking at you and you're picking at me and I don't want to do this. I'm going to stop."

Fred was leaving on a short business trip and instructed his secretary to mail a stack of papers to several different clients. He thought that he'd given very specific directions and stressed the importance of haste. When he returned on Tuesday, the papers hadn't been mailed and he hit the roof in a typical Control Talk outburst.

"What's wrong with you? Don't you care about your job? You were specifically told to get this done. Next time when you come to work, try bringing your mind with you."

When he saw his secretary's eyes begin to water, he realized that he was being very harsh, and he looked for another way to vent his anger.

He could switch to Mr. Nice Guy, burying his feelings in Small Talk:

"Guess you forgot about mailing these papers?"

He could look for an explanation in Search Talk:

"Is there any special reason you weren't able to do this?"

Or he could try to resolve the problem by shifting to Straight Talk:

"Look, I'm really upset that these papers weren't mailed. I'm concerned about the fact that I can't count on you to follow my instructions. I realize I just blasted you and I don't want to do that. What I want is to find a way to avoid this in the future."

Billy, a bright, cheerful eighth-grader, had been expecting A's on his report card, but when the cards were issued, he found B's in English and Social Studies. His average in both classes had been 87. He showed the card to his parents dejectedly, and his father's reaction was an angry Control Talk accusation:

"If you'd studied a little harder instead of watching so much stupid television, you could have gotten better grades. I oughtta restrict your television during the week."

Billy's mother recognized that Dad's style was alienating the boy. She could jump to her son's defense by attacking her husband with more Control Talk:

"Lay off the kid. There's nothing wrong with a B. He did the best he could."

But, if she chooses not to use Control Talk because she doesn't want to demean her husband for his approach, she could shift to another style:

Small Talk: Well, Dad and I will work with you so you'll do better next time. Now, how about some dinner?"

Search Talk: "I wonder if you have any ideas how come you didn't get the grades you expected?"

Straight Talk: "I'm disappointed, too, that you got two B's, but I am pleased that you came so close to getting A's. That tells me you have the ability. I'd like to look at some specific things you could do next marking period, like improving the way you study for tests and perhaps cutting down on the TV."

The Olsens and Gregorys belonged to the same swim and golf club and had been acquaintances for several years. Through sheer coincidence, they built custom homes on adjoining lots. During the construction stage, Jim Gregory needed two feet of land from Pete Olsen's property to complete his driveway. At first, Olsen agreed to give him the land; later, he changed his mind. Angry words ensued. The Gregorys felt betrayed by a friend. Pete Olsen behaved as if nothing had happened.

One sunny Sunday morning shortly after they'd both moved in, Karen Gregory walked outside in a pair of shorts to pick up the paper. In Small Talk, Pete Olsen cheerily called over,

"Hi, Karen. You've got a great pair of legs. Gorgeous day, isn't it?"

Karen was still smarting from Olsen's attitude toward the property altercation.

She could choose to slough over her feelings and join him in Small Talk:

"Thanks. I'm going to do some gardening later. Do you need any tulip bulbs?"

She could vent her anger in Control Talk:

"You sure are friendly now that you got your own way."

She could handle her feelings in Search Talk:

"I wonder how you're able to be so friendly when it seems to me we might still have some things to settle."

Or, Straight Talk:

"Pete, it's awfully hard for me to just smile and say hello to you as if we'd never had words. I'd really like to talk seriously with you about the property thing. I don't think you realize how hurt we were."

Although we are obviously committed to encouraging people to consider Straight Talk, the choice of style to use in any given situation is entirely yours. If you want to fight, go to it. If you choose to explore, fine. If you want to keep things light and lively, that's okay too. And, if you decide to connect by sharing your awareness, we applaud you. All we want you to remember is that you *do* have a choice of styles, and when one isn't working, you can switch to another.

MIXED MESSAGES

Combining styles can be a problem when you couch a Control Talk message in any of the other three styles. We call this a mixed message, and it occurs whenever you say something that can be taken either of two ways. One part of the message appears to be an innocent Small Talk, Search Talk, or Straight Talk remark, while the less obvious aspect seeks to accuse, blame, or manipulate. Obviously, such messages are not conducive to clear communication because your listeners have to decipher which of the two meanings you really intended to convey.

Mixed messages can be very subtle, but they always aim to denigrate or control others. Because the cutting edge of the Control Talk sword is disguised in another style, the Control

Talk intention slips by. And there's a Catch-22 aspect to these messages: no matter which part of the message the listener responds to, the sender can always back off by saying, "Oh, I meant it the other way."

"For a smart girl, you do some dumb things," is a typical Small Talk mixed message. If the receiver takes offense, the speaker can say, "Hey can't you take a little ribbing. I was only kidding. I wouldn't have said it if I didn't think you were really bright." On the other hand, if the receiver accepts the remark as light poking fun, the speaker might say later, "You never take me seriously when I talk to you. I wasn't kidding before."

"I wish I knew why you are so nasty to me," is a mixed message shrouded by Search Talk. Although couched in speculation, the intent is to accuse, and the label "nasty" is an assumption. Unscrambled, the same message might be: "I couldn't understand why you just walked away without saying a word. What was that all about?"

Straight Talk isn't immune to mixed messages either. "I'm excited that I stopped smoking. I really feel proud that I haven't had a puff all week. Don't you think you'd be better off if you stopped too?" The first part of the message is upfront and self-aware. The tail is a typical Control Talk closed question zinger.

For timid types who are uneasy about expressing their feelings or wants, mixed messages offer a way to raise issues indirectly. A wife whose husband leaves his dirty clothes on the floor might not be comfortable saying, "Look, I'd like you to pick up your own clothes and put them in the hamper." Instead, as she stoops down she'll say sarcastically, "Boy, listen to my bones crack. I'm getting too old for all this bending down and picking up." Then later, this woman might complain to a friend, "I tell my husband how I feel but he never takes me seriously." Unfortunately, this type of communication can all too easily become a pattern.

UNSCRAMBLING MIXED MESSAGES

You can train yourself to pick out mixed messages by becoming aware of their typical characteristics.

Watch for "yes, but" mixed messages, when someone seems to agree with you, then tacks on a disclaimer:

TED: I think buying a computer instead of renting one is simply too rich for our budget.
HARRY: You're right, but we can find a way to work it out.

Don't be hooked by people who use the closed questions we described in Chapter 6 to appear flexible when their minds are actually sealed shut:

"I think we have more important matters to discuss here than this nomination. Don't you think you could just accept the man I recommended so we can move on?"

Be wary of messages that say yes when they mean no, and vice versa:

JOE (*in an obviously sarcastic tone*): I can't think of a single thing I'd rather do this Friday than go to dinner with your boss.
KATE: Well, you don't have to go if you don't want to.
JOE: I just said I'd go, didn't I?

Look out for presumptions; any statement in which someone claims the X-ray vision to read your mind:

"I wonder why you didn't like the flowers I sent."

Tone of voice can be another clue. Is the speaker whining, sarcastic, or demanding?

Mark was telling Mimi why he couldn't help her move into her new apartment. She paused when he was finished and, in a sharp, curt tone, said, "All right. That's enough. I believe you." Her words said one thing; her tone indicated another. Had she unmixed her message, she would have said, "I believe you, but I'm disappointed just the same. I was counting on you."

Similarly, question a facial expression that doesn't match what's been said, such as a complaint voiced with a smile:

Connie had just won an audition for a leading part in the spring show. She saw her friend Ellen in the hall and bubbled her good news. Ellen, with a long face, said, "Gee, that's wonderful. I'm really glad for you." Connie was puzzled. "You say you're glad but your face sure doesn't show it. Is something wrong?" This time Ellen was straight. "I guess I'm jealous. I wanted that part myself."

Check out the language itself. Certain kinds of "you" statements, "shoulds" and "oughts," absolutes like "always" and "never," closed questions and "why" questions—the earmarks of Control Talk—often turn up in mixed messages:

Mixed: "Why do you always insist on doing things your way?"

Clear: I get upset when you insist on doing things your way. Just now I wanted ice cream for dessert and you ordered fruit salad for me."

When you receive a mixed message, halt delivery by recognizing the conflicting signals and sorting out your response to each one:

JILL: Gee, I wish you'd show me how to con guys into paying me as much attention as they give you.
BARB: I'm not sure if you're asking me for advice or putting me down for the way I act when we go to a party together.

And don't be afraid to ask for clarification:

MIKE: I don't suppose you could find time to type this newsletter for me?
LYNN: Whoa. I get the message you've jumped to the conclusion that I'm too busy for you, and I also hear a request for help. Could you straighten out what you said?

On the other hand, if you are sending too many mixed messages, you can cut down by tuning in to your intentions and your feelings, and expressing them carefully. Don't mix Style II and IV:

"I love you, honey, but sometimes I want to murder you. You put me in a horrible bind today."

State your feelings and intentions completely in Style IV:

"I love you, honey, but sometimes I want to murder you. Today, when you told my folks about my job transfer, I felt very uncomfortable. I didn't want to tell them until we had talked first."

At certain times, mixed messages add a great deal of sparkle or wit to our conversations. When Groucho Marx tapped his cigar, wiggled his mustache, and leered at a pretty young lady, "Come up and see my etchings some time," it was fairly clear it wasn't his art collection that he wanted to show off. Naughty mixed messages, like Groucho's, are fun. Life would be dull without urbane double entendres that allow us to be suggestive without being lewd. When we want to kid around or purposely have others guess our intentions, the banter of veiled meanings becomes a marvelous game of matched wits.

Mixed messages are far too common to banish from our daily lives. But it's important to know how to recognize them, especially when, instead of enlivening communication, they muddle it by creating confusion and uncertainty because people aren't sure which part of the message they are supposed to respond to: the obvious part or the control part. If you are the sort who regularly disguises your intentions in mixed messages, people will come to mistrust you and view you as unreliable. Little by little they'll tune you out, and when you have something important to say, it won't be heard. You'll become resentful because you can't make yourself understood and you won't know why.

Say It In Style

Styles are a dance of life. When you are waltzing in time with the music and each other, you can connect at almost any level. But if the music suddenly changes to a polka, and you don't know the steps, you may be embarrassed to try it; you don't want to be seen tripping over your own feet. At first, consciously shifting styles or just experimenting with an unfamiliar style may feel as awkward to you as a brand-new dance step. But, with practice and repetition, you will become comfortable with Small Talk, Search Talk, and Straight Talk and learn to use Control Talk appropriately. You will know how to shift back and forth naturally, spot and unscramble mixed messages, and choose the style that says what you really mean.

QUIZ: RESPONDING IN STYLE

For each of the statements below, indicate which style you think the statement represents and then:
   a) respond in the same style
   b) respond with a statement in a different style

Style

1. Looks like rain.   _____

2. Eat your spinach.   _____

3. I'd rather go to McDonald's. _____

4. You never serve me what I like! _____

5. Could our tastes be so different because we grew up in different parts of the country? _____

6. I like the way you greet me. Your eyes sparkle and your voice sounds eager. _____

7. Nine o'clock. Bedtime, Jimmy. _____

8. You're always telling me what to do! _____

9. I wonder if you're cross because of the argument you had with Billy? _____

Answers: 1. I; 2. II light; 3. I; 4. II heavy; 5. III; 6. IV; 7. II light; 8. II heavy; 9. III.

QUIZ: UNSCRAMBLING STYLES

Each of the statements below is an example of a mixed message. Identify the mix. Then, identify the style of the unscrambled statement that follows.

Style

1. I wonder if this happens because you don't pay attention?

   (Unscrambled) All these mixups are caused by your inattention! _____

2. I feel torn. It's so warm and comfortable in bed. I'd just like to sleep in. But you know as well as I do that we just can't miss church today. _____

   (Unscrambled) I feel torn. It's so warm and comfortable in bed. I'd just like to sleep in and not worry about what people would think. _____

3. Wouldn't you rather see a good movie?

   (Unscrambled) I'd like to see a good movie. How about it? _____

4. You probably wouldn't like it if I hounded you to finish the report the way you keep after me.

       _____

(Unscrambled) Stop reminding me about the report. I'll take care of it.

       _____

or

(Unscrambled) The report's not finished and I'm anticipating that you're going to say something critical to me about it. I hope you'll just let me take care of it.

       _____

Answers: 1. III/II and II heavy; 2. IV/II and IV; 3. I/II and I; 4. III/II and II or IV.

10
I Count Me / I Count You: Building Esteem

Self-esteem. Everybody needs a healthy measure of it to feel lovable and important. If others don't value us, we're angry and hurt. And if we don't hold ourselves in high esteem, we're insecure and unhappy. Wouldn't it be wonderful if we could buy self-esteem in an aerosol can and spray it on when our supply runs low? Unfortunately, it's not that easy. Esteem develops only from the inside out; it accrues slowly from the wealth of experience you accumulate over the course of years.

Within each of us there's a very private scrapbook filled with snapshots from our distant past, snapshots forming in the present, and the snapshots we envision for our future.

Look, there's one of you as a child standing in the corner with your head bent, looking guilty. There's another of you proudly receiving the service award at school. There you are with your spouse, beaming in front of the new house right after you got your promotion. Oh, here's another where one of you is crying and the other looks furious. And there you are gray and frail, being visited by your children who are handing money to you. Although you don't leaf through this scrapbook very often, certain recurring images and actions imprint themselves in your mind, and these overall impressions from the accumulated snapshots of your life form the mental picture you have of yourself.

Your mental image is one important element in the development of self-esteem. In addition there are the judgments and evaluations you are continually making about your behavior. You approve or disapprove of your actions; you see yourself one day as successful; another day as unsuccessful.

And on a long-term basis you judge yourself as competent or incompetent; loving or cold; thoughtful or callous, and so on. The third factor in esteem is certain feelings you develop about the inner you over the years—feelings of admiration, shame, confidence, warmth, pride, disgust, etc. When your self-concept, self-evaluation, and personal feelings are generally positive, your self-esteem is likely to be fairly high. But when that mix is burdened with negative images, judgments, and feelings, your self-esteem tends to be quite low.

We all approach life with varying degrees of confidence and we can expect to slide up and down the esteem ladder to some extent. It's useful to be aware that our self-esteem usually reflects how things are going in our lives. It's up when we're up, and it's down when we're down. But are you aware that how well or poorly you value yourself is clearly transmitted in the way you communicate?

Normally we don't associate self-esteem with communication. But there is a strong and crucial link between the two that's demonstrated by your words, combined with your tone of voice, your body posture, your facial expression, and your gestures. These clues to the state of your confidence influence the amount of respect, or lack thereof, that you receive from others. And that, in turn, reinforces your own sense of esteem. In effect, how others treat you is determined by your own sense of self and the signals you send out. If your self-image is negative, you transmit low self-esteem messages:

BONNIE (*monotone, unenthusiastic*): I had an idea about that. Not anything special, mind you. Let me see if I can remember it.

But if you value yourself, you'll come across quite differently:

BEN (*vibrant, buoyant manner*): I just had a great idea. Let me tell you about it.

When your self-esteem is high, you display it by being aware of yourself; by accepting what you see and hear, think and feel; by talking about it; by taking responsibility for yourself and your actions instead of blaming what happens on the weather, the price of oil in Syria, the bank's heartlessness, your husband's stubbornness, or your boss's irrational demands.

Acceptance and self-responsibility have a tremendous effect on the quality of your communication.

Only if you treat yourself with fairness and respect can you communicate openly and treat others with fairness and respect. The goal we repeatedly strive for in this book is the kind of communication in which people demonstrate that they hold themselves and their partners in high regard. Without this basis of mutual respect, you can't truly connect.

Your attitude toward yourself and others is often the most powerful thing you communicate. And, in every situation, you can choose to act in ways that show that you care about yourself *and* others. The capability to build or damage esteem rests in your hands. Although you cannot create self-esteem for your partner, you *can* extend a helping hand and encourage a relationship that nurtures esteem instead of destroying it.

HOW TO BUILD ESTEEM

Although, as we've said, it is natural for your level of esteem to vary, continual high self-esteem is *not* an impossible dream. Even in the toughest of times, you can always value yourself.

It is up to you to build and maintain high self-esteem by accepting reality, even at its ugliest; by acknowledging your contribution to it; and by acting on your knowledge. This process is a variation of the Three A's that characterize Straight Talk. Alcoholics Anonymous offers a good example of this process in action. An alcoholic's first step on the road to sobriety is to acknowledge that he's sunk to the nadir, that his self-esteem couldn't fill a teaspoon. "I can't stand myself. I've got no willpower and I'm a failure." The second step is to *accept* the painful truths of this existence. "My job is in jeopardy. My family life is a shambles." And the third crucial step is *action*. "I can do something to change this. With the help of AA I can get better."

Although alcoholism is an extreme example of the loss of self-esteem, the rehabilitation process, based on the Three A's of Straight Talk—acknowledge, accept, act—can be used to build esteem in any situation.

It is difficult to be straight with others—to communicate openly and honestly—if you're down on yourself. Because you're hooked on only one aspect of your awareness—your self-doubt, your dissatisfaction, your unhappiness—you're likely to perceive comments as attacks and rush to defend yourself. And when you're wallowing in low esteem, it often seems less painful to pin the blame on someone or something else rather than face your own contribution or role in your problems. Instead, you strike out with comments that tend to discount others, shirk your responsibility, and show little self-awareness. In short, when you're down and out, you're most likely to fall into Control Talk and say things like:

"You don't know what you're doing."

"You shouldn't be so quick to make judgments."

"If you paid more attention, things like this wouldn't occur."

Note these "you" statements are focused on someone else's behavior. But, as soon as you move the focus to your Awareness Wheel and speak for self by accepting self-responsibility, the tone of these comments changes completely. The destructive quality vanishes.

"I'm not sure I would have done it your way."

"I'd have called first."

"I jump to conclusions too easily."

"I was so engrossed in our conversation that I wasn't paying attention either."

You can see that you possess immense power to influence the development of esteem and, once you accept that strength, you can use it productively by sending esteem-building messages. These are messages that translate your inner awareness into the kind of communication that honors both your partner and yourself. You declare that you count your partner and yourself when:

- You speak for yourself and take ownership of, and responsibility for, your thoughts, actions, feelings, and intentions
- You listen attentively to your partner
- You take both your awarenesses seriously

Unfortunately, we don't always choose to build esteem by adhering to this "we-both-count" position. Sometimes, we want to dump our hurt or anger on someone else. Sometimes, we want to be coddled or pitied. And at other times, we're caught in the Control Talk trap brought on by low self-esteem. At any given time, however, you actually hold four options for expressing your self-esteem in relation to others. What you say and how you say it—your blend of content and style—can translate as:

> I don't count me/I don't count you
> I count me/I don't count you
> I don't count me/I count you

> or

> I count me/I count you: we both count

Although it's not always easy to maintain an I-count-me/I-count-you position, it's a goal worth striving for. In this atmosphere of mutual respect, you'll benefit in three ways: your own self-esteem will rise; you'll nurture your partner's esteem; and your communication will vastly improve. If you consistently count yourself and your partner, the skills of Straight Talk will become second nature very quickly.

Now, let's take a look at each of these positions.

I DON'T COUNT ME/I DON'T COUNT YOU

This position conveys about as much optimism as a Little League baseball team might feel if they were pitted against the winner of the World Series. Your conversation suggests utter hopelessness. And your words indicate that you have little regard for yourself or anyone else. Listen to the employee in this exchange:

SUPERVISOR: I'd like to spend a few minutes with you discussing your problem of getting to work on time.
EMPLOYEE: Well, I've never been able to get up early. The alarm rings and I fall back to sleep. You're not usually here when I get in anyway.
SUPERVISOR: Sounds like you're not making much of an effort.
EMPLOYEE: I've been late all my life. I'm just a night person.

Although the supervisor is centered in her awareness, the employee is definitely out of touch and operating from a low-esteem position. He puts himself down, passes off any responsibility for his tardiness, and indicates that he has no power to change his habits. In addition, he discounts his supervisor by referring to her lateness.

In the following exchange, note that *both* husband and wife are in an I-don't-count me/I-don't-count-you position.

HERB: I bought two shirts today but, as usual, I was short on cash so I put them on the credit card. I know we ran up a huge bill last month, but what's two little shirts? Wait till you see them.
SALLY: You promised you'd be more careful about impulse spending. I'm certainly not having any luck trying to cut down.
HERB: Well, if you're not going to watch your pennies why should I be deprived and have to watch mine?
SALLY: Neither of us is any good at saving. We'll never get out of debt.

Neither Sally nor Herb is willing to take responsibility for their joint problems of overspending. Instead, each one tries to shift it to the other with Control Talk blaming. There's a sense of hopelessness about their conversation as if some outside force will have to rescue them from the poorhouse because they'll never be able to do it on their own.

This kind of double-negative attitude may be stated obviously in Control Talk, voiced indirectly with an irrelevant Small Talk comment that ignores the issue at hand, or implied in a noncommittal Search Talk promise to think about something later. Whenever the speaker sounds depressed and devalues himself and others, a don't-count message is delivered, with frustrating consequences. Decisions are postponed; issues are avoided. Failure to face a situation reinforces a sense of hopelessness and sets off a downward spiraling cycle: change is impossible, responsibility is avoided, nothing happens, hopelessness increases.

Thus, speaking from a negative position—the double don't-count attitude—produces a self-fulfilling prophecy of ineffectuality.

I COUNT ME/I DON'T COUNT YOU

This is a winner-take-all stance. People who communicate this way believe that there is a right view and a wrong view in every situation and, without question, theirs is right.

PARENT: I've told you twenty times to wash the paintbrush when you're through with it. You'll never learn.

CHILD: I forgot.

PARENT: You always forget. Then I have to clean up after you. I've got a million things to do, and washing out your paintbrush isn't one of them. If this happens again, I won't allow you to paint.

CHILD: Well, you don't have to holler at me.

Parents frequently assume this kind of authority position with their children, but they undermine the effectiveness of their teaching by attacking and over-generalizing. In this exchange, the parent exudes Control Talk. He's blaming, demanding, and threatening. He could accomplish much more by specifically listing the instances when the child neglected to clean the paintbrushes (sense data); by expressing disappointment over the child's failure to follow orders (feelings); and by not taking responsibility to do the child's chore (action).

The I-count-me/I-don't-count-you position is characterized by a clash of wills, as the following exchange illustrates:

JOHN: Boy, you have a big mouth. Why in the heck did you say that in front of her? I'm not callous and you know I wouldn't have deliberately hurt her feelings.

BOB: If you don't trust me, then don't tell me things you don't want me to say. I'm a very honest person.

JOHN: Your kind of honesty can bury somebody.

BOB: I can see I really have to keep a zipper on my mouth around you.

Note that John and Bob defend their own positions and attack each other's without giving either interpretative data or sense data for clarification. The messages are loaded with tension and heavy with force. John wants Bob to admit that he's said something wrong. Bob refuses to concede that he may have overstepped his boundaries. When attacked, he believes, attack back.

The I-count-me/I-don't-count-you position takes two forms. One, as illustrated, relies on the Control Talk putdown, which aggrandizes one person's perceptions, feelings, or actions while denigrating the other's. The goal is to win and the strategy is domination. The other swells from a self-centeredness that casts such a long shadow that it blocks anything in its path. One person's sense of self-importance is so absorbing that others are simply ignored. Instead of launching the verbal torpedoes of Control Talk, such people discount others by behaving as if no one else matters.

Frequently, I-count-me/I-don't-count-you types are accustomed to power positions at work, and they cart their self-importance home with the other papers in their briefcase. Because they don't trust anyone else to handle something as well as they can, they insist that others adhere to their point of view and follow their orders. And when they need help, they don't know how to ask for it or accept it graciously, so they continue to do things their way, slurring the competency of others and reinforcing the sense of omnipotence that led to the imbalance in the first place.

I DON'T COUNT ME/I COUNT YOU

At the end of *Taming of the Shrew*, Shakespeare's marvelous comedy about male domination, the intractable Kate yields to her husband by placing her delicate hand on the floor and announcing, in Passive Control Talk, that she is quite ready for him to stomp on it with his boot. In her way, she tells him, "I am nothing. You are everything. I count for little and I count you above me." Aside from dramatic impact, you might well wonder why anyone would want to demean themselves while aggrandizing someone else, or why so many of our popular songs extoll this most unequal attitude in phrases like, "You're my everything," "I'm nothing without you," "If, baby, I'm the bottom, you're the top."

Quite simply, the world is full of sad people whose self-esteem cowers in the cellar and whose attitude and style of communication keeps it there. Some of them suffer from the misguided belief that by covering themselves with mud, they can please or placate others or, at best, avoid hurting anyone's feelings. Then, there are those who subtly use the pattern of Passive Control Talk to manipulate others into taking over their responsibilities. The I-don't-count-me/I-count-you speaker evokes our pity with his self-deprecation and begs us to rescue him. We normally respond by jumping in like white knights and later feeling trapped. Let's take a look at some fairly typical exchanges in this mode.

DEBBIE: You do everything so well. You work and manage your family and you're even a great cook. Every time I try something fancy, it flops.

PAT: Thanks for the compliment, but you're not fair to yourself. You made an exquisite spinach and mushroom soufflé the night we were over with Sue and John.
DEBBIE: Oh, I was just lucky. I probably couldn't do it over and over like you do.

Poor Debbie. Pat is important and clever and she is not. Pat is valued; she is not.

CONNIE: What would you like to do tonight?
JIM: It's up to you.
CONNIE: No, I'd really like some suggestions from you.
JIM: You know I never have good ideas like you do. Everything you come up with is so much more interesting.

By refusing to check out his feelings and wants, Jim denies his awareness, denigrates his ability to be creative and, at the same time, tries to please Connie by flattering her. The whole exchange is off-balance.

ANDREA: I'm worried about the way we discipline the children. When we started talking last night about my punishment for Cheryl's poor grades, I heard your voice getting loud and I thought I was being blamed for being too lenient. I felt frustrated and a little inadequate, and I'd like to talk about how we could handle these things jointly.
PHIL: You're absolutely right. That kid drives me nuts. Maybe that's why I lose control. You're better with the kids than I am anyway. You have more patience and understanding. You handle Cheryl and I'll keep out of your way so these situations won't happen.

Phil is using a mix of Control Talk and Search Talk to deprecate himself and build up Andrea. But something else is going on. In the act of praising Andrea, Phil has shifted the burden of responsibility onto her shoulders. How do you think Andrea feels being subtly manipulated into a role she may not want? In essence, Phil is telling her that she *must* take charge of disciplining the children. She has no choice in the matter. He is too inadequate.

MOTHER: I guess you've been too busy to stop by this week. I know how important your job is and you always have so much on your mind. It doesn't matter that you can't find time for me. I'm just an old lady who's pretty boring to be with.
DAUGHTER: I don't think you're boring, Mom. I enjoy our conversations.

MOTHER: Of course it's dull for you here. I don't go out much. I watch a little TV, and my cooking isn't even good, so I can't promise you more than a cup of tea and a cookie. I'm sorry I said anything. With all your responsibilities, I shouldn't be an extra burden.

DAUGHTER: I don't consider you a burden, Mom.

Although mothers are the stereotypic martyrs, anybody in the I-don't-count-me role can slip into the Passive Control Talk martyr mold. And the listener will feel annoyed or irritated. Such feelings hardly promote effective communication because, although they appear to count you, they are, in reality, very subtle put-downs.

The I-don't-count-me/I-count-you position initially appears complimentary to someone else, but the consequences are rarely warm and gratifying. The I-don't-count-me speaker conveys feelings of incompetence, dependency, and powerlessness that the esteemed other is supposed to erase. The message is, "Here, you take over and everything will be fine." The esteemed person feels that he's been taken advantage of, or finds himself in the uncomfortable role of rescuer. Both people feel lousy—one, neglected and incapable; the other, used.

I COUNT ME/I COUNT YOU:
WE BOTH COUNT

When Matt and Meg, a couple in their mid-thirties, began a Couple Communication course, they concentrated on ways to show a we-both-count attitude. First, they set aside one day a week to meet for lunch, away from the kids, the house, and other friends, a plan that clearly signaled their esteem for each other and their relationship as a couple. Then, they worked to bolster their talk with action. One Saturday, when Meg had to study for a test in accounting, Matt whisked their daughters off to the zoo so she could have a quiet time to work. Meg told us: "That felt good. I was counting myself by taking a Saturday afternoon to study and Matt was counting me by taking charge of the girls. He didn't just say, 'I value your need to study.' He did something about it. Talk can go only so far. I think you need action too."

The we-both-count position is supported by an attitude that says: "I'm valuable and you're valuable and I don't want to make myself feel worthwhile at your expense. We're both important and we can work things out together." This tricky combination of independence and interdependence allows couples to face issues directly and confidently and find solutions that work for both of them. When people are committed to *full* awareness and the Three A's of Straight Talk, they are in a position to take charge of their own lives—and that extremely positive feeling conveys and fosters self-esteem. After all, chance does not rule your destiny; you do.

A we-both-count approach should be a part of all your dealings with people. When you speak from a we-both-count attitude, you immediately establish a rapport with a child, a co-worker, or the man who comes to fix your roof. In personal relationships, a we-both-count attitude may be all that's necessary to make things click. It tells someone: "Although your problems are not my problems and I can't shift your burdens to my shoulders, I can see you're struggling. I'll listen and I'll try to understand."

For Meg this came through in a small but significant gesture from Matt that solved nothing but gave her the support she needed. After Meg's father died, her mother remarried and the family fell apart. Matt didn't get along very well with her new stepfather and so Meg was reluctant to ask her mother over often, although she saw those invitations as a way to stimulate a better relationship. When she voiced her concern to Matt, he listened carefully and said:

"I can't tell you how to solve this but I know it's important for you to be close with your mother and I'll back you up as much as I can."

His words contained no great insights, but they carried that important we-both-count attitude. He might just as easily have said, "Do whatever you want. It's your mother. It's not my problem."

SENDING WE-BOTH-COUNT MESSAGES

We-both-count messages can be delivered in the social chitchat or the spontaneous hyperbole of Light Control Talk: "Boy, we look terrific as a couple tonight." You cannot count self and other in Heavy Control Talk, but you can in the meaningful discussions of Search Talk or Straight Talk.

ELAINE: I'm excited about the prospect of starting this business with you, but I'm worried because our temperaments are so different. I'm so hyper and you're so laid back. I'd like to talk about it.

NADINE: Am I glad you said that. I've been walking around feeling uncomfortable with you and not knowing why. I'd like to deal with it too.

In smooth situations, we-both-count messages flow back and forth naturally. But when a rock on the road upsets the apple cart, the temptation to switch to another position rears its ugly head.

Suppose you are on your way to the airport to catch a plane. Your partner is driving and misses the exit on the freeway. Now you will have to take a longer route and you might miss the flight. Several thoughts race through your mind: "I should have called a cab. What will I do if I can't get another flight? We've been to the airport a hundred times. How careless can you get?" You are upset, angry, uptight. There are four possible ways to verbalize those feelings:

I Don't Count Me/I Don't Count You: "Boy, was I dumb to let you drive." (Limited awareness—interpretations only)

I Count Me/I Don't Count You: "Why didn't you watch the road? Now you made me miss my plane." (Pure Control Talk)

I Don't Count Me/I Count You: "Don't feel bad. It won't be the first plane I've missed." (Passive Control Talk)

We Both Count: "I bet you're feeling as lousy as I am that we missed the exit." (Note the feelings)

"I want to catch that plane." (Note the intentions)

"I think we're cutting it awfully close to take the longer route." (Note interpretations) "Let's take the next exit and circle back to the shortcut?" (Note actions)

The first three undesirable messages stem from limited awareness and result in the blaming and complaining characteristic of Control Talk. By drawing on the Awareness Wheel, the fourth we-both-count message is straight Straight Talk: complete, clear, and nonaggressive. Now let's put the shoe on the other foot. Assuming you chose one of the first three messages, how might your partner respond to your tongue-lashing?

I Don't Count Me/I Don't Count You: "I do stupid things like this all the time. Your being late didn't help either."

I Count Me/I Don't Count You: "If you'd been ready we

wouldn't be rushing so and you wouldn't be making me a
nervous wreck. I don't make mistakes when I drive without
you."

I Don't Count Me/I Count You: "I know you must be anxious and it's all my fault.

We Both Count: "I feel terrible about missing the exit. But I
also resent your yelling at me." (Note the feelings) "I'll do
my best to get you there because I know it's important that
you catch this plane." (Note the intentions, actions, and interpretations)

Now let's assume that your partner took the bait and retorted with one of the three don't-count retorts. You can still
turn the exchange around. You don't have to play follow-
the-leader. It will depend on the position you choose. You
can:

Discount Both of You: "There's no point in discussing this."
Count Yourself and Discount Your Partner: I'm willing to
make peace, but you probably aren't."
Count Your Partner and Discount Yourself: "I can see that
you are upset about this. I never should have yelled at you."
Count Both of You: "I feel lousy about losing my temper."
(Note the feelings) "I'd like to leave for this trip under better terms." (Note the intentions) "Let's get back on a better
track." (Note the actions)

These dialogues illustrate several points. First, always
remember that you have choices. Next, recognize that the
three negative positions spring from limited awareness, which
inevitably surfaces in active or Passive Control Talk. Whenever you disregard your feelings, intentions, or actions, you
are not counting yourself and your partner. Third, note how
Straight Talk usually leads to a we-both-count position by
bringing in all the dimensions of your Awareness Wheel and
allowing your partner to do the same. Together, your attitude
and your style pack quite a wallop. Recognize that you have
the power to destroy esteem by using any of the three don't-
count attitudes and Control Talk. But you also have the
power to support and build mutual esteem by using a we-
both-count attitude and Straight Talk.

PUT-DOWNS DON'T COUNT

Developing the kind of attitude that leads to a we-both-count position takes time and effort. Attitudes, once formed, change gradually, not overnight. But you can precipitate an immediate difference by eliminating all forms of discounting from your conversations. Discounts often poke their ugly faces into unbalanced relationships. When you're dissatisfied, you tend to focus on everything that's wrong with your partner, beaming your spotlight on *his or her* faults, evaluating *his or her* behavior, pressuring or demanding that *he or she* make changes. In the process *you* fade into the background and you ignore your own contributions and reactions. When you recognize that you're playing a one-sided offense, call timeout, examine your own actions, wants, and feelings, and include these self-discoveries in your communication and behavior.

The quickest way to improve the general quality of your interactions is to do away with all forms of put-downs. Putdowns kill mutual respect, whether you aim them at yourself ("Gee, I'm clumsy; I never should have dropped that plate")—or someone else ("You're always dropping things. How come you're so clumsy?"). And they have a nasty tendency to perpetuate themselves because when somebody zaps you with a discounting remark, your natural response is to blast back in kind:

JANE: Hey, that was really stupid.
CHARLES: Well, you're not exactly Albert Einstein.

If your intention is to fight fire with fire, the Albert Einstein retort is as good as any. But if your aim is to show an I-count-me/I-count-you attitude, there are more useful rejoinders. One alternative is:

CHARLES: Ouch, you got me. What you said stings.

The second choice clearly indicates that you value yourself, that you don't appreciate the verbal parry, and that you are in touch with your reaction to it. In this age where so much is discounted, let's leave discounts where they serve a purpose—in the retail marketplace, not in human relationships.

Asking you to count yourself and others doesn't ignore the fact that there are times you don't particularly like yourself or feel good about things you've done or said. When you're down on yourself or disgusted with others, your negative feelings do not automatically have to destroy your sense of esteem. Of course, when you're hurt or angry it's particularly difficult to maintain the we-both-count attitude. Try to steer clear of all Control Talk messages that blame, defend, or demand. And closely tune in to your intentions. What do you want for yourself, immediately and in the future? What do you want for your partner? In such cases, he who hesitates rarely loses. The pause you'll need to consider these questions can prevent clashes that wound esteem and devastate relationships.

THAT'S THE SPIRIT

In the last twenty years, communication has developed from an art into a science. Books pick apart the structure of language, create systems, and teach skills to make people more adept at communication. Most of the concentration to date has been on the behaviorial part of a message—what you say and how you say it. But if that's all you learn, you become at best a skillful manipulator. You will know what to say to get what you want, but you will miss what we believe is at the core of connecting: the spirit of goodwill.

Spirit is the unspoken force that breathes life and hope into our words. When we talk about a we-both-count position, it's the spirit of goodwill—despite harsh words and awkward phrases now and then—that marks this attitude as a special one and makes it central to connecting. In the best of all worlds you would find your heart and head joined in purpose, your spirit soaring, and your skills well mastered. But our worlds are more than likely to be flawed, so it's important to remember that if you come away from *Straight Talk* with only a slight improvement in your skill as a communicator, you can still change your life significantly by introducing the caring spirit of I-count-me *and* I-count-you.

11

The Roots of Conflict:
Issues and Answers

The invitation was lying in a stack of mail that Harry rarely bothered to check. This particular evening, he happened to absentmindedly leaf through the pile while he was waiting for dinner and his eye was caught by the heavy cream paper and the silver letters:

> *Mr. and Mrs. Wilfred Sheilds*
> *request your presence*
> *at the marriage of their daughter,*
> *Andrea Lee,*
> *to Alan Wilby, son of . . . .*

The nerve of them, he thought. We haven't seen those cousins in years. They never call us when they come to town and they know full well we'd never travel from Milwaukee to San Diego for that wedding. This is nothing but an invitation for a gift.

Calling to his wife in the other room, he said indignantly, "Betty, I found this Sheilds' invitation. Don't you dare send them a gift. I know all about your philosophy of being mannerly, but this is a rip-off. I never liked that branch of the family anyway."

Betty strolled in from the living room where she'd been watering a plant. "I figured you'd react that way, so I already bought the gift and mailed it." Harry was livid. She patted his arm, "Don't get so upset. It was the only proper thing to do."

Obviously, this is not the way to deal with an issue, as Betty and Harry learned in Couple Communication after thirty-seven years of marriage. The wedding gift is a typical example of the kind of issues that snag the fabric of our daily lives, demanding attention that they don't always get.

An issue can be anything that concerns one or more people and necessitates a decision that affects everyday life, personal growth, and/or the development of a relationship. It can be as major as deciding whether or not to have a third child, or as minor as choosing between a weekend at the mountains or the seashore. It can involve both partners in a dispute over their different needs for private time, or affect only one partner trying to decide about a night school course at the community college. It may be a heavy, emotionally laden issue involving a couple's trust for each other, or a light issue such as making arrangements to kennel the dog during vacation.

Issues are an integral part of our lives, looming inordinately large when they are current and troublesome, fading away as they are resolved, or gathering like rain clouds to dampen our future. Fortunately, most issues are fairly ordinary. They surface at work, at home, with the children or friends, and we handle them easily and skillfully in Small Talk or a combination of Small Talk and Light Control Talk. Since you and your partner are basically in agreement about your roles and expectations, most routine issues—stopping at the bank, picking up the boys after basketball practice, having the in-laws to dinner, working late—can be solved with little or no hassle and rarely disrupt the pattern of your lives.

However, from time to time certain issues break our habitual stride because they can't be handled in a routine fashion. Generally, such issues arouse strong feelings in one or both partners, and a number of choices and differing points of view may have to be considered. Sometimes, those choices are hazy and a solution is not readily apparent among the various options. Sometimes, the possibilities are overwhelming, or you and your partner have different expectations about the best outcome. And sometimes, the issue itself is cloudy and relevant information is missing. In short, nonroutine issues are characterized by a great deal of uncertainty which is best explored in Search Talk or Straight Talk.

Issues also vary in importance and intensity. Some bring tension to a rolling boil; others are settled smoothly. Some may stretch out over an extended time period; for example, altering your life-style with a career switch; finding a new activity to replace tennis after back surgery; developing a consistent disciplinary approach with your unruly teenager.

Others may be short and sweet: can we afford a new bike and how much should we spend; should we have Thanksgiving at home or take the family to a restaurant.

THREE TYPES OF ISSUES

Depending on their focus, all issues fall into three broad categories, as the following sketchy lists indicate.

I	II	III
housing	self-esteem	sex
friends	identity	trust
career	values	jealousy
money	energy	affection
children	responsibility	commitment
leisure	success	decision-making
contraception	appearance	control
drugs	goals	communication
work	habits	boundaries
clothes	health	closeness/distance
time	recognition	cooperation

First, there are *topic* issues, which include things, places, events, ideas, and people—any of the strings that tie you to the world around you. Topic issues cover anything in Column I, and there are a number of particular issues that may develop within these broad categories. Under money, for example, you and your partner may be concerned about staying within the household budget, your use or abuse of credit cards, or how much to spend on a new couch.

Next, there are *personal* issues of the sort listed in Column II. These issues concern you or your partner as an individual—the way you define yourself, what you want for yourself. Under the general category of health, you might have to decide whether or not to enroll in a weight-loss program, find time to exercise, wean yourself off sleeping pills.

Finally, there are the *relationship* issues listed in Column III. These involve areas of joint importance to you and your partner, your impact on each other, and how you experience each other. The decision-making issue might crop up in a variety of ways: whether family decisions should be made jointly or singly; how to set aside more time to spend alone with your spouse; your belief that your partner is not adequately supporting your personal decisions.

We have divided issues into these categories because it's important to realize that all issues are not alike. Some are obviously tougher to deal with than others. Take a moment to study the list and consider whether you have the awareness and skill to handle all three types. For instance, most people can tackle topic issues, but if that is as far as they go, their conversations are bland and their lives are burdened with unfinished business at the other two levels. Discussion of personal issues has been greatly facilitated by the self-analysis of the ME decade. But relationship issues continue to be a source of particular difficulty for most couples because intimacy and risk increase proportionately as one moves from the topic to the personal to the relationship level. Because relationship issues are often touchy, they can easily deteriorate into a Control Talk blaming attack. And the sad irony is that what couples most want to talk about is also what they most fear talking about: those issues that concern them as a pair.

DEFINE ISSUES CAREFULLY

Because relationship issues tend to be sensitive, they are frequently cloaked in the guise of topic issues and, as a result, can never be completely resolved. A couple might argue repeatedly about the topical issue of spending money when, in fact, the heart of the matter may be their distrust of each other's judgment about spending, or their inability to agree on who should control the family purse strings. The issue hovers at the topic level because it is less disturbing to focus on money and to complain that your mate fritters away hard-earned income on expensive clothes than it is to confront the more delicate personal issue of excessive vanity, or the relationship issue of differing values.

In Tony's office a topic issue arose over who should wash the dirty dishes and coffee cups that mounted like a tower of blocks in the tiny kitchen sink. Generally, the dishes would accumulate until somebody who couldn't stand the mess would wash them. Nobody wanted the job and there was continual grumbling by the people who grudgingly did it. Finally, the staff got together and dug beneath the topic issue. At the personal level they talked about each worker being responsible for his own mess, and at the relationship level they discussed the issue of respect for fellow workers. The result was a voluntary sign-up chart assigning "dish duty" to a different person each day. Had the group remained at the topic level and failed to look at the deeper issues, the dishes still would be cluttering the sink.

A seemingly routine matter may, in fact, only be the tip of the iceberg. Harvey had been kidding Kate about treating the choice of a new wallpaper as though her life depended on the outcome. Every night for two weeks he'd arrive home to find another swatch taped to the wall and Kate anxiously waiting in the hallway for his opinion. His reaction was, "This is silly. What's the difference? They've all got green in them. Pick whatever you like."

Kate was troubled by her indecision so she turned to her Awareness Wheel for insight. And she discovered that there was more involved than the topical issue of selecting a stripe, a floral, or a solid paper.

"I realized that there are some people who are always fixing up their homes, but we redecorate maybe once in twenty years because it's a nuisance and an expense. That started me thinking that the reason I've always been so conservative in my decorating is that I choose something bland so that I can live with it for a long, long time. I'd like to break that mold and be a bit bolder, but I'm afraid, and that's why I'm looking for support from Harvey."

By considering the personal and relationship aspects lurking beneath this topic issue, Kate gained a new perspective, talked to Harvey about it, and shortly thereafter, they picked a paper together.

AN ISSUE IS NOT A PROBLEM

Hardly anybody lives happily ever after. As Sleeping Beauty and Prince Charming rode off into the sunset, they were probably debating where to spend the night. He wanted to head back to the castle; she wanted a romantic interlude at the little inn on the edge of the forest. Issues, you see, are unavoidable, but trivial or serious, we manage to manage them. Only when issues escalate into problems do we feel backed against the wall with no way out, and this happens when:

- An issue is never identified
- An issue is recognized but ignored until it festers into a problem
- An issue is handled but never effectively settled because a solution is arbitrarily imposed rather than mutually worked out

Most differences still can be discussed at the issue level regardless of the category involved. But at the problem level, when an impasse seems insurmountable, you'll hear comments like, "There's nothing to talk about here" or "This is beyond the talking stage." These clues indicate that you've entered problem territory, probably unconsciously, because an issue can ripen into a problem very easily.

Making a dinner reservation can be an issue. It becomes a problem when there's a battle each time you go out because neither partner has taken the initiative to choose a restaurant until the last minute.

Deciding whether to buy a new car is an issue. It becomes a problem when you are late for work every day because your car is unreliable and you haven't replaced it.

Thinking about leaving the teaching profession for another field is an issue. It becomes a problem when you've changed jobs three times and still haven't found anything you enjoy.

Making plans to spend time with your parents when they come for their annual spring visit is an issue. It becomes a problem when they arrive and you haven't adjusted your schedule to be with them, and they are hurt.

Trusting your twelve-year-old son to ride his bike at night to a friend's house is an issue. It becomes a problem when you withhold that permission without ever offering an explanation or an alternative.

Feeling angry with your partner about something he or she said is a common issue. It becomes a problem if you continually feel angry toward your partner and you don't express it.

It's quite important to differentiate between an issue and a problem because learning to spot the former helps prevent the latter. Few issues will disappear independently. You can't ignore them and it doesn't pay to store them.

HOW ISSUES ARISE

Research has shown that healthy relationships are characterized by the manner in which you recognize and deal with issues. Honing your ability to identify issues is like installing an early warning system in your life, and the first step in that direction is learning and understanding how issues arise.

Awareness Wheel Clues

Your awareness Wheel is a very reliable indicator. Whenever you are in a situation that's not progressing quite as you expected, check your Wheel. There may be a clue in your *sense data:*

> "I can *see* this report is missing some of the charts and graphs I had expected."

There may be a clue in your *interpretations:*

> "I *think* you've been ignoring me by not returning my calls."

There may be a clue in your *feelings:*

> "I'm *annoyed* that Bill hasn't gotten back to us with an estimate."

There may be a clue in your *intentions:*

> "I was sure the guy I met at that party would call me but he hasn't yet. *I'd like* to call him but I'm embarrassed."

There may be a clue in your *actions:*

> "This is the third Saturday in a row that I've had *to do* work I brought home from the office. Maybe I need an assistant, or maybe I have to look at the way I use my time."

Clues from your Awareness Wheel are not always clear and concise. A thought or feeling may be nothing more than an uneasy hunch that something's wrong. But on the premise that where there's smoke there's fire, pay attention to your hunches and check them out.

Pinch Clues

An issue can force its way into your consciousness by means of an internal "pinch"—a nagging thought that won't go away until you accept it and deal with it. And an issue can reveal itself when someone "pinches" you with a complaint: "I'm not going to wait the next time you're late. I'll take my own car and meet you." "I'm bored. We never do anything exciting." "You could bring home more money if you worked overtime."

Unexpected Clues

Frequently, issues pop up without warning. Your sister calls to tell you that she's won a trip as a sales bonus and would like you to take care of her baby while she's away. You're at home in your pajamas watching TV and a friend calls with an extra ticket for a show. Can you be ready in an hour?

Children are likely to explode issues at the most inappropriate times. You have dinner company and there's been some Small Talk at the table about your fourteen-year-old son working with Dad the next day since school is closed for a holiday. Suddenly, in front of your guests, the boy asks for a pay raise. There's an awkward silence. Dad says, "I don't think so." Your son persists, "Why not?" Dad says, "We can talk later." But your son is stubborn. "Well, I want to know if I'm going to make more money, otherwise maybe I'll just stay home." By now Dad feels pressured, the boy is frustrated, and the guests are uncomfortable. Dad can squelch the issue by putting his foot down. "No, you're not getting a raise and that's that." Or, he can identify the issue and postpone it. "I can see we have some talking to do about this and, when dinner is over, you and I will go into the den and settle it. Right now, though, I want the subject dropped."

Buildup Clues

Issues can be generated by an excessive dose of life's normal complications or some new pressures that are added to the existing heap: a parent's illness, a new baby in the house, increased responsibilities on the job. These kinds of issues often simmer unattended on the back burner for a while until they explode to the surface in a sudden and unexpected emotional outburst: a torrent of tears; a Control Talk attack. It's not unusual for issues to build up gradually without making their presence felt until the stress reaches flood level.

Pat and Jerry had a peppy, undisciplined Irish setter whose antics wreaked havoc in the family. Somebody was always yelling at or about the dog. She nibbled at Pat's hanging plants and begged for food at the dinner table. Guests in the house were subjected to her friendly but unwelcome licking. She even learned to open the sliding door with her nose and run off. Finally, Pat reached the end of her tether and announced that the dog had to be given away. Only at that point did anybody realize that the dog's behavior was an issue to be reckoned with. The family immediately decided to enroll her in an obedience training class at the local high school.

Intuitive Clues

Many issues can be anticipated with some certainty and identified in advance. If you know there's an impending event or change that is likely to create conflict, you can sally forth to dismantle it.

June had a sixth sense that her first business trip would create trouble in the family. Although she was thrilled when her boss asked her to spend four days in San Francisco managing the company display booth at a convention, she knew that her husband would not entirely share her excitement. He would have to remain at home caring for the children, and he'd probably feel a mixture of jealousy and nervousness about June on her own in a glamorous city. Rather than pretending that none of these feelings existed, or biding time until they built up and exploded, June peered into the future and raised the suspected issues before they actually surfaced.

Indirect Clues

Sometimes, clues to the presence of an issue can be extremely indirect. Physical symptoms like headaches or heart palpitations may indicate that stressful issues are not being recognized or handled. A bout of depression, a brief unhappy mood, or long periods of tense or strained silence can say as much about a suppressed issue as a verbal outburst or a strong hunch. Whether the clues are subtle or blatant, train yourself to recognize them as the first step in dealing with issues.

ISSUES CAN BE THREATS
OR POSSIBILITIES

Jan and Bruce had been going together for nearly a year and, while they joked about living under the same roof, they never talked about the subject seriously. Although Jan really wanted to move in with Bruce, she was scared to rock the boat by suggesting it, so she avoided the issue. Bringing it up was too threatening. Bruce, on the other hand, saw the issue as a chance to make a choice. He thought that living together was the next logical step in their relationship and, although he was unsure if Jan would be willing to give up her apartment and put her wineglasses on the shelf next to his pottery mugs, he wasn't afraid to talk about it. Thus, he was the one who brought the issue to a head by saying to her one night, "I think it's time we talked about living together."

Many people, like Jan, view issues as threats and fearfully turn away from confrontation. Others, like Bruce, don't court showdowns, but *do* view issues as possibilities. Whether you approach an issue as a threat or a possibility depends to some degree on your confidence in your partner as well as your confidence in yourself: can he or she join you in a discussion rather than reject you; can you raise the issue in Search Talk or Straight Talk, and can you follow it to a conclusion without losing your temper or dissolving into Control Talk.

There's no doubt that confronting issues can be risky, especially when you are committed to a relationship and fearful that the issue might create distance or damage. When you're apprehensive about the risk, ask yourself these questions: What's the best thing that could possibly happen from the confrontation? What's the worst thing? What can I do to prevent the worst from happening?

Appreciation/Criticism Ratio

Whether you tackle issues with optimism or pessimism hinges on the ratio of appreciation to criticism in any relationship. In viable relationships, the balance noticeably tips in favor of appreciation and approval, and the strong foundation built on the expression of positive feelings makes it possible to examine negative issues with the assurance that the relationship will not crumble. If, on the other hand, too many of your interactions with a partner have a Control Talk critical tone—"You're always so slow; You should try to be more considerate; You'd look better with your hair shorter; Whatever happened to the funny person I married"—then any issue you bring up is potential dynamite.

Too often, we're quick to throw stones and slow to say thanks. A forthright "You really were there when I needed you"; a pat on the back for a job well done, "You sure know how to throw a party"; or a supportive comment, "I'm proud that you teach at the Sunday School"—all show a partner that his or her actions and behavior are appreciated and affirmed.

The next time you're about to discuss an issue with someone close to you, look at the appreciation/criticism ratio in your relationship. Do the number of dissatisfied comments outrank the number of verbal strokes? Do you mistakenly believe that if you point out your partner's faults often enough, he or she will get the message and shape up? If there is no balance between the carping and the caring, if you are hooked on a pattern of mainly negative disclosures that may be why you are not resolving issues.

SAYING TOO MUCH; SAYING TOO LITTLE

In any of your relationships—working, loving, playing—once you've identified an issue, the next logical questions are: Should I say something about it; How much should I say? There are no hard-and-fast rules for measuring what constitutes too much or too little disclosure. Although you can err in either direction, research suggests that selective communication is preferable to a see-all, know-all, tell-all approach. Basically, your common sense must be your guide. First, study the risks and the nature and quality of your relationship, and decide whether the appreciation/criticism ratio is sufficiently balanced to support a dispute. Then, consider the following questions.

How Big Is the Issue?
No matter how pressing a concern may seem, bear in mind that all issues are not equally important. Moreover, an issue that's very important to you may be less important or totally

unimportant to someone else. Some people fail to distinguish major issues from minor issues. Consequently, they treat every ripple like a tidal wave and their genuinely serious issues drown in a morass of nonsense. It's fatiguing to be around someone who constantly points out what's wrong. And it's confusing to be with someone who makes no distinctions between mountains and molehills.

Jack, a customer service representative for a utility company, had difficulty getting his supervisor to respond to the situations he encountered in the territory he covered until the supervisor finally told him why. "One of my problems dealing with you, Jack, is that I never know how important a situation actually is because you use more qualifiers than anybody I know. Everything is either *very* or *extremely* or *terribly* serious or *highly* complex or *quite* pressing. I'd like you to try to talk to me without using a single adverb."

If you exaggerate repeatedly, or if you chatter on whenever you're uncomfortable, you are probably exhausting your companions by saying too much. Rate all issues on a mental scale of one to ten and, when an issue falls low on the scale, let it pass. Forgive and forget. You cannot possibly iron out every wrinkle in your life. Attend to an issue when your antenna pick it up for a second or third time, or when you cannot comfortably drive away thoughts or feelings associated with it.

What Are Your Intentions?

Your intentions stage-direct every issue you bring up, guiding and controlling your handling of it with unseen power. Tune in to your intentions when you raise an issue and ask yourself what you really want from the conversation: to blame, to persuade, to discover, to brainstorm, to resolve, to embarrass, to complain, to discredit, to understand, to be understood? Your underlying intentions can run the gamut from positive to negative. They determine how you bring up an issue, the manner in which you discuss it, as well as the final outcome.

If your hidden intention is to trap or accuse someone, you'll raise the issue in Control Talk and, since you have an axe to grind, you'll probably grind it hard. If you discuss an issue with the intention of forcing your solution on the other parties, that will affect your approach and propel you into Control Talk. If your unconscious goal is to embarrass, you

may raise the issue in front of people who should not hear it.
Even if your intentions are honorable you must consider the
ramifications carefully. If you really do want to work on an
issue, are you willing to participate in possible changes, or do
you expect others to make all the changes? If your intention
is to connect, are you prepared to deal with an issue, to put
aside the idea of winning and substitute understanding for
agreement?

Before you bring up an issue, evaluate your intentions honestly. Positive intentions usually produce satisfactory results,
while negative intentions—which we all have—tend to take
us by surprise and steer us into choppier water. "Now I'm
really into it. I never expected she'd react like that." If you
don't kid yourself about your intentions, you will, at the very
least, be prepared for the outcome.

Does the Context Fit?

An issue may be important, your intentions may be just
and fair, but if the context is inappropriate, the outcome
could be disastrous. Do you recall the example of the boy
who wanted a pay raise from his father? The issue was valid
and his intentions were clear, but the time and place—at the
dinner table in front of guests—were all wrong. Because the
context didn't fit, the issue suffered.

Everybody has had the unpleasant experience of wanting
to talk about something and running up against a stone wall
instead of a willing ear. When this happens, people tend to
assume that their partner isn't interested in the issue and
probably never will be. Spouses are especially sensitive to
being ignored or rejected. "What do you mean you don't
want to talk about this now? You can see I'm upset. You
can't love me very much if you aren't willing to deal with
this immediately." With thoughts like these you have no
choice but to drop the subject and sulk while you seethe in-
wardly, or pick a fight to get the attention you are looking
for. What you've done is confuse interest in an issue with a
willingness to talk about it at a particular time and place, and
the two are not identical.

Many perfectly reasonable issues are spoiled because
they're raised in an improper context. It may seem absurd to
you that a spouse would bring up a sexual or a financial issue
at a dinner party, but it's amazing how many people have
little or no sense of time or place. Because many of us lead

frenetic lives, we deal with the issues when it's convenient instead of appropriate. For example, it would not be appropriate to raise an issue of jealousy during a car trip to a party. That's sure to ruin the evening ahead. On the other hand, if you are concerned that your spouse might find the company dull and embarrass you by wandering off to watch TV, it might be a good idea to talk about it in the car so you can resolve the issue and enjoy the party.

While some issues demand immediate attention—a defiant child might have to be reprimanded in front of company— most things can wait until tempers cool. Hot issues are almost impossible to resolve when you're embroiled in them. Take a break and consider the procedure-setting techniques outlined below. Remember that every issue has its boundaries. Use discretion and try to avoid impulsive outbursts.

BEFORE YOU PROCEED, THINK PROCEDURE SETTING

It's 7:30 in the morning. You and your mate are rushing to get to work. You're blowing on your coffee to cool it faster when your mate says, "I think we go to bed too late. Last night was a perfect example. Instead of turning off the TV after the news, you watched the late movie. I can't sleep when you have the TV on and I'm beat this morning." You stop blowing for a second. "I'm not tired. I slept great. You know what a sucker I am for old Westerns." Your mate answers, "That's fine for you but what about me?" You put down your coffee and say, "Gotta go. I'm late for work. We'll talk later." Your mate mutters, "Sure we will. Just like we always do. Never."

Unfortunately, this type of exchange is fairly typical for many couples, and it's one of the main reasons why many issues are not successfully resolved. One partner launches into a heavy disclosure while the other is halfway into the bathroom or late for work. Neither party has the time or the intention to get fully involved so the outcome is bound to be disastrous. Either the issue will be sloughed over and left dangling until it becomes a problem, or it will be clouded by a battle as one party vents his or her frustration.

You can give your major issues the attention they warrant by using a tool we call Procedure Setting to insure that everybody concerned is ready and willing to hash things out. You wouldn't plan a business meeting or a conference without an agenda, nor should you plunge into a serious issue before establishing certain criteria.

What is the issue: First of all, clarify exactly what you want to talk about and use the clues from your Awareness Wheel to establish whether it's a topic, a personal, or a relationship issue. You can waste valuable time and energy, for instance, discussing your desire for your wife to be more independent when the real issue isn't her independence at all, but your need to unload some of the burden of making all the family decisions yourself.

When can we talk: Timing is extremely important to the mood and quality of a discussion. Trying to force an issue into an inadequate or unsuitable time slot generates tension and dissonance. Couple Communication graduates have found that there's magic in the direct question, "Is this a good time to talk?" It either is or it isn't, and if it isn't, try to set up a time that would be better.

Sometimes, you are too harried to give an issue the attention it requires. At other times, you are too pooped for a hassle, or one of you is primed but the other isn't. Maybe you are the impulsive sort—what's on your mind is on your tongue—and your mate is a ruminator who prefers to mull things over before airing them.

In the example on page 228, morning obviously was not a good time to bat around the bedtime issue. The tired mate should have opened with an Awareness Wheel statement: "I want to talk to you about our bedtime. I think we go to bed too late. When would be a good time to talk about it?" However, too often people get into an issue without realizing it, and one cuts it short. In this case, the disgruntled partner should not have responded to the mate's offer, "We'll talk later," with the sarcastic comment, "Sure we will. Never." The preferred response would have been, "Okay. I'm going to hold you to that. How about tonight right after dinner?"

A bank manager told one of our groups that she developed her own twist on timing. She inevitably chose an inopportune moment to remind her husband about chores or obligations, so instead of telling him she began to leave what she called "honey-dos" on his dresser. These were little notes listing things that needed to be done: "The garage door is broken again"; "The airline tickets have to be picked up by the end of the week." Because he could read the notes when he was in the proper mood, she avoided the accusation of nagging.

Whose issue is it: Ask yourself, "Is this issue mine, yours, ours, Aunt Minnie's, or the Joneses'?" When you establish "ownership" of an issue it is easier to stay within boundaries. If an issue is yours—should you fire your manager or give her another chance—you may want to point out to your partner that, although the issue does not directly concern her, you'd like to involve her as a consultant. When you are having a personal crisis or wrestling with a difficult decision, a mate or a friend can be a useful sounding board.

Who is to be included: This depends on who is involved in the issue as well as who is not. With whom do you want to share the information that's likely to arise out of the issue? If there's something your children should not hear or your friends should not share, don't bring it up when they are around. And consider whether the issue might embarrass someone in front of others, even if *you* don't care who hears it.

Don't bring up issues involving people who are not present and should be. If two people in an office have a beef about a third party, the issue should be aired by all three. On the other hand, if you have a dispute with a co-worker, don't go to your superior to discuss it if you haven't told the worker. If your daughter is using the car and repeatedly neglecting to refill the gas tank, it doesn't make much sense to handle the issue with your spouse in your daughter's absence. If one of your students calls out continuously in class, would the issue benefit from an airing in front of his parents?

Where should we talk: The water fountain is not the place to ask for a raise; the dance floor is not the place to examine a marital problem. Obviously, some places are conducive to focusing on issues, while others are distracting or even destructive. Heavy issues are best avoided in bed because they disturb both sleep and sex. Go into the living room or hassle over tea in the kitchen. Private issues should not be dissected in groups. Often, it's wise to discuss an issue away from the atmosphere that produced it. If you have a conflict with someone at work, thrash it out over lunch or coffee in a neutral surrounding.

How will we talk about it: Small Talk is inadequate for handling significant issues because it eliminates feelings. Control Talk heats up issues instead of cooling or resolving them.

So, if you are not prepared to air your issue in Search Talk or Straight Talk, or a combination of the two, it might be best to put off the discussion until you are. Establishing a style for handling issues is particularly critical in intimate relationships because spouses know each other's Achilles heel and are cruelly capable of inflicting wounds there. Recognizing that strike capacity and agreeing not to use it makes peaceful negotiation possible.

How long will we talk: Don't tell someone, "I'd like to talk to you for a minute," if you sense that the discussion will require a half hour. While some issues can be cleared up in ten minutes, others may require lengthy deliberation, so before you begin, try to estimate how much time you will need and make sure you both have that amount of time available.

Can we stop the discussion: Suppose you are in the midst of a major issue and suddenly it's time for the Monday Night Football Game? Or suppose the issue has wandered into forbidden territory and you can feel the onset of a three-aspirin headache? There are any number of reasons why it might be judicious to halt a discussion, and it's important to agree in advance that you both have this right. Some issues actually benefit from a rest period in a holding pattern while circumstances shift; others become boring when too much is said. When enough is enough for the time being but the issue hasn't been settled, consider rescheduling it. Partners who know they can stop a discussion with the certainty that they will return to complete it develop trust in each other and confidence in their ability to work things out.

How much energy is available: The solution to an issue may be related to the energy you're willing to expend to deal with it. It's unfair to both of you to dig into an issue when one is tired or depressed or in too playful a mood to be serious. If your energy level is low, your exchange is likely to frustrate both of you. It's preferable at such times to say, "I don't have the energy to tackle this" than to pretend you're interested and play along half-heartedly.

Procedure Setting is not the general all-purpose wrench to reach for every time an issue arises. Use portions of it—setting a time and place—on a routine basis, but save the complete process for particularly significant issues. Even if an issue is not going to be handled immediately, it can be a tremendous relief to know that it's listed on the docket and will get a fair hearing. Procedure Setting is also useful when an issue becomes a log-jam, because it can provide the missing perspective to break the impasse and get things moving.

Identifying and defining issues and Procedure Setting take you through the preliminary rounds to the main event, resolving the issue itself. Before you begin, coach yourself into an I-count-me/I-count-you frame of mind. Make a supreme effort to use Straight Talk or a combination of Search Talk and Straight Talk. And, if talking together isn't sufficient, use the Problem Prevention Process described in the next chapter.

12

Talking Out Problems
to Creative Solutions

Although Straight Talk is usually sufficient for settling issues, there are times when an issue just can't be talked out. Generally, people reach an impasse because they can't find a way to understand or accept an opposing point of view or make their own view understood. And if they do reach a plateau of understanding, very often they can't climb any higher to an agreeable course of action.

The Problem Prevention Process—PPP—is a systematized approach designed to resolve just this sort of blockage. In essence, it's the Awareness Wheel in action. In Chapter 4, you learned how to use the Awareness Wheel to thrash out a personal issue or handle intense feelings. With PPP, you follow much the same procedure. You and your partner each *share* the information from your Awareness Wheels, discuss all the dimensions in Straight Talk, and use your multiple skills to arrive at a jointly acceptable solution to a pressing problem.

PPP should not be used routinely because it is time-consuming and requires serious thought, commitment, and a true willingness to discover a mutual solution. Save it for the recurring or complex issues that generate considerable conflict and widely divergent perspectives. PPP can be used for issues involving two people, to handle a conflict within a family, or even to settle a group problem at work. It is especially effective when you're uncertain about a course of action, or when you truly have no idea where to go and need to poke around for a path to follow. In such cases, PPP provides an orderly method for finding a solution that suits everyone. And because it creates solutions instead of imposing them, it draws

on a we-both-count position in those sticky situations that are
likely to arouse negative feelings and unpleasant accusations.

STEP BY STEP

PPP consists of five programmed steps that gather and share
written and oral information based on the Awareness Wheel
in order to develop a mutually agreeable solution to a conflict. When using PPP there's a tacit understanding that nobody's ideas, wants, or feelings will be censored; no one will
argue over who's right or wrong; nobody will assert their superiority or insist on a particular solution. People cannot
truly work together if they are privately committed to their
personal outcomes.

In Step 1 the participants gather all the relevant information surrounding an issue with the express goal of creating
understanding for both parties. At this point, solutions are
not even considered. In Step 2, both parties look at their intentions for themselves, for each other, and for their relationship, as a foundation for exploring solutions. In Step 3, they
move from general intentions to the specific actions that each
one is seriously willing to undertake to resolve the issue. In
Step 4, each party selects one or two of those actions and
commits themselves to implementing them. Step 5 is a fol-
low-up, in which both parties review the actions chosen, evaluate their efficacy, and if they aren't working, search for
alternatives.

To show you exactly how PPP works, we've included a
sample exercise worked out for us by a couple named Jill and
Jeff. They've been married nine years. He is a thirty-four-
year-old CPA who works as a comptroller for a plumbing
supply company. She is a thirty-year-old teacher who is not
working at present in order to care for their two daughters,
aged five and seven.

A recurrent issue in their lives was their mutual difficulty
in maintaining their budget and controlling their spending.
Although Jeff made a decent living, their expenses were high
and they were chronically short of cash. Both of them wanted
to find a way to cut back and tighten their belts without
feeling deprived. After months of petty arguing and grumbling, the issue they selected for PPP was "maintaining a
budget." As they sat down to work on it, Jill laughed ruefully

and said, "We do have a budget of sorts. We just can't seem to adhere to it."

They each took a sheet of paper and placed the issue at hand in the center, in this case "the budget." (See the diagrams on pages 212–13.) Now they were ready for Step 1.

STEP 1: CREATING AN INFORMATION BASE:

The purpose of this step is to produce a solid information bank so both parties can clearly understand their own point of view as well as each other's. You will recognize the similarity of Step 1 to the Acknowledging and Accepting phase of the Three A's. By writing down your subjective responses to the sense data, interpretations, and feelings pertinent to an issue, you acknowledge your contribution and accept your responsibility. Your partner does the same. Then you share your individual information by attentively listening to each other and you begin to develop the understanding that's crucial to reach a solution.

To complete this step, as Jill and Jeff demonstrate, draw four pie-shaped wedges around the issue in the center of your paper, labeling each of them as follows: Past/Current Actions; Sense Data; Interpretations; Feelings. Then, using key words or phrases, fill in each dimension and include whatever you consider relevant. Later you will decide what is actually useful.

A. Past Current Actions

JILL'S:

1. Try to stick to grocery list; successful 25 percent of the time.
2. Try to think twice about frivolous purchases; are they necessary?
3. Get carried away with the credit card when there isn't any cash.

JEFF'S:

1. To subtly hint that we should watch it.
2. Get downright moody when money gets short.
3. Continue on with my old spending ways.

You can see that in completing this dimension, you focus only on your own behavior and what you have done in the

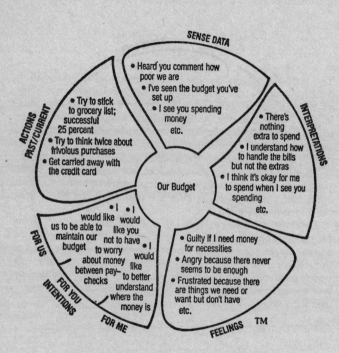

JILL'S PROBLEM PREVENTION WHEEL
—STEPS 1 and 2

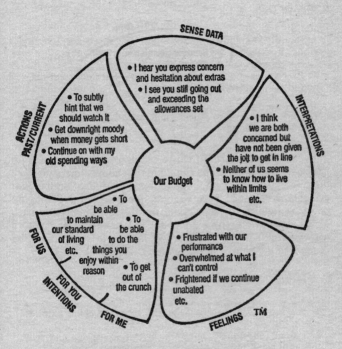

SENSE DATA

- I hear you express concern and hesitation about extras
- I see you still going out and exceeding the allowances set

INTERPRETATIONS

- I think we are both concerned but have not been given the jolt to get in line
- Neither of us seems to know how to live within limits etc.

ACTIONS PAST/CURRENT

- To subtly hint that we should watch it
- Get downright moody when money gets short
- Continue on with my old spending ways

Our Budget

FOR US
- To be able to maintain our standard of living etc.

FOR YOU
- To be able to do the things you enjoy within reason

FOR ME
- To get out of the crunch

INTENTIONS

FEELINGS ™

- Frustrated with our performance
- Overwhelmed at what I can't control
- Frightened if we continue unabated etc.

JEFF'S PROBLEM PREVENTION WHEEL
—STEPS 1 and 2

past or are currently doing in relation to the issue. Don't dig into ancient history unless it's clearly relevant. You might want to note which actions were successful or unsuccessful, which ones contributed to settling the issue, and which ones impeded progress. Do not include any possible future actions.

B. Sense Data

JILL'S:
1. Heard you comment how poor we are, that there isn't any money in the checking account for the next two weeks.
2. I've seen the budget as you've set it up on paper.
3. I see you spending money. Last week you took a subscription to an expensive travel magazine.

JEFF'S:
1. I hear you express concern and voice hesitation about extras.
2. I see you still going out and exceeding the allowances set.

In this dimension you focus on what you've seen others do and say. It's helpful to be more specific about time and place than Jeff and Jill were, and to remember to describe, *not* evaluate. Evaluations are part of interpretations. First, you have to establish the sense data that leads to interpretations. Your descriptions might include facts or events you've witnessed. For instance, Jeff might have noted the amount he deposits in the bank and the amount Jill spends.

C. Interpretations

JILL'S:
1. We are really in bad shape and there's nothing extra to spend.
2. I don't understand how the budget is set up and how much money I have to spend from payday to payday.
3. I understand how to handle the bills but not the extras.
4. I think it's okay for me to spend when I see you spending.

JEFF'S:
1. I think we are both concerned but have not been given the jolt to get in line.
2. I think we both want some action to change.
3. Neither of us seems to know how to live within limits.

In this category, include all the thoughts generated by your sense data. You might make evaluations, note your impressions, beliefs, or assumptions, give your reasons or opinions. Remember that interpretations are not based on some hard-and-fast reality but on personal perceptions and, as such, are not debatable.

D. Feelings

JILL'S:
1. Guilty if I need money for necessities.
2. Confused at times.
3. Angry because there never seems to be enough.
4. Frustrated because there are things we need or want but don't have.

JEFF'S:
1. Frustrated with our performance.
2. Overwhelmed at what I can't control.
3. Frightened if we continue unabated.
4. Apprehensive about starting a new plan.
5. Confident we could do something.

When you write down your feelings, include *all* your emotions, both positive *and* negative.

E. Sharing

After you have filled in all these dimensions, share what you've written. Let each person speak for self. Don't deny, dispute, or criticize each other's awareness. What is, is.

Listen as Jeff and Jill talk about what they've written.

JILL: I'll start with my past or current actions. First of all, I try to stay within the grocery allowance that I'm given, but I'm only successful about 25 percent of the time. I try to think twice about anything that might be frivolous. I'm even getting to the point where I ask myself, Do I really need this? Is this something I want? Can I do without it? One of my negative actions is that I sometimes get carried away with credit when there isn't any cash in my billfold.

JEFF: Okay. My actions have been things like subtly hinting we should watch our spending. When that doesn't seem to work, I get, not depressed, but down and moody. However, I still continue on in my old ways—doing things like going out for breakfast after church. For a while there, we were doing that every week and it got to be a little much. Or buying lunch at work rather than bringing something. I would figure: To heck with it; I'm going to buy something different. Or getting the car ready for the trailer, full steam ahead, forgetting what it's going to cost. Those are my old ways. Let's move on then to what I've seen and heard.

What I've seen and heard is that both in the past and currently you express concern and voice hesitation on extras. But I still see you going out and golfing, doing things that require an extra outlay. And my impressions are that we are both concerned, but we haven't really had a significant enough setback to jolt us into knuckling under, getting down there and staying with a set budget. Granted, we haven't got much allocated for extras. I think we both want some action to be taken from what I've seen and heard, but we're too used to not having any limits, and going off and doing what we want.

JILL: Well, what I've seen and heard is your saying to me that we don't have any money in the checking account from pay period to pay period, and you've shown me that on the books. But I have a very difficult time understanding that. I guess my interpretation of what I hear you say every paytime is that we are really in bad shape. We have no extra money to spend. And *then*, I see us falling back into our old pattern of spending money after you've already told me that we don't have any money, and so I think that's a go-ahead for me. That's when I go out and spend. Moreover, when you show me the budget, I do understand the bill part of it. You show me where all the money's going for the bills, and you also show me where the leftover money has got to be applied for next time. So I look at that and I think there is no money, and I don't understand how we can manage. When I hear you say that there's no money, I feel guilty if I have to go out and get a haircut. I get angry, too, because a haircut is no big deal. I also feel frustrated because there are a lot of things that I would like to do and yet can't always do for lack of money. Like my golfing. I guess I am really feeling frustrated because I think there is no money for golf or lunch at a nice restaurant with my friends. And as far as the budget goes, even though you have explained it to me, I do get confused. I guess that's all.

JEFF: Okay. At first I went down and listed my feelings without any reasons why, and I wrote: frustrated, overwhelmed, frightened, apprehensive, and incompetent. Then I started thinking about them and went back and wrote: I'm frustrated because of our performance. I know it can be better. I'm overwhelmed when I see prices skyrocket on things we have to buy, like food, and and I have no control over them. I get frightened at the prospect of what will happen if we don't sit down and do something, and yet I'm apprehen-

sive about starting to knuckle down. I'm also confident that
if we really set our minds to it, we could do it.

JILL: I feel overwhelmed sometimes, too. Even panicky, because I feel I have no control over the situation either.

STEP 2: LAYING OUT INTENTIONS

For this step, draw another dimension and add it to the
Wheel on your paper, labeling it "intentions." Then list the
general intentions you have for yourself, for others (partner,
friend, etc.), and for the relationship. By exposing your intentions, you bring an honesty to the issue and point the way
toward potential solutions by creating a framework of possibilities. Steer clear of specific proposals (that comes next),
and be sure to focus on what you want *for* others, not what
you want *from* others.

Thinking in terms of what you want from others automatically places you in an exchange position in which you each
offer to swap something to get something else. The aim of
Step 2 is to bridge the differences you have over a particular
issue, and that goal is fostered by the collaborative position
of what you want *for* others and *for* the relationship. There is
something quite affirmative about hearing someone voice support and concern for your interests. Thus, the collaborative
orientation of "for" cements people, while the exchange orientation of "from" separates them.

JILL'S INTENTIONS:
What I want for me: I would like to better understand
where the money is going so I won't feel guilty about my
spending.
What I want for you: I would like for you not to have to
worry about where the money will come from between pay-
checks.
What I want for us: I would like us to be able to maintain
our budget so we will be freer to do the things we enjoy.

JEFF'S INTENTIONS:
What I want for me: To get out of the crunch so I won't
have to just get by.
What I want for you: To be able to do the things you enjoy
within reason, without feeling guilty, frustrated, or angry.
What I want for us: To be able to maintain our standard of
living and do the things we both enjoy. To change our negative feelings about budgeting to positive ones.

Include in this dimension any of your wants, wishes, goals, and objectives, and remember that your wants do not have to be explained or defended. Knowing and accepting both your intentions and your partner's eliminates the danger of hidden agendas and provides a realistic starting point for a workable solution. Bear in mind that Step 2 is merely a list of your intentions, without any commitment to implementation. Thus, you are free to express all your wants without the fear that you'll have to follow through. And remember to include your negative intentions as well as your positive ones—what you *don't* want as well as what you *do* want. When you've both finished writing, share your notes.

STEP 3: SAYING WHAT YOU WILL DO

The purpose of this step is to list what you *are* willing to do and what you're *not* willing to do to resolve the issue. Building on the background awareness of Step 1 and the intentions declared in Step 2, you are now ready to list the feasible possibilities you'd consider undertaking. You are not yet making a specific commitment, just developing a pool of choices. To begin, take a fresh sheet of paper, place your issue at the hub, and draw a new dimension labeled: "What I am willing to do/not to do." (See the diagrams on pages 220–21.)

JILL'S POSSIBLE ACTIONS:
I am willing to:
Destroy my credit cards.
Do the books in order to understand them better.
Stay within my grocery allowance.
Curtail some of my fun activities involving money.
Think when I buy, Do we need this now or can it wait?
I am not willing to:
Give up my weekly golf commitment.
Give up a fun night out with you once in a while.

JEFF'S POSSIBLE ACTIONS:
I am willing to:
Sit down and explain my theories on why I do things and how I do them.
Actually establish a budget and stick to it.
Let you do the books to get an idea of what exactly is involved.
Expand my side tax business.
Quit watching TV and get better organized.

Restrict my spending to necessities.
I am not willing to:
Let go of the financial control completely.

When you've completed this dimension, share what you've written once again.

JILL: Here's what I'm willing to do. Don't laugh but I'm willing to destroy my credit cards.

JEFF: Are you serious?

JILL: Yep. Next, I'm willing to keep the books just to see where the money goes. I'm willing to stay within my grocery allowance, to curtail some fun activities involving money. And I'm also very willing to think before buying, such as, do we need this now or can it wait? And, I am not willing to give up my weekly golf commitment, and I do not want to give up a fun night out with you maybe twice a month.

JEFF: The credit card thing, I can't get that out of my mind. I think I should put that down under what I am *not* willing to do. I am willing to sit down and explain my theories on what I am doing and why I am doing it as far as the budget is concerned. To actually establish a budget and stick to it, because what we've got now I don't really think is a budget. Another thing I might be willing to do is to expand my side tax business to bring in extra cash and I might be willing to let you do the books to get an idea of exactly what is involved in it. It'll be hard but I am willing to restrict my spending to necessities. And another one I put down might be to quit watching TV and get better organized—on important things. That might go beyond the budget issue. What I am not willing to do is to let go completely of control of the checkbook. And I did not put down the credit cards. I am not willing to *completely* destroy them. I mean, we can put them someplace where we can get at them . . . like the safe deposit box.

STEP 4: COMMITTING YOURSELF

Draw a final dimension and label it: "What I actually will do." Now you are ready to make specific choices from the possibilities listed in Step 3. Think small. Don't over-commit yourself. Select two or three actions that you realistically believe you can fulfill and build from there. It's best to keep your commitments short-range and manageable, rather than long-term and overwhelming.

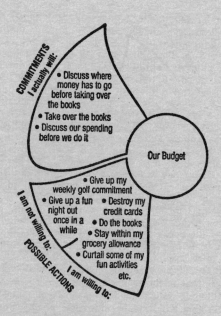

**JILL'S PROBLEM PREVENTION WHEEL
—STEPS 3 and 4**

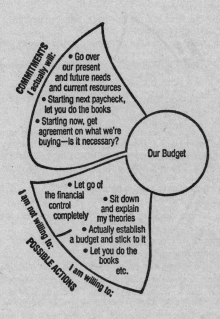

JEFF'S PROBLEM PREVENTION WHEEL
—STEPS 3 and 4

JILL'S COMMITMENTS:

1. Discuss where money has to go before taking over the books next payday.
2. Take over the books with your help but with the understanding I can do them my way.
3. Discuss our spending before we do it.

JEFF'S COMMITMENTS:

1. Set aside an evening to go over our present and future needs and current resources.
2. Starting next paycheck let you do the books with my help.
3. Starting now, get agreement on what we're buying—is it necessary.

After you have selected the actions you are prepared to take, share them with your partner.

JILL: I really would like to maintain the books, because I enjoy doing that, and I think that's about the only way I will understand where the money is going. You can explain it to me, but unless I'm actually doing it, it's pretty difficult for me to understand.

JEFF: Well, as long as I could watch. I don't think I could let go completely.

JILL: You let me do it those two weeks when you were out of town.

JEFF: Right, but I don't think I could go months without knowing where our finances stood.

JILL: Well, I'd like your help. Even with you standing over my shoulder and me being able to ask you questions, I would really like to have a sense that I'm doing it myself.

JEFF: Okay. What do you think of really establishing a dollars-and-cents budget? So much for this and so much for that, and if it's not there, that's too bad. That's almost as bad as taking the credit card away.

JILL: I'm willing to do it.

JEFF: Do you think that's feasible?

JILL: Yes.

JEFF: Do you think we can do it?

JILL: I think we could.

JEFF: Do you think we *would* do it?

JILL: I don't know if we would, but I think we could.

JEFF: Let's stick to what we actually would do.

JILL: Okay. I'm ready to take over the books.

JEFF: A good time for that would be next payday.

JILL: Okay. That would work out.

JEFF: So next payday you could pick up the disaster where I leave off.

JILL: I have a question. If I take over the books, can I kind of do it my way? With help from you, with certain limitations? Because I don't know if I'd maintain them the same way you do, 100 percent.

JEFF: Well, I think that would be all right.

JILL: I think another thing that we're both very guilty of and we could change is to think before we buy. You know, ask is it necessary? Can we do without it?

JEFF: Well, we can start right away to discuss what we are buying before we do it.

JILL: I can't see having a conference with you every time I get the impulse to buy a magazine or a lipstick.

JEFF: We could discuss bigger items and try to be conscious of curbing our impulse spending.

JILL: I could certainly agree to that.

JEFF: I'd like to go back to the budget again. How about if, before next payday, we actually sit down and establish a budget by looking at our present and future needs and being realistic about our resources?

JILL: That would be fine with me. I don't think, though, that I'll dispose of the credit cards.

JEFF: Then let's look at just what we're committed to: set aside time to go over our future needs and resources; beginning next payday to let you do the books; starting right now to get agreement on what we are buying, whether it's necessary or can it be postponed?

JILL: That's pretty much my list, too.

JEFF: It's hard to be thinking this is actually what I will do and to be so positive and approach this so systematically instead of in our usual haphazard way.

JILL: I'm a little nervous, too, but I think the key word is willing. We've said what we're willing to do and looking at all these "willings" really opens up possibilities and expands your thinking. There's just one more thing for me. Kind of a contingency. When I do the books with your help, I'd like, with reason, to have some of my own control.

JEFF: Sure.

JILL: Good. I feel better about that now.

STEP 5: REVIEW

Allow a few weeks or a month to implement your actions, then check your progress informally. A short ride around the Awareness Wheel is a good way to make a quick assessment.

About a month after their commitment to change, Jill and Jeff did this update:

JILL: Well, I've been doing the books for nearly four weeks now and I'm sure glad I didn't become an accountant. It's a thankless job. But I think it's accomplishing a purpose. I do have a better sense of how much we have to spend and I feel more responsible seeing it in black and white. I'm glad you left me pretty much on my own to work out the errors. I never was a math whiz but the more I do this, the more competent I feel.

JEFF: It hasn't been easy for me to keep my mouth shut, but I see you're trying hard and I don't want to undermine that. I felt a little like a kid asking permission when I came to you to talk about ordering cable TV. Before, I probably would have just written a check. I was relieved when you agreed. I think having a budget to see how we would manage the monthly payments helped make the decision easier.

JILL: How true. I passed up a suit I saw on sale last week because I knew it would throw the budget out of whack.

JEFF: I'd say then, for me, that I feel satisfied with the path we chose. I see both of us working to keep up our end of the bargain and I think by following a plan we're avoiding some of the bickering we used to have. I'd like to continue as we are.

JILL: Fine with me. And won't you be surprised when I tell you that my astute bookkeeping gave me an extra twenty dollars this week to put in our vacation fund.

If, like Jill and Jeff, your Straight Talk appraisal shows that your issue has been settled and your solutions are working, celebrate your success. If, however, the forecast is still cloudy and your solutions aren't working, put the issue back in the hub of the Awareness Wheel and recycle it through PPP again, with special emphasis on why the current actions failed and how you might amend or supplant them.

We hope the communication skills you've learned in this book will iron out most of your issues before it's necessary to engage in the Problem Prevention Process. However, when you're reached an impasse, don't hesitate to use PPP as a structured approach to solving major or recurring conflicts.

PART III
Connecting

13

Connecting in Bed

In recent years sex has been subjected to the intense research once reserved for fatal diseases, making people like Masters and Johnson our contemporary Pasteurs. The sexual act has been examined, analyzed, and classified into neatly labeled stages: excitement, plateau, orgasm, resolution. Sex manuals have become as popular as creative cookbooks and you don't have to ferret out sleazy bookstores to buy them. The public library has all the books you need to tell you everything you want to know about sex, many complete with lavish illustrations.

Clinical exploration of sex and sexuality has vastly improved our sexual climate and washed away much ignorance and rigidity. But this concentration on what happens in bed has obscured the other significant facet of sex: what happens out of bed. The joy of physical coupling is a transitory high unless nurtured and supported by communication beyond the bedroom. As one woman told us, "You can't matter in bed unless you matter over the breakfast table, when you come in from work, or when you're sick with a cold." Connecting out of bed is crucial to connecting in bed, and the way two people behave toward each other between sexual encounters may be the most overlooked aspect of the sexual cycle.

When Roy was first divorced he met a woman with whom he had the best sex he'd ever experienced. "She thought I was fabulous. She liked everything I did and I really got off on her adventurous spirit. But before we made love and after we finished, we didn't have that much to say to each other and after about four months we broke up. We had great sex, but there just wasn't any real closeness to keep us together."

Despite the firecrackers, physical attraction alone cannot maintain a relationship. In order for sex to be satisfying time after time, year after year, a couple has to click not only physically but in four other areas of their life together: intellectually, socially, emotionally, and spiritually.

A couple connects intellectually when they can share their thoughts, exchange ideas, and sense that their opinions are understood and appreciated, even in opposition. Neither Sally nor Joe excelled at chitchat and their marriage was relatively low-keyed, but they shared a passion for boating and scuba diving. Their conversations about these sports were so animated that it was hard to tell where one left off and the other began. And this one common interest provided the basis for an intellectual connection.

A couple must be able to connect socially. Do they have friends in common? Are they satisfied with the amount of time they spend socializing? Do they get a kick from being together at parties? Bill and Connie had an active social life and a wide circle of friends, but for their twenty-fifth anniversary they opted to spend a simple evening at home with three couples who'd been their dearest friends. "Actually," Bill told us, "we designed the evening to show them how much we valued their friendship. Connie cooked a fabulous dinner and later we sat in a hot tub we'd just installed in the back yard, sipping wine and reminiscing about the crazy times we'd had over the years. I felt there was no place in the world I'd rather be at that moment and no people I'd rather be with. Connie later told me she felt exactly the same way."

Partners must be able to connect emotionally. When we settle into a relationship, we escape from the frozen smiles of singles' bars and superficial connections with casual friends to the refuge of that one person who truly cares about us, who wants to be with us, who understands our feelings, who laughs at our jokes and shares our troubles. When emotional needs are not met, either because a couple is not tuned in to each other's feelings or is unable to freely express their own, the relationship crumbles.

A couple should also be able to connect spiritually. This does not mean that they need to commune on a mystical level, but rather that they respect each other's values, ideas, and beliefs, and agree in some major areas while accepting their differences in others.

Cathy and Alan argued endlessly over a basic split in their attitude toward material possessions. Cathy had been raised by parents who considered it immoral to care about owning things. Alan, while not frivolous, came from a background centered on the idea that life was to be savored, and one way he translated this message was into a fascination for big, fast cars. Cathy was truly embarrassed by the flashy cars that Alan bought, and she cringed every time she had to sit her plain cloth coat against the plush leather upholstery of Alan's latest "pleasure boat." After years of trying to force their separate value systems on each other, they gave up the struggle and rejoiced in other values that they shared—in their case, a common view of God and morality.

And finally, a couple must be able to connect physically, both in private and in public. Marriage counselors report that they are seeing more and more people who have sex regularly but are starving for affection and, as a result, their sex isn't fulfilling. Both men and women complain that they are hungry for physical attention. Although their mates are involved in sex, they're not interested in touching and there is very little warmth or loving outside the bedroom. In contrast, those couples who greet each other with a hug and a nuzzle, who hold hands in the movies after several years together, who walk arm and arm, are constantly demonstrating physical connections. They develop the kind of ongoing physical closeness that culminates in intercourse, but doesn't depend on it.

Satisfying sex results from magical clicks—nonsexual orgasms, if you will—at all five levels. Relationships need a variety of the marvelous moments when you sense that you and your partner occupy exactly the same space, either emotionally, intellectually, spiritually, socially, or physically, and that being there together is indeed very special. Without these other connections, sex can be just a mechanical release of tension instead of an intimate, ultimate experience.

TIME AND TALK

While there's no easy formula for connecting out of bed in order to connect in bed, there are two important ways to increase your opportunities: time and talk. Every couple needs time to be alone together, to revel in each other's company without demands or expectations. And every couple needs to get beyond the light reporting of Small Talk to the deeper thoughts, feelings, and wants of Straight Talk. Closeness comes from good times and good talk. Yet, because of the multipressures of work, family, and outside activities, too many couples drive their lives in parallel lanes, wondering why their lovemaking has fizzled to a Saturday night special.

A study done in Philadelphia showed that the critical difference between happily and unhappily married young couples is the amount of free time they spend together. The happy couples reported they spend at least one third of their available time with one another, while those who were dissatisfied with their relationship spent less than 20 percent of their time in common. Furthermore, the happy couples consciously arranged the time to be together.

We plan almost everything in our lives—dental appointments, church meetings, ski weekends, jogging, but how often do we program private uninterrupted time on a regular basis, simply to be with our mate? Could you imagine a successful business partnership without regularly scheduled meetings? Instead of haphazardly snatching a chance to talk or laugh when you happen to be alone, consciously make a date with your mate to meet privately at least once a week.

Steve, a copywriter with an advertising agency, and Roxanne, a housewife and part-time student, found themselves so busy pursuing careers and the kids that they barely had time to pursue each other. They decided to schedule a weekly rap session. Each Sunday night they'd check their calendar and choose a day to meet for a leisurely lunch—away from the house and the clamor of the children. When the weather was nice, they'd take a walk or have a picnic. And it didn't seem to matter whether they chatted casually about their daily routine or discussed something special. Being together was what counted. Although their "dates" were not planned to improve their sex life, they discovered some months later that they frequently had intercourse on the night they'd had lunch.

Wayne and Carmen had more specific intentions. They set aside Wednesday as "our night to make it" and agreed that once the kids were in bed, they'd cuddle on the couch, watch TV, or read or talk together. "We intended to spend this hour as a warm-up to sex, but sometimes we'd get so heavily into a discussion that we'd be exhausted from talking and go to sleep lying in each other's arms. Oddly enough those talks were as fulfilling as if we'd made love."

Private time creates the context for intimacy, but healthy

dialogue binds couples together. Wonderful as it is to hear "I love you" in a burst of passion, it's more valuable to share a whole spectrum of moods, thoughts, likes, and dislikes on a daily basis. When Rod looked back on his brief three-year marriage, he saw that one of the problems was his *lack* of communication. "I thought she had no sex drive and that I was some kind of sex maniac because I wanted to make love every other night. Now I see it wasn't the sex drive at all. I should have made her feel more important, more noticed, more appreciated. I didn't give her recognition and gratification out of bed, so she didn't want to gratify me in bed."

Too often, people only communicate when they have to deal with issues, and they forget the simpler joys of sharing fondness or showing appreciation. If you think that your wife is the best stockbroker on Wall Street, has a terrific body for a mother of three, or makes better chicken soup than your mother, don't be embarrassed—tell her. If you think that your husband is a superb lover, looks dashing in three-piece suits, and has a brilliant way of analyzing complex political situations, don't assume he knows that—tell him. Appreciation warms a relationship. Everybody needs verbal stroking, and the remembrance of a compliment can flower into physical tenderness when you're in bed.

Relationships dry up without the intimate exchange of thoughts, feelings, and wants. Today, Muriel looks back on the desert of her marriage and wonders how she stayed with a man she could never talk to for twenty-five years. "There was no real communication in our marriage," she recalls. "None. Sure we talked about our three kids and his problems building a business, but we never talked about ourselves as a man and woman. All our conversations were either searching or academic. We never discussed anything emotional, and I craved that kind of intimacy. I wanted to talk about little nothings—tell him that I didn't sleep well, that my bunions ached, that I worried what I'd do with my life when the kids grew up. But all he could talk about was world affairs."

When the children grew up, Muriel found the courage to leave. She enrolled in a master's program at a local college and, on a blind date, met a widower, an engineer, who, like herself, used words as building blocks. They liked each from the start, and on their second date, Muriel had no qualms saying so. "I really like you," she told Sam. "And I don't expect you to answer that. I told you for myself. It's just so good to feel again." Sam, on his part, had lots of other things to say. He'd become so bored with the ritual of dating that he joked he was going to make a tape of his life story and send it to his dates in advance to avoid the tedium of talking about himself over and over. "But with you, it's different," he told Muriel. "I want to tell you everything and I want you to know me." So she talked and he talked, and because he accepted everything she said, she opened up even more.

The first time they made love, Muriel wept. After so many years of emptiness, she was overwhelmed to discover that she was still alive and capable of loving. Soon the two of them began to talk about sex just as they talked about everything else. Sam noticed, for instance, that Muriel rushed their lovemaking. She'd been in the habit of hurrying with her husband before he lost his occasional urge. Sam told her, "I'm not a wham-bam-thank-you-ma'am kind of guy. You don't have to rush me." He encouraged Muriel to express what gave her pleasure. "I want us both to experience every possible good feeling and we don't know what we both like unless we tell each other." And when he sensed that his uncharacteristic silence during sex puzzled her, he explained, "I'm a silent lover. It's like I'm in another world then, and words break my mood. Don't take my silence as a criticism of you."

Muriel and Sam were recently married. On the certificate her birthdate appeared as 1927, his as 1925; remarkable proof that age has no bearing on the potential to communicate. It's easy to imagine these two in twenty years, holding hands as they rock on the front porch, still talking. Barren for so long, Muriel has discovered with Sam the delicate interdependency of love and like. She says, "For us, the talking is the liking. If that liking isn't there, then the love wears down and the sex isn't good. That's what happened with my first husband. We didn't talk. We're not that young anymore, so we'll probably love less often. But as long as we can talk, the liking won't ever go away."

CONNECTING IN BED

Just as talk binds couples intellectually, emotionally, and spiritually, it is also the glue that cements their sexual relationship. How sad that this most special act of sharing is often shrouded in silence. Two people mate, each with their own sexual fantasies, expectations, and preferences, but they do not tell each other what these are. One may go on for years doing something he or she doesn't especially enjoy to please the other, yet reluctant to say so and seem prudish or selfish. And the other may wish for a certain kind of caress without ever daring to request it. Embarrassed, afraid to appear critical, unable to ask without demanding, he or she cannot find the language to talk about sex on a personal rather than an abstract level.

Before, after, and even during sex, there are all sorts of emotions you feel, things you want to say and things you yearn to hear, questions you'd like to ask, preferences you'd like to voice. All this is perfectly natural, and expressing yourself in all these areas is how you and your partner connect in bed. Intimacy is an intricate combination of what couples *do* with each other and what they *say* to each other. When sex therapists work with people who have functional problems, they teach more than simple arousal techniques; they also teach them to talk about sex because, without words, sex is empty.

Nancy and Ted were medical students married less than three months when Nancy came to a sex therapist questioning her sexuality. "Here I am a newlywed," she sighed, "and I don't look forward to going to bed with my husband. Something is missing." That something turned out to be verbal. Their physical parts were functioning, but Ted was so wrapped up in the demands of his hospital residency that his mind was miles away from Nancy, and their sex was speechless and cold. She felt as though she was making love to a machine and, like many women, she assumed something was wrong with her ability to respond.

You can add the caress of verbal intimacy to your sex life by taking your Awareness Wheel to bed. When you are lying next to your mate, tune in to what you are thinking, feeling, and wanting at that very moment and begin to express these things out loud. "I think it's exciting when you leave a light on." "I feel very secure with your arms around me." "I'd rather you rub my back than my legs." "I'd like to do something different tonight. Got any suggestions?" When you speak up for yourself out of your inner awareness, you open yourself up to your partner and pave the way for mutual sharing. "Hmm, so you like this soft, feathery kind of massage. I always thought you liked the same kind of hard rub-bing I did." Couples can learn to appreciate and please each other only when assumptions are cast aside and replaced by statements based on tuning in to self and tuning in to other.

People who share the sheets actually know very little about what goes on in each other's heads. Because of the silence that so often surrounds sex, most of us have become amateur mind readers, quick to make judgments on what we think we perceive. We mix up our thoughts with our feelings, and we think we're expressing feelings when we're really swapping judgments. "I feel you never want to make love" is a judgment, not a feeling. But, "I feel unloved and think I'm unappealing when I ask you to make love and you tell me night after night that you're too tired," is a bonafide uncritical expression of feeling. Unlike the judgment, there is no subtle accusation that your partner is at fault for making you feel terrible. Since sex is such a sensitive subject, it's essential that you speak for yourself, be responsible for yourself, and learn to separate feelings from judgments.

ASK FOR WHAT YOU WANT

Many people find it supremely difficult to ask for a hug, to request a kiss, to say, "Touch me here" or "I like it when you . . ." When you're unable to ask for what you want, you are forced to settle for what you're getting, and consequently you may feel cheated, deprived, or just plain angry. Unfortunately, our society is fraught with stereotypes and unspoken rules that zipper up the mouths of men and women.

Etta and Bud were typical. Etta felt that she had absolutely no right to ask Bud to please her. If she made a request she'd be imposing; she'd become a burden. Furthermore, she believed that nice women don't ask. If you have a good husband, he'll know what you want. Men are supposed to know everything before they get married. As for Bud, he considered it unmasculine to ask for anything, much less to indicate what he liked. He could murmur, "I love you," but he could never say, "I like it when you nibble my ear," or "I love it when you crawl into bed without a nightgown."

Like most couples who can't talk about sex, Bud and Etta communicated nonverbally by gentling pushing each other's hands from one place to another to indicate what they wanted. When Etta was angry with Bud, she wouldn't tell him; instead, she'd touch him in all the places that she knew he didn't like, and their sex would be quick and unsatisfying. One morning after a mechanical session, Etta asked Bud if he knew what she had been trying to say to him the night before. He replied that he sensed something was vaguely wrong, but he couldn't put his finger on it. Etta burned. She'd put so much effort into making him feel awful, and he hadn't even gotten her message. It's fine to talk with your hands, but if you don't back up gestures with words, you're likely to be misinterpreted.

There is nothing selfish about wanting certain pleasures or preferring a particular caress or position, and it is perfectly legitimate to ask your partner for what you want instead of assuming he or she will know. What's essential is that you both make an effort to know and to satisfy each other. Remember, what is sexually exciting to one person may be dull or distasteful to another. While you should never be ashamed to refuse a discomfitting request, you need not buffer your refusal by demeaning it. Maintaining an I-count-me/I-count-you attitude is one way to avoid judging or denigrating those sexual preferences that do not appeal to you.

Feedback and discussions of sexual likes and dislikes should be educational, not critical. Avoid Control Talk statements such as, "Don't do that," or "You've got weird taste," or "Couldn't you force yourself to do it just for me." Instead, accentuate the positive and emphasize what you'd like with Awareness Wheel statements: "What would turn me on is . . ." "What I'd really like is for you to . . ." "I feel so good when you . . ."

In many relationships, asking for sex is a continual issue. Few people have equal sex drives or even the same affectional needs, and the more active partners often becomes the initiator. However, when this develops into a pattern, when one partner always asks for sex on the assumption that, even if given the opportunity, the mate will never ask, the relationship suffers. The mate, denied that opportunity, can't ask, and inevitably the couple winds up fighting:

SHE: You never want to make love.
HE: That's not true. You want it too much. I can't keep up with you.
SHE: Well, if I didn't ask, we'd never do it.

HE: How do you know? You never give me the chance. You always ask first.

The real issue, a normal difference of sexual appetites, is diverted into the battle of who's right, and both go to bed angry. Unfortunately, sexual response cannot be operated like a light switch, and long-married couples are not always going to be at the same place at the same time. Don't hesitate to ask for sex when you are in the mood, but ask for *yourself.* When you phrase your request as a closed question, "Wouldn't you like to come to bed now?" you box your partner into a corner. When you ask by speaking-for-self, "I feel horny and I'd like to make love tonight," you remove the onus of compliance and the guilt that inevitably accompanies a refusal.

HOW TO SAY NO

In twenty years of marriage, Debbie never once initiated sex with her husband, which frequently put her in the unpleasant position of saying no or using denial as a weapon.

> "When we've had words or he's been harsh with the kids or upset the tone of the house so that I'm angry at him, I don't want to make love. It's not that I love him any the less when I say no, it's just that I'm not in the right frame of mind. Instead of telling him that I'm angry, or why I'm angry, I hide it, and when he rolls over in bed, I'll say I'm too beat or I have a headache. He goes to sleep, and I lie awake angry with myself for rejecting him."

Debbie's silence made it impossible for Dick to differentiate between her anger and genuine exhaustion. He interpreted her unqualified and unexplained "no" as a personal rejection and fought back by reverting to Control Talk to gain the upper hand. After Couple Communication, Debbie recognized that she'd been hurting Dick. She admitted, "I do too much thinking about what he's thinking and why he acts a certain way. I have to concentrate on verbalizing my own feelings." That meant telling Dick when she was mad and when she was glad. If she thought about him during the day, she began to call his office and, instead of her old "What's new?" she'd say, "I was thinking about you and I called to say hello." When she wanted to be with him, she learned to say, "I'd like to have dinner alone with you tonight." She used to say, "How would you like to take me to dinner?" and get angry when he'd invite another couple and enlarge her twosome to his foursome. And finally, she summoned the courage to ask for sex when she wanted it and to experience what it felt like when Dick said, "No. I'm just too tired." And for Dick, the chance to refuse now and then helped him understand that people often say no for their own reasons, not to wound their partners.

There is nothing inherently wrong with denial. It's perfectly reasonable not to be in the spirit for sex, not to want to participate in certain sexual behaviors. The point is to say no in a manner that doesn't equate refusal with rejection or substitute excuses for truth. It's possible to talk out the anger that puts distance between you and your mate. It's even possible to accept rejection—if it's expressed honestly, in a nonaccusatory fashion. "I'm not over our argument yet. I don't want to talk about it. I want to be left alone, and I want to be angry at you."

Similarly, if you don't know why you're not in the mood for sex, be clear about your confusion. "I just don't want to make love now and I'm not really sure why." On the other hand, if you do know why, use your Awareness Wheel to express your reasons, and try to focus on them without attacking your partner. "I'm angry with you because I wanted to go out tonight and you said you were too tired. But you played Ping-Pong with Jimmy and split logs for the fireplace. I don't think you're tired at all and I'm annoyed that you didn't put some of your energy into doing something with me."

The most powerful way to say no can be frigidity or impotence. For instance, a man who is unable to verbalize refusal may unconsciously shut himself off and let his inability to have an erection speak for him. To establish equality in a relationship, it is vital that both partners learn how to say no, and become comfortable enough to deal with personal inhibitions honestly by saying, "I'm embarrassed to do that in front of you." The awareness and expression of your own feelings is as much a part of intimacy as the willingness to stretch them when and if you want to. Lovemaking is a series of choices, and if you don't believe that you have choices, what you do out of duty or compliance won't feel very good to either of you. If you can't say no to your partner, how can you freely say yes and mean it?

Barry and Jean show the positive power of saying no in this dialogue they taped for us after Couple Communication.

BARRY: Honey I'd like to share something with you. All day, I've been feeling extra good in an unexpected way. Remember this morning when I was kind of excited—you know, sexually aroused—and I wanted to play around a little and you didn't want to? Well, ordinarily I would have felt terrible about your saying no, and today I didn't. I think what's happened is that we've been able to talk about this enough and share feelings so that instead of your old grunt or groan, you now come out and tell me, "Uh, gee I just don't want to now." When you can be upfront with me I understand what you want. My intention is not to bully you or say, "Hey, give it to me, lady," but rather to have something we can share and feel good about. So I would just as soon have no sex as sex, and I feel really terrific that I've come so far.

JEAN: I used to think that you were supposed to know what I wanted and didn't want without my telling you, that sex wasn't something to talk about, and if I made motions, you'd understand.

BARRY: Yeah, oh yeah. Me too.

JEAN: But when I did that, my actions were often misinterpreted.

BARRY: Well, I really didn't know what you wanted and I often interpreted it as my problem—that I wasn't being an adequate lover; that I'm not doing it right; that I should go back to the sex manual and find out what's wrong so you'll be happier and I can turn you on. That kind of thing.

JEAN: I had a lot of mixed feelings about myself when I wasn't talking. I'd think there's something wrong with me because I can't respond right now. But I couldn't express that. That's why I'd keep quiet and make some kind of motion to pretend I wasn't interested. I'd do anything but say, "You know I don't want to make love right now." But the more we've been able to talk, the easier it is to say no and know that doesn't mean there's something the matter with me.

BARRY: Or me either.

JEAN: Right. Or you either.

BARRY: And I think that's where the good feeling comes from. Instead of going to work and feeling lousy or crummy over what happened this morning, I can face you tonight feeling fine, that we're still friends, that our relationship hasn't been battered. In fact, it's kind of cemented because there's a sharing here.

JEAN: The nice thing for me is that when we do agree now that we both want to make love or play around or whatever, it's good because we both want to do it.

Being able to say no without guilt or rejection demonstrates esteem for yourself as well as your partner, and that is the essence of the important I-count-you/I-count-me attitude in bed.

HOW TO SAY I CAN'T

For some men and women, "no" doesn't automatically mean "I'd rather not." It can be an excuse for "I don't think I can." Both sexes may experience problems with impotency. A female who has trouble achieving orgasm can, if she chooses, go through the motions, but a man having difficulty holding an erection simply cannot fake it. In either case the easy way to avoid potentially disappointing intercourse is to offer a terse "not tonight" comment and turn a cold shoulder to sleep on.

Although Straight Talk won't cure impotency, it will reduce the pressures that may lead to it. Particularly if you are a man, your fear of giving an impressive performance in bed could be part of the cause of your failure to do so. Some of that tension can be reduced by discussing your problem in advance. While you're getting undressed or just lying in bed, tell your partner about the difficulty you've been experiencing, how demands frighten you and often prevent you from doing what you really want. Say that you would like very much to cuddle in each other's arms and just see what happens. Then ask your partner to tell *you* what he or she thinks you said.

You may recall this as the skill of shared meaning, a technique to use when it's important that your listener receive the very same message that you sent. You'll probably find that this delicate message—understood by anyone as awkward to deliver—will be received with compassion. Often the shared meaning triggers other kinds of sharing. A partner appreciates your honesty instead of your rejection, feels your pain and responds with the understanding comfort you need most. Shared meanings backfire only when you wait too long to use them. When you're in bed, excited and suddenly unable to finish is no time to say, "Oh, I've got something to tell you." At that point your partner is likely to feel angry or cheated and assume the blame for your inadequacy. "Something's wrong with my body. I can't turn him/her on." "It was something I did that he didn't like." "I shouldn't have rushed her." The value of a shared meaning is its ability to impart sensitive information about a potential problem *before* it is a problem. The key to its effectiveness is to use it *before* the possibility becomes the reality.

In contemporary society, sex has become a primary way for couples to connect with each other. Unquestionably, sex has the potential to light the spark of connecting. But sex alone isn't enough. A couple must be able to talk to each other, first out of bed and then in bed. Sex creates moments of intimacy; only talk sustains them.

14

Connecting with Kids

A journey down a warm, dark passage. A burst of light, a blast of cold air. A snip of a scissors and a new member of the human race takes its first independent breath. Nothing quite matches the joy of a mother and father at the birth of their child. And nothing quite prepares them for the conflicts that periodically mar that joy as the child grows.

How fine life would be if we could rekindle at will the intimate bonding of those early days after childbirth! Although we always want to connect with our children, to be close to them, to show them our love, we find that it gets harder and harder. As soon as they are able to talk, they begin to talk back. They defy us; they act in ways that we dislike or disapprove of. They make us proud one day, blow our dreams to dust the next. They fail a test; they win a prize. They smash the car; they sneak drugs; they close themselves behind the locked door of their bedroom. Then they surprise us on our birthday with breakfast in bed and a tender poem. How can we connect with these extensions of ourselves who irritate us, aggravate us, then turn around and captivate us?

A father, who was going through a period in which one of his two teenage daughters would barely speak to him, told us, "If I had it to do all over again, I'd still have children. But I wish I'd known what it was going to be like. We've had wonderful times, to be sure. We've also been through hell, and I certainly didn't expect parenting to be so painful."

Being a parent isn't easy! Fathers and mothers straddle a seesaw trying to achieve a balance between connecting with their children and controlling them. Often, the control seems more natural than the connecting; parents are supposed to manage their children's lives. Our parents learned that from

their parents and taught it to us. Control is so much a part of
handling children that some kids, between home and school,
hear nothing but control messages: sit still; stand straight;
lower your voice; feed the bird; clean your fingernails; don't
eat so fast; don't walk so slow; finish your homework; try
harder; don't get upset so easily; stop moping. Although control has its rightful place in child-rearing, it can be overem-
phasized, and when it is, connections are impaired. Yet many
parents believe that loosening control is tantamount to losing
control, which, once gone, is impossible to retrieve. So they
hold on tight, afraid to step down from the throne of authority.

Actually, connecting with kids is every bit as natural as
controlling them. In the long run, the more connections you
invest in your child's emotional bank account, the less dent
the control withdrawals will make in your relationship.

Connections with children happen whenever an adult and a
child join momentarily and link like meshed gears, and you
can't predict when, where, or how you'll click. Connections
don't crop up automatically at church on Sunday or every
Thursday on the way to ballet school. They aren't guaranteed
by taking your child to the circus, the museum, or the baseball game. It's unlikely that you'll connect if, like a good father, you cart your son to the playground but read the paper
while he swings. And don't expect to connect when you are
physically present but psychologically absent, when your
body is sitting by the side of the bed reading a story but your
mind is fishing off the coast of Florida.

Connecting will often creep up and surprise you in an activity as ordinary as a bike ride, a game of checkers, or toss-
ing grass seed on a winter-weary lawn. The event itself is less
important than what you both bring to the event. What are
your intentions? How are you feeling? How do you express
yourself?

More often than not, when one of you wants to connect,
the other isn't available. You walk in the door at dinnertime
and your child is watching television. You walk over, hug
her, and try to chat a bit, but she's glued to the tube. You
barely get a "hi." She's not available. So you begin to thumb
through the day's mail and get involved reading a letter. The
show ends, she clicks off the TV, comes over to you, and
starts talking about school. Now, you're not available. "Just a
sec," you say, "let me finish this last paragraph," and by the

time you look up, she's off again. Some parents and children go on and on like this, just missing each other.

Establishing a pattern of hits among the misses requires consistent and not always rewarded effort. You may have to do the lion's share of reaching out, and you'll be likely to catch little more than air if your idea of connecting is to force a child to come into your world and accommodate to your plans. "Come shopping with me now. I have a few minutes and we'll talk." "Aw, gee, Mom. I hate to shop. Do I have to?" While there's nothing wrong with that kind of invitation, you'll be far more successful if you try to enter your child's world and look at life momentarily through his or her eyes. Share your children's anger over a lost intramural game, their delight with a compliment from a teacher, their conflict over whether to wear the green slacks or jeans to a school dance, their hysteria because their nose has a pimple or their current love hasn't called, their desire to be left alone, their doubts about whether God hears their prayers.

By crossing the invisible threshold from your grown-up reality to their youthful perception of it, you automatically increase your chances of connecting. It takes but a few moments for a direct hit, and hits tend to produce more hits, while misses are also sadly self-perpetuating.

LET KIDS LEAD YOU

The snow fell all through the night, layering the streets and lawns with thick vanilla icing. Sheila cannot wait to take her two-year-old son, Kenny, sledding. As soon as she finishes the breakfast dishes, she takes out his snowsuit, sits him on the floor, and pushes his chubby legs into the quilted pants. She eases his arms through the sleeves of the jacket and zips it up. Kenny pulls the zipper down. She zips it up; he pulls it down again, giggling. She puts on his little wool hat. He pulls it off to play peekaboo. Sheila gets impatient. She doesn't want to play. She wants to get outside in the snow. Kenny doesn't understand her irritation. He's having a fine time doodling with his zipper and hat.

Later that morning, Sheila is on the phone when her ten-year-old daughter, Stacy, rushes in for lunch. "Quick, Mom. You gotta get my sandwich." Sheila puts her hand over the mouthpiece and says, "You've got a whole hour. What's the hurry?" Stacy answers, "I'm starving, Mom. I lost my recess snack and I'm starving. I have to eat right away." Sheila says, "Go watch TV for a few minutes. I'll be finished soon."

Parents and children have a different sense of time. Children live in the now, in the moment. Parents tend to focus on the future, on finishing the tasks of the present to move to something else waiting ahead. Because they are goal-oriented and time-limited, parents usually don't realize that time stops for children, that what they are thinking, wanting, and feeling right now is all that matters to them. Sheila wants to hustle Kenny outside where she anticipates a grand time pulling him through the snow. Kenny's interest doesn't extend that far ahead. He's happy playing with his zipper and hat. Stacy really thinks she's starving and she wants her urgency at least to be recognized, if not attended to.

Wrapped up in their own wants and feelings, parents frequently don't bother to tune in to their children's reality, so they don't connect with them. Take the time to use your Awareness Wheel to check out what your child may be thinking or feeling, and you'll quickly come together. Hank told his Couple Communication group how surprised he was that changing focus changed a situation with his daughter:

> "Sunday afternoon the kids and I were outside playing with the dog, and Carrie, our youngest, started to whine and act crankly. I caught myself getting impatient, about to say my usual 'Stop whining' or 'If you're going to act that way, get in the house.' Instead, I decided to check out what I saw and reflect her feelings. I said, 'It looks like you're getting tired.' That acknowledgment was all she wanted. She stopped whining and stayed and played. That fast, it was over."

Once you begin to tune in to your children, you can reap the rewards of letting them lead you by joining them wherever they happen to be and savoring that moment with them. If your pre-schooler is building a tower of red and blue blocks, squat down on the floor and join her. If your pre-teen is dressing a Barbie Doll or snapping together Lego pieces to make an airport, join in. If your teenager is stretched out on the bed listening to music, take your needlepoint to his room and listen with him.

Seven-year-old Rebecca was not permitted to operate the family stereo system. After dinner she asked her dad to put on her favorite record and her feet were tapping even before the music started. Her lithe little body swayed and dipped like the disco dancers she saw on TV. Drawn into her pleasure, Dad began to dance, too—not really with her, but next to her. Her baby brother toddled in and Dad picked him up in the air to include him in the rhythm. Soon all three of them were whirling unself-consciously around the den, laughing out loud. The connection lasted perhaps five minutes. It never would have happened had Dad turned on the stereo and left to read the evening paper.

It's tough for parents to abandon themselves and follow the flow of their kids. Try it. Invite yourself to a tea party or a game of cops and robbers and see how long you can play without having to leave to make a phone call, offer a suggestion, change the rules, or exert your influence. How long can you walk with your daughter before you begin to direct the route? How long can you play touch football without quarterbacking? How long can you talk to your kids without giving advice or changing the subject to something you find more interesting?

When you allow yourself to join children in their space, you demonstrate an I-count-me/I-count-you attitude. Your actions and behavior say: "I, as an adult, take you seriously. What you are doing or saying matters to me. I like you and I want to be with you." Stepping into a child's realm at any age and letting the child establish the direction of the play or the conversation is a significant act with great potential for connecting.

THE BUILDING BLOCKS OF ESTEEM

The four I-count positions that build or destroy esteem affect your relationship with your children in much the same way they affect your relationships with other adults. When your dialogues with your children reflect your own self-esteem, you provide them with a healthy role model. At the same time, if you show esteem for them, you develop their ego and enhance their self-respect.

Twelve-year-old Willie thought he needed a bigger allowance. He approached his dad for a raise, pointing out that he was getting only half as much money as his friends. His dad could respond in one of four ways:

I don't count you/I don't count me: "There's nothing I can do to help you. We don't have money now for that kind of thing."

I count me/ I don't count you: "I've got enough financial troubles of my own without you asking me for more money."

I don't count me/ I count you: "Well, you know things are really tight around here now. I don't know where I can cut back, but I'll find a way."

I count me/I count you: "It's tough to need money. I've been there myself. Let's see how much you need and how we might be able to work this out."

The party for Debbie's dad's birthday was in full swing. Most of the forty guests had arrived and the canapés were parading from the kitchen in a steady stream. Suddenly, Debbie, a fifteen-year-old, tugged anxiously at her mother's elbow. "I've got to talk to you," she said. "It's important." Her mother was in no mood for a heart-to-heart. How could she respond?

I don't count me/I don't count you: "How could you even bring up something at a time like this. I just can't cope now."

I count me/I don't count you: "Don't bother me now. Can't you see how busy I am? Here, pass these hors d'oeuvres."

I don't count me/I count you: "I'm awfully busy, but if it's that crucial to you, I'll stop what I'm doing."

I count me/I count you: "I'm feeling pressured right now with this party. Could we talk afterward? You do look upset though. I don't want to put you off if it's urgent."

To let your kids lead you, you must be sensitive to their green lights. If either you or your children complains, "You never want to talk when I want to talk, and when I don't want to talk, you do," *you* may be flashing a red light too often. As uncommunicative as many teenagers are, if you listen to *whatever* it is they are willing to discuss, you will have a clue to what they're thinking, which you can use to enter their world.

DON'T GIVE UP YOUR AUTHORITY

Allowing your kids to lead you does not mean abdicating personal authority. Parents have definite responsibilities for and toward their children, and there is no question that your authority should be exercised. The question is *how*. Parent power is frequently abused on a captive population. Kids know who's boss and realize that parents can't be impeached. Jack laughed as he told us how he'd once stomped into his daughter's room and sternly ordered her to put out the light because it was a school night. His son, hearing the executive decree, yelled from his room, "Right on, Dad. Veto power in action."

Authority is not a synonym for coercion. Still, many parents govern by the motto, "As long as you live under my roof and I pay the bills, you'll do what I tell you." The trick to effective parenting is to exert authority without becoming a dictator, without blaming, shaming, belittling, or demeaning your children. That means recognizing that your control over your offspring is only temporary. Gradually, you must relinquish authority and replace it with influence.

When parents recognize exactly what they can and cannot control early on—in other words, the limits of their authority—this process evolves naturally. This means that you have no authority whatsoever over your children's thoughts, feelings, and wants, tough as that may be to swallow. Unfortunately, many parents commonly issue orders as if they had such control:

You should feel sorry for Aunt Grace.

Don't worry so much about your appearance.

Be grateful for what you have and stop complaining about what you'd like.

Why do you want a new bike? There's nothing wrong with your old one.

You'll eat it and you'll like it.

You can't possibly believe it was the coach's fault that you didn't make the team.

However, parents can legitimately exercise control over their children's actions. When they confine their authority in this way, they are less likely to alienate their children and diminish their chances for connecting.

Mike had a haircut appointment for 5:00. At 4:30 he dashed in the house and announced that he wasn't going. His buddies had come over and they were playing basketball in the yard. His mother calmly said, "You made the appointment. You are going to keep it." Mike said, "No way," and ran outside.

At 4:50 his mother walked into the yard and said to the group, "Sorry, boys. You'll have to come back another day. Mike has a haircut appointment." Mike slammed the basketball into the ground, burrowed into the back seat of the car, and glared at his mother. "Oooh. You think you can make me do anything you want." "Mike," she said, "I'm making you keep this appointment because I want you to recognize an obligation. The barber makes his living on his time. If you cancel at the last minute, he can't fill your appointment and he loses money. I know you're excited when your friends come over and you'd rather play ball, but you made this appointment and that's the way it is."

Mike's mother chose Light Control Talk as an excellent mode for expressing authority. It's efficient, forceful, and non-abusive. However, many parents handle their children with nothing but Heavy Control Talk which, over a period of time, cuts off communication and fosters resentment.

Avoid closed questions that try to manipulate a child and invariably produce the very result you don't want:

"Wouldn't you like to finish your spinach?"

"No, I wouldn't."

"What kind of smart-aleck answer is that?"

Stay away from demands as well:

"It's after ten and you forgot to do the dishes again. Do them immediately."

Instead, issue a mild Light Control directive:

"Hey, it's almost bedtime and the dishes are waiting for you."

When an order meets with major opposition, consider switching styles. Move into Search Talk to inquire why your child is resisting, or into Straight Talk if your viewpoints are truly polarized. Sometimes, kids resist out of obstinancy, to see how far they can push you. Use Style III and IV to gather information about the source of their recalcitrance. Tune in to your own awareness and tell them what you feel and what you want. As a parent, you hold the aces and can ultimately insist on getting your way. Use insistence as a last resort and, in the meantime, consider the above alternatives. By steering away from Heavy Control Talk, your authority can be both obeyed and respected.

TALK WITH YOUR CHILDREN, NOT AT THEM

Parents spend far more time than they realize supervising their children: Where are you going? What time will you be back? Wash your hair. Don't slurp your soup. Hurry up or you'll miss the bus. And as a result, they spend much less time than they realize actually interacting with them. For a study on parent/child interaction, a team of New York psychologists asked a group of middle class fathers to estimate the amount of time they spent playing with their year-old infants each day. The average answer was fifteen to twenty minutes. But when the fathers were actually observed, the time was shockingly less. The mean number of interactions per day was 2.7 and the number of seconds for each involvement rounded out to thirty-eight. Less than a minute a day for so much as a koochy-koo.

It's sad enough that some parents hardly talk to their children and sadder still that when they do, so much of what they say is a directive or order in Style II. While a good bit of Light Control Talk is necessary for child-rearing, if it isn't diluted with other styles the opportunities to connect decrease. Parenting has two vital aspects. On the one hand, parents are expected to be teachers, authorities, evaluators, and guides, and they can perform this role admirably in Light Control Talk. Use Style II judiciously when it's necessary to separate from your child to talk *at* him from your position of maturity and knowledge.

The flip side of parenting supports and nurtures. While parents are quick to comment to control, they are less likely to speak out to support. Don't assume that your children know that you love them, appreciate them, and take pride in their accomplishments. *Tell them.* Kids need to hear the good things you think and feel about them—just as we adults do—and not as a mixed message either: "I love you, but I wish you'd work harder to pull up your math grades." Fur-

thermore, don't be embarrassed to apologize when you've
goofed or hollered at them because you were uptight about
something else. Saying you're sorry shows that you're human
and makes it easier for kids to admit their own faults.

Because Small Talk, Search Talk, and Straight Talk stem
from equality and strive for togetherness, they are ideal for
expressing affection, appreciation, and apology. Including
them in your repertoire will add depth and warmth to your
relationship with your children. It's not unusual, however, for
parents to Small Talk easily at work with friends or over a
back fence with neighbors, yet have difficulty chatting with
their kids. If you fall into this category, try to create an atmosphere that promotes conversation. An hour around the
Monopoly board provides a great opportunity for Small Talk.
Looking at old photograph albums or family slides can be a
terrific bridge to intimacy. The pictures evoke memories, the
memories stimulate anecdotes, and soon the children are participating in an unknown part of your life. One mother we
know has great talks with her kids while watching old movies
on TV with them. She says, "When there's a Bob Hope and
Bing Crosby 'road picture' or a Judy Garland epic, I call everybody into the den because I want them to share things I like.
Pretty soon watching the movie leads to talking about the
'olden days' and we have wonderful chats."

Frequently, family activities or outings begin with high
hopes for connecting but rapidly deteriorate. A trip to the
zoo starts buoyantly and ends angrily. An afternoon set aside
to build a birdhouse with your son winds up with the two of
you barely speaking. When events sour and good times
crumble, check your communication. Control Talk is probably the culprit. How can you have fun at the zoo if most of
your conversation is authority-based: "Don't eat so many
peanuts, you'll be sick." "Don't run so fast, you'll trip."
"We've watched the lions long enough." And when any project with a kid turns into a session of strict instruction and
criticism, the chance to connect in Small Talk or even
Straight Talk is lost.

Some parents assume that kids are incapable of Straight
Talk, but they are wrong. Often, some outside event—the
death of the family dog, a best friend who is moving away, a
grandparent undergoing surgery—triggers an emotional response in a child. Listen for a feeling statement as a clue that
the child is ready to talk with you, then sidle in.

Talking *with* children offers both of you the opportunity to air feelings and express opinions. Often, the direction and continuation of a conversation depend on the questions you, as a parent, ask. Do you encourage sharing with "what" or "how" questions: What happened at your Scout meeting today? How did you feel about that? Or do you shut off communication with "why" and "when" questions: Why didn't you wipe your feet? When are you going to learn? We can't point out often enough that *why* questions put anybody on the defensive, children, in particular, because they are so often called to account for their behavior.

ASK YOUR KIDS QUESTIONS

As a rule, kids dislike interrogation, especially when parents question them with the accusing tone of lawyers pressing witnesses. What kid hasn't smarted under: "Why did you do that?" "How could you be so foolish?" "When do you think you can spare a half hour to mow the lawn?" These are not the kinds of questions we advocate. We do recommend genuinely exploratory questions that seek information and give a child the chance to explain his reasons for doing or not doing something.

Lynn told her group an amusing story about the time she asked her six-year-old son whether there were any black children in his class. He nodded and said, "Yes." She then asked if he played with them and he said, "No." Assuming he was acting out of prejudice, she gave him a long lecture on racial equality and tolerance and he squirmed the whole time. When she was finished, he gave her one of those "boy-are-mothers-dumb" looks and said, "Mom, we don't play with her 'cause she's a girl."

A few well-placed questions may be particularly useful when you find yourself in a power struggle with a child.

Roz had taken her seven-year-old daughter shopping before school began to select some dresses that Christine could wear as an alternate to daily bluejeans. But after the first week of school, the dresses hung in the closet and Roz found herself quite annoyed. She'd spent a lot of time picking out those dresses and asking Christine, "Do you like it and will you wear it?" The little girl had been quite enthusiastic, showing her new purchases to Daddy as soon as they came home. Now, each morning when the alarm rang, Roz and Christine argued about the dumb dresses. Roz would complain about having spent time and money on them, reminding Christine of her promise to wear them. Christine would cry. It would get late and Roz would relent. Finally, it occurred to Roz to ask Christine why she didn't wear the dresses. The child looked embarrassed and finally said, "The boys pull up our skirts to see our underpants." It was that simple. Roz wanted to kick herself. "Well, what could we do about that?" she continued. Christine replied, "I'll wear the dresses if you let me wear shorts underneath." That night Roz laundered some summer shorts and Christine took off her jeans.

Asking questions, even the right ones, doesn't mean you'll get the right answers. With teenagers you may not get any answers at all. But don't let that deter you. If you ask because you're sincerely interested, *not* because you want to prove your case, an I-count-me/I-count-you message will come through. Should the response be silence, respect it and back off. Perhaps the timing isn't right and you would be better off using the Procedure-Setting Plan in Chapter II. Choose a mutually agreeable time and place to talk, and when you do, rely on Search Talk to ask your questions.

DON'T ASSUME YOU HAVE
ALL THE ANSWERS

Pete's father typically assumes the worst of his son. One afternoon there was a garage sale in the neighborhood and Pete strolled over to poke around. When he returned, his dad was sitting on the front porch and Pete rather clumsily tried to sneak by him, obviously hiding something behind his back. His dad called out, "I bet you bought some of that junk over there. Boy, you'll never learn the value of a dollar." Pete didn't answer. His father went on, "You wasted your allowance again, didn't you? Another toy you'll just throw in the corner and forget about. Let me see what you bought." Pete blushed and reluctantly revealed a pair of bookends. "They're for you, Dad. For Father's Day."

Because all parents are former children, they tend to assume that they're experts at diagnosing kids' behavior. When Pete doesn't do what he's told, his parents are certain that they can explain his motives: he's in a rebellious stage; he's being spiteful; he doesn't care; he's looking for negative attention; he's lazy; he's selfish. While it's entirely possible that any one of these bad motives may be the actual cause, it's unfair to assume. There are three other plausible explanations that are just as likely to account for a child's misbehavior.

A. *The child may not have known what was expected.*
Jenny was told to pick up the puzzle pieces scattered on the floor. An hour later, Jenny was still stretched in front of the television and the pieces had not been moved. Her mother scolded her angrily, "Why haven't you done what I told you?" The child looked surprised. "You told me to pick up the puzzle but I didn't know I had to do it right away." Be clear and specific about your expectations. Tell your child exactly how and when you want an order followed and don't assume you've been understood.

B. *The child may not be capable of performing the task.*
Parents easily overestimate the maturity as well as the physical prowess of their children and fail to adjust their standards accordingly. If every time wee Willy sweeps the kitchen floor, you sweep it over again because you aren't satisfied with Willy's work, Willy will stop sweeping the floor when he's told to.

C. *The child may not have heard the order, may truly have forgotten it, or may have a legitimate excuse for failing to do it.*
Andy and two cousins went off hiking in the hills during a family Fourth of July gathering. Almost immediately after the boys left, Andy's father whistled for him—the established family signal to return home—but Andy was already out of earshot. An hour later when the boys trudged back, Andy was whipped for disobedience. Although his cousins stood by his story, his father would not believe that he hadn't heard the whistle.

It's important to get in the habit of checking out these three possibilities before impugning a child's motives. First, you'll avoid making false assumptions. Second, the labels you pin on your children are less likely to become a reality as they begin to accept your accusations as truth and match their behavior to fit the picture you've painted. To restrict your assumptions, pay attention to your sense data—what exactly do you see and hear? Then check out what you think and avoid hardening of the categories by treating your thoughts as possibilities rather than self-evident truths.

LET KIDS SOLVE THEIR OWN ISSUES

Parents are natural problem-solvers. From the vantage point of their vast experience they consider themselves eminently equipped to solve most of the conflicts children lay at their feet. At one time or another, they've probably been in a similar situation and worked their way out of it. Despite their best intentions, when parents handle issues for their children they actually stifle their kids by preventing them from developing independence and self-reliance. What happens when mom or dad isn't there to tell the child what to do? Although there are times when it's necessary to impose your solutions, get in the habit of helping your children find their own way to handle conflict. Slip into Search Talk and guide them in seeking information from which they can draw their own conclusions.

Laura came home from third grade and threw herself in her mother's arms, sobbing. "My friend Brett is going to be absent all week. She has the flu. I have to have my table changed. Without her I'm the only girl in the group. I can't talk to all those boys." Her mother, Jane, sympathetically patted her hair and asked, "What do you think you could do about that?"

Laura wept. "I don't know. Maybe you could write a letter to Mrs. Percy, my teacher." Jane said, "No, I won't do that. If this is important to you, I want you to learn how to handle it. How could you change this situation?" Laura wiped her eyes. "I guess I could ask Mrs. Percy to change my table." Jane said, "You could do that. She might not say yes, though. Would you like to practice and pretend I'm Mrs. Percy?" Laura liked that suggestion. She cleared her throat. "I don't like anybody at my table, Mrs. Percy. Could you change it?" Her mother smiled. "How might you say that more accurately?" Laura thought a moment. "Brett will be absent all week and I'm the only girl at my table. None of the boys are my friends. Could you change it?" Jane, playing Mrs. Percy, replied, "Well, Laura, I don't know. If I change your table, I might have to change everybody who's unhappy. Could you try it for a day or so and if you're still uncomfortable, we'll talk tomorrow."

Laura seemed satisfied and went out to play. The next day Jane eagerly awaited the school bus to see how her Style III exploration had worked. "Well, Laura, what happened?" Laura shrugged. "I didn't do it. We're having a contest for the quietest table and our group is ahead by ten points so I decided not to leave."

When Search Talk isn't sufficiently precise, turn to the Awareness Wheel and use it as a roadmap to help lead your child to a solution.

Cindy, a somewhat shy fifteen-year-old learned through the grapevine that her former boyfriend was angry because she had snubbed him at a dance. Cindy felt terrible. She moaned to her mom, "I don't want him to be mad at me. I didn't mean to hurt his feelings. What should I do?" Her mother asked, "Could you call him to talk about it?" "Are you crazy?" Cindy said. "Well, how about a letter?" her mother continued. "I guess I could do that," Cindy replied. "But what would I say?" That's when her mother brought out the Awareness Wheel. "Could you start by telling him what you saw at the dance?" "You mean that I saw him across the room but it was very crowded and when I looked again I couldn't find him." "Something like that," her mother said. "Then how about telling him what you thought when you heard he was angry." Cindy paused. "I thought he misinterpreted why I didn't say hello." "And how did you feel about that?" her mother went on. "I felt terrible." "What did you want to do?" she asked next. "I wanted him to know I hadn't intentionally snubbed him and I would never want to hurt his feelings." "Do you think you could put that in a letter?" her mother asked. Cindy nodded. "I think I could now that you've helped me to say it. I just didn't know where to begin and how to get the words straight. Thanks, Mom."

TELL KIDS WHAT YOU EXPECT

The thorny path of parenthood is strewn with broken expectations. Our children can't possibly be all that we expect them to be. But often, children fail to meet expectations because they weren't told what those expectations were.

Fran had an appointment with a doctor whose office was near a shopping mall. Rather than leave her ten-year-old son and his friend squirming in the waiting room, she decided to drop the boys at an amusement arcade in the center. When they arrived she found she had nothing but a $10 bill, which she gave the boys, telling them to have it changed to something smaller. About an hour later she picked them up and asked for her change. There wasn't any. Fran was furious. "You should have known not to spend all of it. Don't you know the value of a dollar? If that money had come from your piggy bank you wouldn't have spent it all. I trusted you to know better."

It's easy to understand Fran's anger, but, in truth, she had never told the boys how much to spend. She'd simply expected they would know.

It is important to be as specific as possible about your expectations. At a family picnic, Sam tells little Sally, "Don't wander too far." She goes to the edge of the water to feed the ducks and Sam spanks her. What is too far? Is it the park bench, the barbecue pit, or the swings? Be clear. And when you're angry with a child because he or she misbehaved or failed to follow instructions, take out your own Awareness Wheel and check out your expectations and how clearly you expressed them.

Being definite about what you expect is, of course, no guarantee that your expectations will be met. However, if your expectations are reasonable and you've checked that your child understands them clearly, then *your* obligation is fulfilled. If Tom has soccer practice at 5:15 and the carpool picks him up regularly at 5:00, it is not your responsibility to drive him to practice if he's consistently late and misses his ride. Meeting expectations and accepting the consequences for a failure to do so is a valuable part of learning to grow up.

With younger children it's a good idea to anticipate situations and give them some advance coaching in how you expect them to behave to spare them the embarrassment of public rebuke because they haven't performed properly. If grandma is coming to dinner, tell Muffy that you expect her to finish her homework after school so she'll have free time to spend with grandma after dessert. If you're taking your son to a show and you want him to wear a sportcoat and slacks, let him know in advance so that he doesn't emerge from his room in jeans as you are ready to depart and say, "It's not my fault. You didn't say I had to dress up."

Letting children know what you expect from them is one side of the coin. To be fair, also let them know what they can expect from you with strong I-statements. Andy was home from college for summer vacation and had made no move to find a job. Ed, aware that his son wasn't earning any money, was worried that he'd be unable to contribute his share of college expenses in the fall. One approach would have been a Control Talk attack:

"You'd better get off your duff and find a job. I'm not paying for your whole education, you know."

Instead, Ed, speaking for himself, told the boy clearly what help he could anticipate from his family:

"I want you to know, Andy, just what you can expect from me financially this fall. I plan to pay for your board and tuition, but not for your books or your spending money."

The following week, Andy found a job.

FOCUS ON THE ACTION, NOT THE KID

Like adults, children fashion their sense of self partially from what other people think of them. If a child is told often enough that he's selfish, careless, fresh, or moody, he begins to believe *he* is his *label*, and the label becomes a straightjacket from which he can't wriggle free. "If that's what Mom and Dad think I am, I guess it's true." It's awfully hard for anybody to change what they are, and attacks on people rarely have the desired effect of improving character traits.

What can be changed, however, is behavior. Not only is it less painful to accept criticism for what we've done than what we are, it's easier to do something about it. All too often, though, as parents we gloss over an action or an event that offended us and we pounce on the child instead. Rather than look at what the child did, we assail their self-worth. You can avoid this trap by using the skills of documentation. Be specific about time and place. Say what you saw or heard. Provide a frame of reference. Stick to the facts and steer away from personal assaults.

When Peter came to Couple Communication, he became aware of his tendency to belittle his children when he disapproved of their behavior. If his son spilled his milk, he'd call him "clumsy." If his daughter complained that she had too much homework to rake the leaves, he'd label her "lazy." One night at the dinner table Peter commented rather sharply that a curry dish his wife had made was too spicy and he couldn't eat it. His daughter, jumping to her mother's defense, piped up, "You never like it when Mom makes anything new. If it's not something you like, you put down her cooking."

Peter hit the ceiling. "You little pipsqueak. You stay out of this. Who do you think you are telling your father what he can and cannot say. You're nothing but a little kid with a big mouth. When I want your two-bit opinion, I'll ask for it." There was a stunned silence at the table and one by one each family member stalked off, leaving Peter's wife alone to pick at her food and seethe at her husband.

Toward the end of Couple Communication, Peter replayed the incident with his wife so he could use the skill of documentation to zero in on his daughter's behavior rather than his daughter. And his response was very different:

"Hey, I don't like you commenting when your mom and I are having a hassle. This is between your mom and me, and I prefer she speak for herself."

If Peter had known the technique of documentation when the incident had occurred, he would have been able to appropriately vent his disapproval without squashing his daughter's self-esteem.

DON'T SHOOT KIDS' DREAMS

To dream the impossible dream is a privilege of youth. To see clearly all the obstacles blocking fulfillment takes the eyes of an adult, and there are times when it pays for an adult to keep his eyes half shut. When you are fortunate enough to have your child daydream aloud to you, don't destroy that willingness to share by bringing up all the reasons why a dream can't come true. Control your impulse to confront a fantasy with your mature view of reality, especially when it seems threatening.

For example, your sixteen-year-old son announces, "Next summer I'm going to hitchhike across the country." You could respond, "Like heck you are. It's too dangerous for a kid your age to travel like that. I'd never permit it." Or, your seventeen-year-old says, "I think I'm going to put a rock band together." You could respond, "It would cost a fortune for equipment and you don't have any money. Besides, where would you practice? They'd never allow that kind of noise in our apartment building." Or your five-year-old gets a new truck, looks at the rest of the series pictured on the box, and says, "See these, Daddy. I'm going to get every one of them." You could respond, "I doubt that. We couldn't afford all those trucks."

All of these Control Talk answers shut off the possibility of sharing and discourage communication. Instead, try a Small Talk or Search Talk response to show interest in your child's ideas and acceptance of his or her feelings and wishes: "It would be exciting to travel all over the country." "You'd feel like king of the mountain with your own rock band." "You'd really enjoy having all those trucks."

PREPARE YOURSELF FOR BAD NEWS

Opening communication within a family is like taking the lid off a jack-in-the-box. You can never be sure what kind of information will pop out and, once it's out, you won't be able to stuff it away again. Although we are firm believers in the benefits of shared communication which encourages children to speak freely (although not freshly), we are aware of its liabilities. Children often don't understand the boundaries of propriety, and a remark such as, "I don't like the color of your nail polish" might be acceptable to mom but shocking to a teacher. Moreover, you will undoubtedly become privy to information you'd be just as happy not to have. A mother who works hard to establish a good rapport with her teenage daughter could still be unnerved when the girl comes to her asking for birth control.

Even more common are those situations in which you seek full disclosure, and the answers you get put you in the awkward position of disciplining the child for being honest. Alan found himself in this dilemma:

"We're trying to cut down on the sugar in our diet, and when our little girl goes to her friend's house they always have lots of candy and cookies around. I'll ask her what she's eaten there and she'll be honest with me. It's always far more sugar than I'd like her to have. I value her honesty but

I also want her to regulate the sugar. If I rebuke her for being truthful, she won't tell me the truth in the future."

Another danger to open communication is that you're likely to hear painful criticism of your own behavior.

Leon told his kids he'd take them skating after dinner, but at the table their continual bickering needled him to the point of explosion: "I'm not going anywhere with you. I can't stand to be around your noise. I just want to be left alone in peace and quiet." He picked up his coffee cup and moved into the den. His children followed him. "Just a minute, Dad. You can't cut yourself off from the family and go into your shell routine. You're a part of us whether you like it or not. You made a promise and it's not fair to change your mind because you're uptight."

When, as a result of healthy two-way communication between parent and child, you are faced with unpleasant or disturbing truths, try not to overreact in Control Talk. Reach for Search Talk or Straight Talk to explore or acknowledge what you've heard.

DON'T FIGHT FIRE WITH FIRE

We've talked a good deal in this chapter about the destructiveness of clubbing children with Heavy Control Talk. Yet often, the weapon is in the other hand, and parents are the victims of their children's Control Talk barrages. Sometimes, the parent is a convenient third party for a child to dump on; sometimes, the parent is the object of an attack. What should you do when you are on the receiving end?

When you are the hapless third party, it's helpful to use the skills of attentive listening to diffuse the anger and find out what's going on underneath it. Is it a mask for fear, distrust, embarrassment?

Dan stomped off the school bus, slammed his books on the kitchen counter, and launched into a diatribe against his social studies teacher. "I hate her. She's so dumb. And mean too. She picks on me. One of these days I'm going to tell her she's an ass."

Dan's mother easily could have fired back in Control Talk, "How dare you use such langauge. That's no way to talk about a teacher." Instead, she moved to interpretative listening to pick up sense data on what triggered Dan's reaction and to help him see the incident in a broader light.

MOM: Something must have fired you off. What happened?
DAN: Billy was telling me something and she caught me answering and said if I was out of turn one more time she'd send me to the principal.
MOM: And how about Billy?
DAN: That's just it. She didn't say a word to him.
MOM: And you're pretty sore at her.
DAN: Darn right. I'd like to fix her wagon!
MOM: That might get you in worse trouble.
DAN: Probably. I just wish there were some way I could get her off my back!
MOM: So you'd really like to get her off your case—and you haven't come up with a way yet. Would you like my help in figuring something out?
DAN: Yeah, okay, but not right now. Jimmy's waiting.
MOM: Okay, let me know when you're ready for us to sit down and have a "teacher management" session.

When a child smacks you with Heavy Control Talk, don't lose control of yourself and smack back:

Nancy was preparing breakfast and making Small Talk in an attempt to connect with her teenage daughter. She asked, "Does Mrs. Ames still have the same frizzy hairdo she had last year?" The daughter snapped back, "Of course she does. Do you think she'd care that you noticed?" Nancy, stung by the sharp response to her offhand remark, might bark back, "Don't be so flip. You're talking to your mother." Or she might think to herself, "This is a moody fourteen-year-old. It's a passing phase. I'll keep quiet." Or she could say, "I don't like you to give me flip answers." Or, if the time and place seemed fitting, she could go a step further and say, "I'm hurt when you talk to me like that, kind of flip and arrogant. I think this has happened a lot lately between us. Have you noticed it too?"

Try to be aware that you do have choices, that you do not have to follow the leader. As a parent you will naturally want to criticize the inherent disrespect of Control Talk. Although it may seem demeaning to you *not* to respond in kind, bear in mind that Control Talk begets more Control Talk unless someone changes the track. Stick to speaking for yourself and reflecting your thoughts and feelings instead of biting back. You'll provide a far better example if you say, "I don't want to be talked to that way," than if you snap, "Don't give me your wise answers." You can't teach your child other styles if you consistently answer their Heavy Control Talk with a sting of your own.

DON'T LOOK FOR MIRACLES

Children have long memories. If you begin today to change the way you communicate, you will not find tomorrow or the next day markedly different. But in a month or so you should see glimmers of change. Attitudes alter slowly, as we've seen before, and old patterns are hard to break. If you respond to a child's Heavy Control Talk with a feeling I-statement, or try to connect in Straight Talk, or ask a caring question and nothing happens, don't say to yourself, "I didn't think it would work." It won't work once and it won't work all the time, but it *will* work eventually, as long as you are using your skills to understand and not to force compliance.

What makes raising children so tough is their constant need to establish their own identity—a need which frequently puts them in conflict with their parents. By acting against your wishes and challenging your authority, they develop independence and self-control, and this rarely happens without painful struggling on both sides. How you communicate during these struggles may determine whether you separate in a stalemate or connect and grow from the experience.

The rewards of quality communication accrue slowly but leave permanent impressions, and they create connections at the oddest times. We received this letter from a woman who had taken Couple Communication and resolved to use the skills to improve her stormy relationship with her teenage daughter. Apparently it worked.

"I wanted you to know how I've turned around my difficulties with my daughter by consciously paying attention to my communication. Last week I took her shopping on a Saturday to find a party dress. We dragged through two shopping malls and nothing pleased her, but I was very careful not to slip into Control Talk to voice my frustration. When we came home, I was visibly tired and I said I was annoyed because now I'd have to do my weekly marketing on Sunday. I expressed how I felt, but I didn't attack her as the cause. She put her arms around my waist, hugged me, and said, 'Thanks, Mom. I know you hate this kind of shopping. I'm sure we'll find something next week.' You can't imagine what that little gesture meant to me. Six months ago we could hardly talk to each other."

15

Connecting at Work

Brriinngggggg. The alarm clock shakes you from slumber. You stretch under the covers, open your eyes, and begin getting ready for the single activity that consumes the bulk of your adult life: work. There are currently 104 million men and women in the labor force and a high percentage of them complain about their jobs. More often than not, however, it isn't the work that they don't like, it's the atmosphere of the place where they're working.

Every job—whether it's in a store, factory, office, or service industry—has two basic components: one is the work or product itself; the other is the people performing the work and their relationship with one another. Usually tension at work is generated by a conflict between these two forces. Instead of a harmonious meshing that values both task and people, one takes paramount importance at the expense of the other. And all too frequently, the task gets the lion's share of attention and the people get the shaft.

Most of us want from our work the dual opportunity to be productive and to relate to others, which requires coordination between task and people. And the foundation of coordination is a we-both-count esteem position that counts people as well as task. People can't be happy in a work situation that consistently places what they do above who they are. And on a practical level this balance can be achieved through effective communication.

Although Small Talk and Light Control Talk are routine labor language, pack Search Talk and Straight Talk in your briefcase or lunchbag, too. These styles are used much too infrequently for handling job-related conflicts, pressures, and misunderstandings. Keep your Awareness Wheel handy as well. When you use it to gather information, you'll be less likely to jump into situations or make quick, inaccurate decisions that later require rethinking.

Because so many businesses are conducted in a highly pressurized environment, clear and complete information is too often overlooked in the rush to get things done. Feelings are viewed as inappropriate or insignificant. Intentions are bypassed for terse orders. Yet, of all the arenas in which we operate, our jobs are the most dependent on full information and, because of time pressures, the least likely to get it. Frequently, couples who take our course tell us how pleasantly surprised they are to discover the benefits they receive when they transfer communication skills from the home to the office. And that doesn't surprise us at all.

THE COMPLAINT DEPARTMENT: DEALING WITH DISSATISFACTION

Complaints, whether they come from employees or customers, are a routine part of business. Disgruntled people feel pinched and a complaint is their way of saying ouch. It's easy to discount complainers because we don't want to become involved in other's hassles. We tend to pooh-pooh their grumblings or respond directly to their anger without seeking to understand the cause of it. Unfortunately, unhappiness can't be ignored and it can't be stored. It must be dealt with.

Employees may not always be direct about expressing dissatisfaction. If you are in a management role, train yourself to pick up early warning signals in the form of Passive Heavy Control Talk. Excessive or uncharacteristic carping, placating, hinting, whining, prolonged silences, sarcasm, little jokes with poison punch lines, may all be clues that an employee is unhappy. Check it out. Good administrators should be amateur detectives looking beyond symptoms or bogus complaints to get at the truth.

Jenny is an industrial nurse who, after taking Couple Communication, began to use the Awareness Wheel to treat many of the backaches and headaches that drifted into her infirmary. "Instead of simply asking people about their pain," she explains, "I'd go around the Wheel to get information about the cause. First, I'd have them go through the motions of their job so I could see how they're operating with a back-ache. That would be my sense data. Then I'd question them to get more interpretations: Does your manager expect you to do more? Is this task new or difficult? I'd ask them how they feel about their work and what they'd like to change, and often I'd find their back is only part of a bigger picture. What they have isn't a medical problem but a personnel problem. So we'd make an appointment with personnel, and that's where the cure was.

Donald's real estate firm was expanding from the Midwest to the coast, and he assigned the task of finding and furnishing the branch office to Helen, who had been asked to head the new operation. The target date for opening was November. All through September Helen complained that she'd never be ready on time. This wasn't going right. That fell through. People didn't deliver what they'd promised. Donald was about to blast her with Control Talk, "Why the hell isn't this office ready?" when his Couple Communication training interceded. "I called Helen into my office and said, 'I'm disturbed that we're way off the timetable for our new office. I suspect something else is going on here. I'd like to be more confident about you than I am right now. What's happening?' Helen looked relieved. 'To tell you the truth, I've been moving awfully slowly because I'm having second thoughts about my ability to handle the new place on my own. I was too embarrassed to tell you. There are so many broader demands than what I'm doing now.' That got us into discussing whether she was ready for this promotion and we eventually decided to send someone along to open the office with her."

When complaints are loud, clear, and angry, be particularly careful to avoid the trap of Active Heavy Control Talk. To resist, make a concerted effort to adhere to an I-count-me/I-count-you attitude, backed up by the three A's of Straight Talk. *Acknowledge* what you hear. *Accept* it at face value for the moment without making judgments. *Act* on it by using the skills of Attentive Listening to invite the disturbed employee to give you more details. This approach is atypical for many bosses who are, by nature, action-oriented problem-solvers. Listening is not their instinctive response. If you fall into this category, resist your tendency to explain away the concern, give advice about solutions, or negate it by defensively counterattacking. Instead, encourage more information.

Angry Employee: "This is a job for a moron."
Discounting Response: "That doesn't say much for you."
Attentive Listening Response: "Do you think your ability is under-used here?"

Angry Employee: "I've spent this whole day tracking back orders. Just because somebody else screwed up, I can't get my work done."
Problem-Solving Response: "Let the back orders go. Fill the current orders. They're more important now."
Attentive Listening Response: "I can see you're steaming. Tell me more about what happened so we can get to the root and straighten it out."

Angry Employee: "We never have the right stock around here. That guy I was working with on Saturday bought a boat from Flynn's Marina because the one I was selling him didn't have the right equipment."
Counterattack Response: "If you were a more aggressive salesman, you wouldn't have blown the sale."
Attentive Listening Response: "Could you have interested him in something else we had in stock? Tell me what you tried to do."

Angry Employee: "I can't work as hard as you do. This business may be your whole life but it isn't mine."
Defensive Response: "You're darn right I work hard and just look where it's gotten me."
Attentive Listening Response: "I think you're telling me my expectations are too high for you to meet."

Irate customers want your attention, too, and they should be treated with the same care and consideration. Often they see themselves as victims of an unfair or unjust system in which they have no power. So it's particularly important to *avoid* increasing their anger or frustration with *rational explanations:* "The buttons were missing when you gave the shirt to our route man"; *denial:* "We aren't responsible for the brakes. If you didn't ride them so hard they'd hold up longer"; or *defensiveness:* "We can't clear any faster. You'll simply have to be patient."

These very common responses can escalate a minor encounter into a major battle. Instead, meet the customer's anger by *acknowledging* and *accepting* it, and using Attentive Listening to encourage the kind of information that will lead to *action.* Ask "what" and "how" questions: What do you think a fair solution would be? How would you like us to handle this? You may not be able to grant the customer's request, but your questions do affirm his or her point of view and indicate a willingness to negotiate.

Anger is usually a smokescreen hiding fear, hurt, confusion, inadequacy, or vulnerability. More often than not, customers anticipate a fight and prepare themselves by building up a defense and focusing solely on their anger. But with Attentive Listening skills, these pent-up underlying feelings can be aired and hopefully understood, thereby diffusing some of the employee's or customer's irritation immediately. By encouraging complainers to express their thoughts, feelings, and hopes for action, you dismantle the screen to get at the real problem and explore a mutual solution.

STRATEGIES FOR SURVIVING IN GROUPS

In the course of a work day, people confer for all sorts of reasons, in all kinds of groups. Meetings and conferences are a vital aspect of many businesses, yet all too frequently they are ineffective, ineffecient—or just plain boring. When the confab ends, nothing has been accomplished or it's taken three hours to settle a single issue.

Generally, meetings ramble because they are poorly planned. You can introduce efficiency, either as a participant or leader, by using the procedure-setting guidelines in Chapter 11 and organizing any conference around a modified version of the Problem Prevention Process described in Chapter 12. The next time you call a meeting or are involved in one, try to follow these steps:

1. Identify the issues to be discussed by listing all of them and setting priorities.
2. Choose the one issue that involves the greatest number of people present and can make the best use of available time by asking these questions: Are all the people who should be included in the discussion present? Do we have enough time to handle the issue? How much time should we devote to it? There is no point in wasting a half hour on an issue that could be handled by a sub-group.
3. Set your goals. Do you want to just brainstorm ideas and stimulate discussion? Do you simply want to reach a general

understanding of the issue? Do you want to generate several possible solutions for everyone to mull over? Do you want to make a decision now?

4. Once you have set a direction, travel there by using the Awareness Wheel to gather relevant information concerning the issue.

A. What *past* or *current actions* have or haven't worked in relation to the issue?

B. What have people in the room *seen and heard* that casts light on the issue?

C. What do they *think* about it?

D. How do they *feel* about it?

These four points will usually create a broad understanding of the issue and its context. Sometimes, this understanding is an end in itself. At other times, it leads to a breakthrough that can be pursued with the rest of the Wheel.

E. What *intentions* do the people at the meeting have for themselves and for the company?

F. What kind of *actions* is the group willing to take?

There are several advantages to a PPP approach to meetings. First, it tempers the common tendency to jump from interpretations straight to action. Second, it eliminates the pitfalls of limited awareness. For instance, many meetings bog down in a repetitious recitation of ideas and opinions without any reference to the feelings or intentions that could be the key to an action plan. Third, PPP's emphasis on the Awareness Wheel provides the necessary focus to keep the group from wandering off on tangents or crossing into unrelated subjects.

Even if formalized meetings are not part of your work pattern at times, you will surely be involved in group projects or activities. To help you make the most of those times, here are some general guiding principles.

Pay Attention to Intentions. In the "we're-here-to-do-a-job-let's-do-it" atmosphere of work, intentions often fall by the wayside, and this can lead to confusion and misunderstanding. People in groups are often shy about voicing their wants because they're afraid of appearing selfish or being perceived by others as a foolish majority of one. However, without an awareness of intentions it's hard to find acceptable solutions. As a group leader, if you can identify a pool of wants and build a bridge between them, you can literally move mountains. Even as a participant, you can elicit intentions by pointing out, "We haven't really looked at what we all want here."

Zeroing in on intentions often dramatically shifts a group's perspective. Bob was called into a meeting to approve a creative blueprint prepared by a marketing team who planned to present it to the client the following morning. As he read the blueprint he found several points with which he disagreed. Since it was 4 P.M. on Tuesday and he knew that the presentation was scheduled for 9:30 A.M. Wednesday, he asked point-blank, "Do you want me to contribute to this and improve it, or do you want me to rubber-stamp it so you can get it through tomorrow?" The three other men were taken aback. "Well," one said, "I think we were looking for a rubber stamp, but if you've got problems maybe we should put off the client meeting." "I think that would be a good idea," Bob replied. The meeting was postponed.

Use the Awareness Wheel to Organize Your Presentations. Regardless of the brilliance of your ideas, you'll have all the dazzle of a 10-watt bulb if they are jumbled and inchoate. Presentations should be clear, concise, and thorough. Kent, an advertising executive, finds this easy by patterning his presentations around the Awareness Wheel. He's more comfortable having a map to follow, and his listeners are invariably impressed with his accuracy and completeness. He tells this amusing story.

"I was presenting an ad campaign to a company that had recently hired our agency. I began by recapping our last meeting: 'When we got together originally you requested a campaign that would stress your service. We thought that was a very good idea and we've tried to incorporate it. We're quite excited about what we're going to show you today. We want your feedback before we move on it and so on.' When I was finished, one of their guys raised his hand and said, 'I heard you tell me blah, blah. I think blah, blah. I feel thus and so.' I thought to myself, this guy is running the Wheel right back at me. After the meeting, I asked him if he ever heard of Couple Communication, and he smiled and said, 'Yeh, my wife and I took it. You did, too, didn't you?' There was no question that he and I communicated better than anyone in that room."

Take a Shared Meaning Break to Clear Confusion. When you find yourself wondering, "What did he mean by that?" back up before you move ahead by clarifying the comment that perplexed you. Begin by saying, "As I understood what you just said . . ."; then translate the other person's statement into your own words. Time out for a shared meaning prevents dangerous assumptions and unnecessary confrontations.

Lynn was being interviewed by several members of a large accounting firm and, in the course of the conversation, they said they were looking for a person who had substantial real estate experience and could bring in real estate business. Lynn had had some experience, but it could not be termed substantial. "Just a second," she said. "Let's see if I understand what you want. You want someone with both substantial real estate expertise and connections." "Yes, that's true," they said. "Well, I don't fit that bill," Lynn replied. "I wonder if we should continue to talk." "Wait a minute," they answered. "That's our ideal. We don't necessarily expect to get it and you've got other things we want." As a result of Lynn's shared meaning, she saw that she was not out of the picture, and they continued to talk.

Don't Exchange; Collaborate. The competitive nature of work frequently pits people as adversaries, forcing them to bargain from an exchange position: you give me some of what I want and I'll give you some of what you want. Superficially, this may seem fair, but in fact, this exchange position is characterized by an I-count-me/I-don't-count-you attitude that encourages obstinacy and stifles creativity. Amazing things can happen in a group setting when one team shifts from the miserly bargaining of exchange to the collaborative position of we-both-count. The concept that we're in this together—we've got a problem to solve; let's cut the give-to-get and work our way out as a team—neutralizes the atmosphere. People are more apt to yield when the chips are pooled and the push-pull tension is removed.

HOW TO ASK FOR A RAISE

Money is hard to talk about in any context and an employee who doesn't have butterflies going in to a salary negotiation is as rare as a child who doesn't like cookies. Employees generally assume that they want a bigger slice of the pie than the boss will be willing to give and, at the same time, they don't want to appear greedy or ungrateful. Moreover, whether it's true or not, employers are generally considered to be more interested in filling their own plates than in serving generous portions to everybody else. Uncomfortable at best, and uncertain how to be direct, too many employees hang around the back door dropping hints about money. This is *not* the way to ask for a raise:

Sheila had been working about four months as a secretary in a printing firm when she not-so-subtly asked her boss, "Are there any scheduled raises here?" He answered directly. "We talked with our last secretary about every six months." From time to time after that, Sheila would make suggestive remarks like, "Paycheck sure does disappear fast." "It's harder and harder to make ends meet these days." Her boss got the message. "I'm getting the impression you'd like to talk about your salary now." And so they scheduled a meeting in which Sheila continued to play cat-and-mouse. Her boss asked, "How much more money would you like?" She said, "Well, there's a lot more work here than I realized." Frustrated because he asked a direct question and got an indirect answer, he tried another tack. "There is a lot of work here and I'd like to be fair. How much more money do you need?" Sheila hemmed, "It takes a lot to live these days, you know." He wanted a figure to negotiate, and the game was exhausting. He finally opened the bidding. "Do you want three dollars more a day?" "That would be pretty good," Sheila answered. The meeting ended with the sense that it was just beginning. The boss wanted to cooperate, but the employee was so indirect that he was left with the impression that she wouldn't be satisfied for very long. In fact, that's exactly what happened and, after two more similar encounters, Sheila was asked to leave.

While the indirect approach is frustrating for both parties, a direct approach coupled with incomplete information isn't likely to be much more successful:

"Mr. Green, I need more money. My expenses are up. We just bought a house and I need ten dollars more a week to make the mortgage." "Everybody has money problems, Sam. You ought to budget more carefully. Talk to me in the spring."

Although Sam was direct, he didn't support his claim with reasons that would convince the boss he deserved more money. Your personal financial state is not your boss's concern. Your *job performance* is. The best approach is a detailed request organized around the Awareness Wheel. Look at the difference:

Phyllis returned to college at thirty-five and graduated from law school on her fortieth birthday. After one year with the small law firm that had hired her at a fresh-out-of-school-staring salary, she decided she was worth considerably more money. She sat down with her Awareness Wheel and mapped out her approach.

Past Action:
Started with no experience.
Handled several major cases my first year.
Brought in three clients on my own.

Sense Data:
My clients were satisifed and generous with praise. Specifically Mr. T said his settlement was higher than he expected and Mrs. J said I was thorough and attentive. The annual report shows that the firm is busy and making money.

What I think:
I am competent and doing more important work than we thought I would be able to handle.
I bring a mature perspective to the office.
I have shown my capacity to work hard.
The firm could afford to pay me more.
I am being underpaid.

What I feel:
I love my job.
I'm happy here.
I'm proud you've shown your respect for me by giving me big cases to handle independently.
I'm resentful that others here earn much more than I do.

What I want:
To continue with the firm.
To be fairly compensated.
To do more for the firm.
To contribute more to my family's expenses.
A salary increase.

When Phyllis met with her boss, she didn't simply ask for a raise. She laid out her Awareness Wheel and her thorough presentation won her case.

THE CRITICAL DIFFERENCE

As we've mentioned earlier, appreciation is a basic human need. What most employees want to hear from their superiors is that they are doing a great job and are an asset to the company. Unfortunately, criticism is a basic reality of working life, and it's offered much more frequently than appreciation. Criticism stings, no matter how it's delivered, whether wrapped in kind words with pretty ribbons or even couched as "constructive." While there's no verbal novocaine to totally deaden that sting, it can certainly be minimized by avoiding Heavy Control Talk and using the Awareness Wheel as a painkiller.

The most lethal criticism is the garden-variety, on-the-spot, hot-tempered reaction. You see something wrong, discover a costly error, catch a disregard for procedures, and *bam*, you pounce—saying something mean, belittling, and probably far more harsh than you had intended. "How could you be so downright dumb?" "Your mistakes could bankrupt us." "Take that diploma of yours and use it to dry the dishes." No matter how Heavy Control Talk criticisms are worded, they deliver the same hurtful "you dummy" message. And the receiver's ego crumbles like an egg in a bear's fist.

When you must give on-the-spot criticism—and there are times when you have no other choice—steer away from Heavy Control Talk. Hesitate a moment and look at what's behind your anger. Quickly tune in to your Awareness Wheel and state the relevant dimensions. It's essential to begin with documented sense data and an interpretation of what you saw or heard.

"I noticed the bank bag lying on the desk. I think you're careless and that scares me."

"I heard you've been mailing out renewal notices on the fifteenth. I'm surprised you haven't been sending them out earlier after our conversation several weeks ago."

When you document your criticism in this way, you offer others the opportunity to respond to the accuracy of your interpretations. Depending on this checkout, the picture might change immediately. Suppose the bank bag had been left out by someone else. Suppose the computer couldn't have the notices ready before the fifteenth. Documented criticism with Awareness Wheel support encourages explanations and reduces defensiveness. In contrast, Heavy Control Talk criticism shuts off feedback.

Try speaking-for-self whenever you give criticism, and, although it's difficult, strive for an I-count-me/I-count-you attitude by focusing your displeasure on the act, *not* on the individual. Everybody slips up, rarely intentionally. Making mistakes does not make someone a stupid or bad person. Yet, in the buckshot of spontaneous criticism, there are inevitably personal put-down pellets. I-statements, documenting, and we-both-count esteem will clean up your criticism and keep it where it belongs—on the performance, not on the person.

Good criticism can be a learning experience. Although nobody enjoys being told that they're performing poorly, an individual can feel positive about the future if the criticism takes the form of coaching or support. When you have to plan a critique or evaluation—and it's not a bad idea to make a practice of doing this periodically—approach the task as a teacher. Prepare your lesson plan by sitting down with your Wheel and filling in the blanks about the person, including both the good news and the bad. Balance is important in receiving criticism. Rarely does any report card show failure in every subject. The science dud may shine in spelling. Let him know.

By tuning in to your sense data, you will avoid the pitfall of blanket accusations such as, "You don't follow orders," in favor of a documented complaint, "Two weeks ago I asked you to improve your attitude and I haven't seen much change. Yesterday you spent all your time locked in your office. At the meeting this week you sat silently and contributed nothing. My secretary tells me your reports are incomplete . . ."

By tuning in to your intentions you will quickly discover whether you are out to get someone or truly help them.

By tuning in to actions, you can see exactly how you've been helping or hindering the problem.

Giving criticism is never easy, but the Wheel will help you organize it with the least amount of pain on both sides. You will recall that we talked about the criticism/appreciation ratio in relationships in an earlier chapter. Just as couples collapse under excessive carping, employees don't last long in jobs where they are criticized more often than they are appreciated or praised. We all tingle at hearing we've done a good job, but what sustains us in the long run is more than a pat on the back. It's a sense that our presence matters, that our effort for the company makes a difference, that, in short, we are valued for being there. With the protection of that kind of appreciation, when criticism comes along it stains but it doesn't destroy.

USING THE WHEEL TO DEAL

Selling is sometimes defined as the not-so-gentle art of convincing others that you have something they need. The shopworn approach to sales is a high-pressure Control Talk routine, relying on "you" messages, assumptions that aren't checked out, closed questions, and heavy persuasions:

Isn't this a beauty?

You put this carpet in your living room and your old furniture will look brand-new.

I'd take the frost-free model. You could swing the few extra dollars and it's worth it.

You'll want our maintenance service after we finish landscaping, won't you? Everybody takes it.

There's no question that pressure selling sells, but we believe that process selling is more satisfying. In process selling you use the Awareness Wheel and open questions to collect information with the goal of matching the person with the product instead of superimposing one on the other.

To illustrate this technique, let's watch a car salesman in action. First, he seeks background data: What are you driving now? How much are you planning to spend? What have you seen or heard about our product? Do you have any special model in mind? Next, he explores the customer's needs: How many people in your family? How big a car do you think you need? How much driving do you do? Do you have any ideas about how this car should perform for you? Next, he listens for feelings—likes and dislikes—but he doesn't probe too far. Finally, he checks intentions: What do you want from your new car—mileage, flash and dash, comfort, speed? How do you intend to use it—for work, for leisure, for both?

Once the salesman has tracked his customer around the Wheel, he's ready to take over as an informed leader, using some of the techniques of Attentive Listening.

He *encourages* the customer to comment on his or her feelings. If the reaction is negative, he doesn't rush the customer to another model. He asks, "What don't you like about this?" so that his next question isn't a shot in the dark.

He *acknowledges* the customer's comments. "You say you could live with this shade of green on your lawn but not in your driveway." "You seem to like the lushness of the cloth upholstery." Not only are people flattered by hearing their own words, they also feel comfortable when they sense that they are being heard and understood.

He *checks out* what he sees and hears—the positives and the negatives. "I see you're frowning at the price. What are you thinking?"

Process selling doesn't always end with a signature on the dotted line, but at least it eliminates the discomfort of pressure selling. It doesn't scare people off, turn them off, or rip them off. And, because you're more likely to connect with process selling, you can establish a rapport that brings people back to shop again even if they don't buy now.

SIMON LEGREE OR MR. NICE GUY: HANDLING AUTHORITY

"I don't want to be loved by my people but I do want to be understood and respected." Owen is vice-president of a huge insurance company and his comment sums up the dilemma of leadership: how do you properly exercise authority? Too many people in authority positions either abuse or under-use their power because they've never learned how to implement it and they're slightly uncomfortable with it. They may become Simon Legrees, using their desk chairs like thrones to issue orders, edicts, and demands. Or they may retreat behind a Mr. Nice Guy image, accepting sloppy performances mildly because they don't want to ruffle feathers or offend anybody.

That is, until their superior chews them out and they turn into rampaging buffalos.

Authority should not be handled in either of these ways, nor is it a leash to let out and pull back intermittently. Properly exercised authority, the kind that breeds respect and understanding, begins by establishing an I-count-me/I-count-you attitude and maintaining it in *every* conversational style. Because people with authority handle a multiplicity of situations, they need to know how to use all four styles, how to match style to situation, and how to regulate the self-importance that leads to discounting.

First, let's look at some of the common abuses of authority that stem from discounting.

Inappropriate Small Talk: We Both Don't Count. This is the kind of boss who shirks authority. He or she rarely outlines expectations or gives clear directives. Such bosses are easygoing, kind even jovial, radiating the Pollyana hope that everyone knows how to do his or her job and will do it superbly. Unfortunately, this rarely happens, since workers look to their superiors for guidance. And when it's not given, these bosses discount themselves by withholding information and hiding intentions and discount others by making them guess what's expected of them.

Inappropriate Light Control Talk: I Don't Count Me/I Count You. These bosses walk softly, concealing a big stick. Their requests are wishy-washy and ambiguous. In an effort to appear exceedingly considerate, they sacrifice clarity for the sake of caring: "If it's at all possible, could you total these now?" "Would you mind taking a late lunch to cover the phones while I'm in conference?" On the surface these requests sound peachy, but they deliver mixed messages because the boss's hidden intentions is compliance. The counting position, in which the boss seems to esteem the employee and discount self, is purely manipulative. If the request is denied, the boss is plenty peeved. The prefereable mode here is direct Light Control Talk: "I need these totalled immediately. I'm sorry if it inconveniences you. Thanks." "I have a conference that can't be interrupted at noon. I'd like you to arrange to go to lunch later so you can cover the phones."

Inappropriate Heavy Control Talk: I Count Me/I Don't Count You. Offices are littered with the bodies of walking wounded who've suffered the withering attacks of authoritarian Heavy Control Talk. Some bosses are all to quick to blame or belittle when a policy isn't followed or something goes awry. Phil is typical. "I have high performance standards and low tolerance for poor-quality work. I know just what I'm looking for and when I don't see a job done properly, I quickly conclude that somebody screwed up and I demand to know why. I'm a big 'why-er' and I can see I make people defensive."

Heavy Control Talk is deaf. It never listens and it discourages discussion. Leaders who use it may want information, but all they're likely to get is excuses, apologies, or counterattacks.

Inappropriate Search Talk: We Both Don't Count. There are two forms of this kind of Search Talk. One occurs when people in authority are too fearful of outcomes to make decisions so they muck about in Search Talk to avoid commitments. This is especially frustrating for employees who look to their superiors for active direction. The other is a bogus kind of Search Talk in which the boss superciliously says, between clenched teeth, "Let's explore this together. Why do you suppose your account left us for another agency?" In this instance, superiors discount themselves by disguising their anger and belittle their employees by treating them like naughty children.

Inappropriate Straight Talk. Straight Talk can be wasteful, boring, and pedantic when used in routine situations that could be quickly handled in Light Control Talk. A full Straight Talk explanation is recommended only when a conflict or snafu upsets the routine. For example, whenever a floor nurse wasn't Jenny-on-the-spot, it would be ridiculous if the head nurse said to her, "I see 318's light is on. I think we're negligent any time a patient's light isn't answered immediately. I want our patients to feel we care about them. I'm afraid we might be failing them in an emergency. Why don't you get right over there." A direct Light Control Statement would be far more fitting: "318's light has been on for a few minutes. Will you get right over and see what she wants."

In order to exercise authority properly—to direct instead of demand, to command respect instead of merely command—it is essential to operate as much as possible from an I-count-me/I-count-you attitude and to weave all the styles appropriately into your leadership role. Here are some suggestions.

Appropriate Small Talk: We Both Count. Small Talk humanizes the workplace. It gathers routine information:

"How are the orders coming in?"

"When is Lou's vacation?"

"Are we going to meet our quota?"

And it relieves tension:

"Boy, this has been three days in one. The old goose is overcooked tonight."

"If we don't wind up this confab soon, I'll need a derrick to unglue me from my chair."

Chitchat helps develop a pleasant work milieu, generates brief connections, and balances the instructive, directive side of authority. Used properly, it gives the boss the chance to flesh out a Mr. Nice Guy image to counteract those times when he behaves like Simon Legree.

Appropriate Light Control Talk: We Both Count. This is the desirable, efficient leadership style. It meets goals and keeps things moving without belittling, blaming, or demanding. Reread Chapter 2 to refresh your memory on the characteristics and correct usage of Light Control Talk as the best mode to express authority.

Appropriate Search Talk: We Both Count. There are three distinct work situations in which a leader can advantageously use Search Talk.

When something has gone wrong: Jeff didn't show up for work. A directive wasn't followed. A sale was lost. A client is fuming. A report is late. Use Search Talk to explore what happened.

When there are ripples on the pond: Orders are backing up. Sales are slipping. The typing pool is bickering. Accounting errors are mounting. Check them out with Search Talk before they become tidal waves.

When you want to generate ideas for the future without any commitment to a plan, brainstorm with the tentative mode of Search Talk.

Appropriate Straight Talk: We Both Count. In many on-the-job conflicts, people in authority roles try to make informed decisions by relying strictly on facts and figures while neglecting the important inner information of the employees involved. They forget to count both task and people. At such times, Straight Talk is especially fitting. You, as the authority, can use it in tandem with the Awareness Wheel to draw out what others saw, heard, and thought, as well as what they feel and want. Only with this complete data can you implement a plan of action that fits the situation, rather than a hastily imposed solution.

Admitting that you've goofed is an equally valuable aspect of counting self and keeping your authority in perspective. An executive friend of ours puts it this way, "If you do the best you can with the information you've got and you're wrong, then you don't owe anybody an apology. But if you ignore the facts, or the data is there and you just haven't used it or haven't tried to get it, then you look stronger by apologizing than by pretending you're infallible."

WHEN THE PRESSURE IS UP, DON'T LET DOWN ON THE SKILLS

It's one of the nutty realities of life that we're most inclined to speed up when it would be wiser to slow down. This is especially true at work where, even in the most relaxed atmosphere, time means money and now means yesterday. Errors that seem piddling on calm days become catastrophes when the work stew is boiling. In tense or rush situations, people are less likely to listen carefully and more likely to jump ahead with insufficient information. When we're harried, we fly off the handle, blurt out blue meanies we immediately regret, and discount everyone and everything in order to get a particular task done.

Think of the times you've said, "I thought you understood what I wanted" or "I thought we were clear about this." And think about how easily you could have avoided such a situation if you'd paused for a simple shared meaning: "Could you run back for me what I asked you to do?" "I want to be sure you're clear about what I mean. Could you tell me what you heard?" Or think about a time when you were accused of stepping on someone's toes and trying to take over. You could have avoided being misinterpreted if you'd paused to explain that you were doing such-and-such solely to finish the task at hand.

That's why when you're under pressure, when you normally forget communication skills, you need them more than ever. The very act of hesitating to choose the appropriate skill slows you down enough to think about what you're saying and how you say it. That moment is often the turning point between the miss of a mistake and the hit of connecting.

16

The Spirit of Connecting

Once upon a time there was a happily married couple named Jack and Jill. They loved each other and they loved their children. They both worked at reasonably satisfying jobs. Although, like all their friends in mortgaged America, they could have used more money, they managed a good life—vacations, braces, piano and skating lessons for the kids, a new car every few years, membership in a tennis and swim club, and so on. Jack and Jill were active people, busy working, playing, living, and loving to the hilt. Yet, some nights when they snuggled in each other's arms waiting for sleep to come, Jill would think to herself, "We never seem to have time to really talk to each other. Here we are, close as two bodies can be, and still something is missing in our lives." And occasionally, Jack would wonder why he had a restless feeling that their relationship hummed but it hardly ever sang.

A fable of modern life? A spiritual emptiness that has nothing to do with religion. Have you felt it? Have you experienced moments of loneliness within your relationships—not because you are isolated from your partner but because you rarely connect at that spiritual level? Many relationships, successful ones, stop at the point at which they could really begin, never stretching past the mundane to embrace the meaningful. Partners may talk about all sorts of external issues—money, jobs, kids, schedules, politics, health—but they don't talk much about the inner values and core beliefs that give substance to their lives. Running around busily, pursuing our various endeavors, we hardly ever sit down to share a broader sense of what really matters and where we are going.

In the vacuum of spiritual connecting lies a rich soil where relationships can flower. Why do we have such difficulty cultivating it? Partly because we haven't had the tools. Partly because we don't know what's growing there. Most of us spend more time doing things than thinking about them. When we do burn brain fuel, it's generally to solve a problem rather than to explore our personal goals and convictions. Even if we are in touch with our deeper thoughts, wishes, dreams, and insecurities, we usually keep the precious package under lock and key because we're terrified of being criticized, ridiculed, or rejected. We imagine that there are enormous risks in discussing our pipe dreams, our strengths, our inadequacies, the meaning of God in our lives, our expectations, our sexual fantasies, our fears of dying, our need for living. But what is really at risk other than the possibility of discovering that you and your partner may not believe or want the same things? And that is risky only if you depend on agreement for survival.

Surely it's a nice pat on the ego if people agree with our essential beliefs, and we try our darndest to win them to our point of view by generally airing values in Control Talk. We tend to talk about our core beliefs either by arguing about them: "I'm telling you, honesty is the best policy. Pick up the phone and tell her the truth"; or by triggering position statements accidentally: "You spent what? Look, let's have a little chat about the value of money." "We are all going to see your sister in the show tonight. The meaning of family is that we support each other."

What's missing for many of us are the intimate disclosures of beliefs that carry relationships past chitchat and beyond bickering and control to the ultimate connection: when two people momentarily unveil the eternal mystery of their inner being. These beautiful exchanges are the missing ingredient in many otherwise pleasant lives, and they are absent because we've been programmed to deal with values and beliefs in protected styles.

Often you may Small Talk your beliefs at the nonthreatening level of "I like this" or "I don't like that," "I approve of this," or "I disapprove of that." You can and probably do Control Talk your values to gain support for them, although we hope we've convinced you that high pressure, force, or preaching rarely fosters a climate of acceptance. And as long as it's not habitual, it's sometimes valuable to use Search Talk to intellectually tiptoe into sensitive or explosive territory. "I know you've never been much of a believer but I've been thinking I'd like to join a church. Would you consider going with me?" "Rick tells me there is an interracial couple dating in his school. How would you handle it if they were our kids?"

However, we'd like to encourage you to try Straight Talk as a means of introducing spiritual connecting in your life. Move past superficiality, pressure, and speculation and unite with people who matter to you by *sharing* what's important for both. With Straight Talk you can leap past arguments about the best disciplinary action in a particular situation to the deeper issue of what you want to teach your children and the kind of climate you want to provide for their growth and development. Use it to look at your desire to simplify your lifestyle or to reveal your secret ambition to be a tycoon; to strip away your public image and let the private self-portrait shine through.

Something very special happens between two people when they hear each other's fears, excitements, dreams, and limitations in an atmosphere that requires nothing more than listening and understanding.

You may be a little tongue-tied at first. Nervous and shy. How do I start? Do I turn off the TV one night and say, "Let's talk about something deep." Do I suggest a walk in the soft light of a summer evening and say, "I want to tell you something about myself." Yes and no. Timing is a factor, and both partners have to be in the mood to talk and to listen. Sometimes this occurs spontaneously and, when you sense sparks in the air, don't let the fire die by picking up the newspaper or changing the subject. However, it's more likely that you'll have to consciously initiate soul-sharing discussion by unfolding yourself and encouraging your partner to do the same with leading open questions.

The idea of spiritual connecting may attract and frighten you simultaneously. It isn't necessarily heavy-heavy or gut-wrenching, and what seems reflective to one pair may seem banal to another. Discover what works for you, what's bubbling in your private kettle, and fly with it.

We asked a pair of Couple Communication graduates to take a look at their life and tape their conversation as an example of what spiritual connecting means to them. Diane is a program coordinator for a museum. Ben is president of a transportation company. He is forty-one; she is thirty-eight. They live in the city with their two children, ages eight and three.

BEN: I've been thinking lately we're very successful in our lives. You've got a career. We've both had good educations. I've got a good business. We've worked out a life-style where we are each pursuing individual things and I think we have some very good times together and with our family. I feel blessed materially, and as far as I'm concerned we have everything we need in life.

DIANE: I wouldn't say that myself. I think our home is a bit of a shell. I'd like more furniture, paintings, to cozy things up.

BEN: Well, I can see that, too, but for me, I feel blessed. I think we live a pretty comfortable life, insulated from pain and suffering in the world, and it concerns me that we might be taking more than we're giving to people who are in real need. I have a sense—I wouldn't call it a mission because that's too strong a word—that I'd like to do something better for mankind with my life, and often, my thoughts are more concerned with getting than giving or contributing. I'm trying to make a buck or put this or that together. So much of my orientation is to accumulate or to get by day-to-day that I don't have much of a sense of service. I'm also not sure whether we're teaching our children any values about giving and service to others.

DIANE: I'm not really too concerned about service right now. I consider what I do in my work as service, and traditionally, women have done so much volunteer work that I don't aspire to that now. My major interests are my family and my work and they take up most of my time and energy. Like tonight when I was playing with Benji I was aware of how much energy it takes to give quality time to a three-year-old.

BEN: I think that's really true. What I don't see is anything in my life that demonstrates to the children that I care about other people, too. Hey, this is shifting some, but I want to ask you about something. Since I've been meditating and praying and spending some of my time tuning in to non-material things—matters of faith and such—you said you thought my life was different. What's different about me?

DIANE: You're a lot different than you were just a few years ago. Let me see if I can put my finger on it. You have a stronger sense of commitment to me and the family. It seemed to me that you used to think somebody else had to entertain you—this notion of "entertain me or I'll go outside to get my entertainment." Now you seem to be getting more from inside yourself, from what you read and experience. I think you have a different attitude, that life is more than entertainment. It's to know God, to reach some higher consciousness by knowing yourself, being in tune and in balance. In the old days it even seemed that sex was part of the entertainment package. You were angry about your upbringing—blaming your parents' attitude, and yourself for not experimenting more. I even think you saw me as interfering with your experimentation. That doesn't seem too much of a thorn anymore.

BEN: It isn't. It's hard to put my finger on what's changed, but through my meditation and prayer I'm not as desperate anymore. I'm more content. Sometimes I'm on a real high that's joyous and I go through a day carried by joy.

DIANE: That's a whole lot different for you, Ben, that attitude of being blessed and thankful, when you used to think somebody out there had it better.

BEN: For me contentment is that we've got everything we need.

DIANE: That's true, but I still have a few wants.

BEN: Yes, and I don't want to squash your wants. I'm not suggesting that we abandon this world and put on sackcloth or anything. I just have a sense I want to give more than get now. But I want to be careful saying that because I haven't done too much about it yet. It's a different orientation for me. Instead of wondering what's coming next and trying to manipulate and control things, I have confidence that what's necessary will come. I'm going to be alert to it, not hung up on possessiveness, but go with the flow and make a contribution to this world. I want my being here to make a difference.

DIANE: Well, it's made you easier to live with. I like it.

BEN: It's like I've gotten this internal thirst for God and the more I drink, the more I want. I also want you to know I really appreciate the support I get from you in pursuing this. I never have the impression you put me down. It's terrific when you say, "Hey, tell me about that." I was worried you might say, "That stuff is ridiculous" or "You should be spending your time doing more important things." It really feels good that you're behind me.

Religious, financial, emotional, social, physical—there are any number of topics that lead to spiritual connecting if they are viewed in the context of values and beliefs. The potential for meaningful dialogues is by no means limited to your partner. You can engage your parents:

"Dad, tell me what it's like for you to be retired."

"Mom, what would you like your grandchildren to tell their children about you?"

You can talk to your children about your beliefs and explore theirs:

"Maggie, I sometimes wonder what kind of person you admire? What kind of adult would you like to be?"

"Let me explain to you why we won't allow you to serve beer at a high school party. It's not just that it's illegal. It's a moral issue, too."

And you can reach out and touch your friends:

"Here it is your birthday. What kind of year has it been for you? Was anything great? Was anything awful? What would you have done differently?"

"I've been thinking about where I'd like to be in my life in five years. I feel sort of restless. My job's getting boring, but I'm really afraid to chance it on a new career. You know when I was a kid I wanted to be an actress. Isn't that silly? I never had the guts to pursue it when I was in college. It seemed so frivolous and I was afraid I didn't have the talent to make it. Sometimes I wonder if it's too late. Being on the stage is a dream I never quite gave up. Do you have secret dreams like that?"

In our endless search for intimate experiences, we peek under the bedcovers, stare into the limpid pools of our lover's eyes, watch for an outstretched hand or an act of kindness, and rack our brains for things to say that will cut through gristle to the heart of the matter. Yet intimacy is accessible through spiritual connecting, as you share with a trusted other the mysteries of your life.

CONNECTING WITH PEOPLE WHO DON'T HAVE THE SKILLS

Now that you've read this book you have the skills to plumb the depths you've been skimming. You can talk to anybody about anything—especially the beliefs, doubts, and dreams that you've never revealed before. You're emancipated, eager to connect with everybody, until suddenly you realize that many of the people in your life don't have the skills to connect back. Relax. They don't need them as long as you're around. You have a great deal to give to others through your own ability to communicate. You know how to join, to support, to nurture, and to express love. You have the tools to connect with your inner self and help free friends and family to develop along with you.

Connecting will occur naturally when you use your Awareness Wheel to understand yourself and tune in to others. Although you can't drag information out of people, you can help them pan for their own gold by asking open questions: What did you see or hear? What do you think? How do you feel about it? What would you like to do? What do you want? Offer your own experience, draw out parallel Awareness Wheel information with open questions and Attentive Listening, and you will find yourself engaging with people who'd run for the nearest exit if you told them you had some communication skills you'd like to demonstrate.

You'll find that it's even possible to Straight Talk with someone who has no idea what this style is. Simply by using Straight Talk skills yourself, you will discover the magnetism of sincere full disclosure that carries no intent to blame or place demands on others. Lack of pressure attracts people; pressure repels them. The true spirit of Straight Talk is positive; it engulfs others naturally as long as there is no pressure. But if you go out with a lasso in hand and preach your new skills you'll drive everybody away.

* You should really speak for yourself.
* You should tell me what you feel.
* You haven't documented why you think that.
* You've got an attacking manner.
* Let me show you how you discounted me by saying that.
* What you should have said just then was . . .

All these examples employ Control Talk to manipulate someone into Straight Talk. *It won't work*. The worst thing you can do with people who don't have these skills is to play teacher, to act as though you've got the answer to their problems, to look down your nose at the poor quality of their communication or urge them to try what you've learned. What you *can* do is *suggest* that they read this book or quietly but definitely change the way you communicate and wait for the magic to spread. It will take time. But it will come.

Recognize that communication skills do have limits. If, for instance, others do not want to join you in Straight Talk, that is their privilege. However painful that rejection may be, you show the important I-count-me/I-count-you attitude of

Straight Talk by respecting their refusal. "I hear you don't want to talk about this. I'm really disappointed, but I won't push you." And remember that our communication program is *not* a manual to wheel-and-deal. It's a process designed to bring you closer to others, to express your inner self, and to resolve issues—all of which will happen as you weave the principles of this book into your life.

THE POWER AND THE GLORY

It is no accident that over and over in this book we have used the word *connect*. On an everyday level we continually hear men and women talk about their need for or lack of connecting. And on a higher level, we thought the concept of connecting suggested something alive and kicking *between* people. There is always a danger in our work when we introduce the Awareness Wheel that people will confuse centering-on-self to mean self-centered. It has never been our intention to focus people inside themselves at the expense of bcoming involved with others. Quite the contrary. Straight Talk is dedicated to encouraging the infinite variety of connections possible between you and others, and showing you new ways to initiate and strengthen those connections with all the valued relationships in your life.

In the opening chapter we said that communication builds or destroys relationships. While there are many factors that influence the quality and outcome of relationships, we hope you now understand the pivotal role of communication as well as your own ability to develop and enrich your relationships by changing the way you talk. You have seen how damaging Heavy Control Talk is, whether it's couched in the maiming dependency of Passive Heavy Control or the my-way-is-the-only-way independence of Active Heavy Control. You've learned how Small Talk can cripple a relationship if it's consistently misused to dodge issues, and how too much intellectualizing in the what-ifs and possibilities of Search Talk limits relationships by robbing them of zest and commitment.

Those are the negative aspects of the three styles. However, when properly used, they are the mortar that cements relationships. Small Talk is the key to light and easy connecting in everyday activities. You'll want Light Control Talk in your life for management and direction, and Search Talk to hunt for answers when you're not ready to make choices. But to complete your repertoire—to build a solid foundation that can support great heights—you need the special sharing of Straight Talk. We selected Straight Talk both as the title of this book and the name of the style that is so central to our program because it's a phrase people use when they refer to open, honest, and clear communication. The common expressions: "I wish he could be straight with me"; "Give it to me straight"; "I'd really like to be straight with her" all imply the desire for genuine, upfront exchanges, the kind Straight Talk is all about.

We all have a great deal to share with one another and we can share harmoniously as soon as we give up the extremes of independence and dependence for the nurturance of interdependence. At the crux of interdependence is the I-count-me/I-count-you attitude that generates collaborative communication. In the equality of collaboration, individual contributions are not weighed or measured. There are no yardsticks, no self-centered exchange contracts. You toss aside the idea "You do this, then I'll do that. If I get mine, then you'll get yours." Instead you begin from the position of "what's best for both of us." Unfortunately we have lived with a social exchange philosophy for so many years that shifting to collaboration isn't easy. But it may be one of the most important messages you can take away from this book, and we hope you'll try it because it's worth every effort.

We have given you in the pages of Straight Talk the skills you need to connect through communication. But the spirit of connecting—the heart of interdependence—is already within you, asking to be discovered and used. Catch that spirit, tie it to the skills, and start connecting now.

Appendix

How to Find out about Couple Communication Programs in Your Area

The number of COUPLE COMMUNICATION groups being offered by certified instructors throughout the United States and in many foreign countries is expanding. If you wish to inquire about the availability of COUPLE COMMUNICATION in your community or purchase a copy of the COUPLE COMMUNICATION Workbook, please write or call Interpersonal Communication Programs, Inc., at the address listed below.

Other Related Programs

Interpersonal Communication Programs, Inc., also offers other programs, workbooks, and instructor training to strengthen family and business life:

UNDERSTANDING US provides a family experience to help you understand and appreciate how your family operates together as a system, maintaining stability and initiating change through stages of development.

WORKING TOGETHER translates the framework and skills from STRAIGHT TALK into a dynamic program for improving communication and decision-making in business and professional work settings.

For information on programs, materials, and training, write or call:

Interpersonal Communication Programs, Inc.
7201 South Broadway
Littleton, CO. 80122
(303) 794-1764

Index